In a Cajun Kitchen

Authentic Cajun Recipes and Stories from a Family Farm on the Bayou

Terri Pischoff Wuerthner

St. Martin's Press New York

 For information, address St. Martin's Press, 175 Fifth Avenue, New York, N.Y. 10010.

www.stmartins.com

Book design by rlf design

Library of Congress Cataloging-in-Publication Data

Wuerthner, Terri P.
In a Cajun kitchen / Terri Pischoff Wuerthner.
p. cm.
ISBN-13: 978-0-312-34305-7
ISBN-10: 0-312-34305-1
1. Cookery, American—Louisiana style. 2. Cookery, Cajun. I. Title.

TX715.2.L68W84 2006
641.59763—dc22 2006043410

First Edition: September 2006

10 9 8 7 6 5 4 3 2 1

Dedicated to my cousin Eleanor Haggerty Code,
my source of inspiration on many levels

Contents

Acknowledgments

I write this book in honor of past generations, and in the hope that future generations will share in the culinary magic of Cajun cookery. I write this book, also, in honor of the people of Louisiana, who suffered so greatly from the effects of Hurricane Katrina in August of 2005, and Hurricane Rita in September of 2005. A portion of the profits from the sale of this book will be dedicated to recovery efforts of cultural institutions and archival repositories attempting to save and preserve the history and culture of Louisiana.

To my roux-mate, my always supportive husband, Dick. I am especially grateful to him for cheerfully becoming my sous-chef, recipe testing assistant, and dishwasher when I sprained my foot two months before this book was due.

To those who are the sunshine of my life no matter what the weather: my three daughters, Michelle, Dawn, and Diana; my son-in-law, David; and my three amazing grandchildren, Jordan, Kyle, and Lily.

To my sister Lorna for numerous hours of editing of this book in draft form, and for helping me with research, both historical and culinary.

To my sister Bonnie for researching our family genealogy, and for lighting my passion for our Cajun roots.

To my brother, Linus, for his professorial critique of this book in draft form.

To my mother for putting up with the Cajun eccentricities of my wonderfully unpredictable Cajun father.

And to my Cajun father—this one's for you, Dad.

To my supportive and enthusiastic agent, always a pleasure to work with, Carole Bidnick.

To my editor at St. Martin's Press, Michael Flamini, for his belief in this book from the moment he saw the proposal.

To the following Cajun cousins and Cajun friends who readily answered questions and offered feedback: Bill and Roberta Schmaltz for contributing many family stories, and answers to endless e-mails, Charley and Ruth Addison, Shirley and James Bolyard, Tommy Cobb, Phyllis Dumesnil, Adrien Green, Lynn Labauve, Madge Labauve, Raphael Labauve, Rose Labauve, Paul McIlheney, Carol Monahan, Judy Thousand, and Tony Walker.

To Bill Douglas and his children, Shawn Douglas and Paige Douglas Brown, for giving us access to our family farm, which their family purchased in 1972.

To Pete and Mary Boudreau for introducing us to St. Mary Parish and the homes, churches, recreational areas, and graveyards where our ancestors lived, prayed, played, and were laid to rest.

To John T. Edge for sharing his chicken-frying expertise.

To Bonnie Hearn Hill for the time she generously spent helping me with my first proposal for this book.

To Toni Allegra for her creative input.

To the Writers' Colony at Dairy Hollow, Eureka Springs, Arkansas, for providing the seclusion to write.

To Tyson Foods for the 2000 Tyson Fellowship to the Writers' Colony at Dairy Hollow, Eureka Springs, Arkansas.

To the American Egg Board for the 2004 American Egg Board Fellowship to the Writers' Colony at Dairy Hollow, Eureka Springs, Arkansas.

To Dr. I. Bruce Turner for his support of my research, and for writing the foreword to this book.

Foreword

I am not a Cajun, but I have lived in Lafayette, Louisiana, the heart of Cajun Country, for over twenty years and have come to appreciate some things about the Cajun people. One of the core values of their lives is family. Until fairly recent times it was unusual for a Cajun to move far from his or her place of birth. Therefore several generations were in close proximity and interacted frequently. Grandparents and even great-grandparents took part in raising children. Fathers, sons, and sons-in-law worked together; mothers, daughters, and daughters-in-law engaged in domestic pursuits together. Families were so stable that if you knew a family name frequently you knew where they came from. The Vidrine and Fontenot families had their roots in St. Landry and Evangeline Parishes (counties); the Broussard family was from Iberia or Vermilion Parish; the Mouton and Arceneaux families from Lafayette Parish; the Durand and Breaux families from St. Martin Parish. Even with the greater mobility of recent generations and increasing geographic dispersion, family remains at the core of Cajun identity.

Although "Cajun" is a corruption of the word "Acadian"—and the people who came to Louisiana after being forced from their homes in Acadie (Nova Scotia) in 1755 are the start of the culture—many other ethnic groups have contributed. Many Louisiana settlers in the eighteenth and early nineteenth centuries came directly from France to the region now incorporated into Acadiana. At first they were royalist sympathizers escaping the turmoil of the French Revolution, which started in 1789. Later there were followers of Napoleon after his overthrow in 1815. Although separate from the Acadians at first, eventually both elements of French-speaking people melded as Cajuns. New Iberia was founded in the late eighteenth century by Spanish-speaking peoples from the Canary Islands (the Isleños). Germans came in both the eighteenth and nineteenth centuries. African Americans—both slaves and free—and Native Americans contributed to and intermingled with the growing Cajun culture. In the end there were Cajuns named Schexnayder, Waugenspack, Lopez, and Romero as well as Theriot, Declouet and Comeaux.

Other important elements of Cajun culture include the Catholic Church, music, and food. To a great extent these provide opportunities for family and friends to gather together. Church events were not only religious but also social in nature. Music was played at the often weekly dances held in private homes or neighborhood dance halls. Meals provided the opportunity for multigenerational families to come together for fellowship. In many instances these elements reinforced the importance of family to the Cajuns.

One previously important aspect of Cajun culture is dying—the French language. Until the early twentieth century the primary language of every Cajun was French. This began to change for many reasons. The increasing intrusion of Anglo culture through mass communication of radio and then television exposed Cajuns to an English-dominated society. In 1921 Louisiana prohibited the speaking of French at school—either in class or on the playground. Both students and teachers were punished for breaking this law. This led many French-speaking parents to stop using the language at home to help their children become fluent in English. (Cajuns who attended school in the 1920s and 1930s often understand Cajun French but cannot speak it fluently. Their children often have no French exposure at all.) World War II accelerated the decline of the French language. Many Cajuns left Louisiana, never to return. Others spent the war years submerged in an English-speaking society and learned to depend on that language. The growth of the oil industry in south Louisiana from the 1930s on brought many outsiders into the region. Cajuns employed in the petroleum industry had to use English. All these factors contributed to the decline of the French language. Few Cajun youths today can speak Cajun French.

Although modified, Cajun culture continues to survive. In the last twenty-five years both Cajun music and Cajun cuisine have enjoyed great national and even international popularity. This in itself has been a threat to the continuation of traditional practices. Music might be mixed with other genres or utilize other instruments. "Cajun" restaurants in Chicago or London might not follow traditional recipes at all but simply serve any dish spicy hot or blackened and call it "Cajun." Cultures evolve, but this should be done while building on traditional roots and values.

There is one aspect of this book upon which I must comment. The University Archives and Acadiana Manuscripts Collection at the University of Louisiana at Lafayette where I work has a collection of papers the author used extensively—the Theodore A. Labauve and Joseph L. Pischoff Families Papers. Both of these individuals figure prominently in this book. The collection contains personal and business correspondence of both men and their families, financial records, and photographs. The author has cited some of the letters in her text. She also had many of the photographs reproduced when she researched in the collection. Papers such as these are kept in archival repositories so they can be accessible to interested researchers and be preserved. Archivists and manuscript curators are very pleased when a collection in their repository is as helpful to a researcher as this one was to the author.

The author notes that when she and her sisters visited her great-uncle T. A. Labauve's abandoned store, they found many pieces of paper and even some old business ledgers that had been damaged or destroyed by neglect. These items were probably very similar to the materials in the collection at this repository. It is too bad that they were not donated as were the items we have, since they would then have been preserved for future researchers.

The author indirectly documents why research projects such as the one she undertook may be much more difficult if not impossible in the future. Paper documents can be placed in storage and donated to repositories long after they were created. As long as they were not damaged while stored, they can still be used by interested researchers. Benign neglect of paper does not destroy the information it contains. This is not true of information stored in new electronic technologies. E-mail, digital photographs, computer files, and other modern storage methods will be quickly unreadable unless conscious efforts are taken to preserve the information. Technology popular ten years ago often cannot be accessed today because hardware and software has changed so much. The author mentions her exchange of Christmas menus with a relative by e-mail. Unless intentional efforts are made to save that information and migrate it to new formats as technology changes, her grandchildren will never have access to that as she had access to her great-grandfather's letters. The instability of electronic storage devices has frightening implications for the long-term preservation and access of information saved today.

Finally, the author should be commended for dedicating a portion of the profits from the sale of this book to recovery efforts of archival repositories from the two hurricanes of 2005 that struck Louisiana—Katrina and Rita. They wrought a great deal of damage that is still a gaping wound in the fabric of the state. Many cultural institutions including archival repositories were severely impacted. It will take many years to accomplish a full recovery—if that is even possible.

—Dr. I. Bruce Turner
Head of Special Collections
University of Louisiana at Lafayette

Genealogy of the Labauve Family from 1815

Names in bold are featured in chapters in the book

Theodule C. Labauve 1815–1887 m. (1840) Marie Irma Labauve 1824–1899

Their child:

Theodore Stephen Labauve *(Great-Grandpa Theodore)* 1850–1933
m. (1875) Marie Clara Prevost *(Great-Grandma Clara)* 1857–1946

Their seven children:

T. A. *(Uncle Adolphe)*, 1877–1972
Joseph, 1879–1879
Irma, 1880–1967
Victoria, 1883–1965
Oreline, 1887–1975
Alice, 1890–1966

and my Grandmother, **Marie Olympe Labauve *(Grandma Olympe)* 1885–1953**
m. (1908) Joseph Laurent Pischoff *(Grandpa Pischoff)*, 1874–1964

Their three children who survived birth:

Marie Irma Lorna *(Aunt Lorna)*, 1908–1994 **Clothilda Rhea, 1911–1933**
and my father, Joseph Darrell *(Dad)*, 1910–1998
m. (1934) Wandah McDonald, 1910–1942

They had two children, my half sisters:

***Lorna*, b. 1936**
m. (1957) G. Neil Farr, b. 1932

they have three children

Clay, b. 1958; Jennifer, b. 1960; Thomas, b. 1962

and five grandchildren

Shannon, b. 1982; Sean, b. 1990; Olivia, b. 2001
Candace, b. 1984; Matt, b. 1994

***Bonnie*, b. 1940**
m. (1963) John Willacker, b. 1940

they have two children

Greg, b. 1965; Lorna Jean, b. 1967

and two grandchildren

Brett, b. 2002
Luke, b. 2004

Joseph Darrell, my father, married again in 1945 to
Mary Breda Griffin *(Mom)*, b. 1922

They had two children:

My brother
Lawrence Joseph Pischoff *(Linus)* b. 1946
m. (1990) Ying Ma (Jenny) b. 1954

They each have a child by a previous marriage:

Anita, b. 1978 **Benny, b. 1980**

Me
Diana Teresa (Terri) b. 1948
m. (1969) Richard Wuerthner, b. 1944

We have three children:

Michelle, b. 1970 **Dawn, b. 1973**
Diana, b. 1977
m. (2004) David Barclay, b. 1969

And three grandchildren:

Jordon Yorn, b. 1994 **Kyle Yorn, b. 1998**
Lily Barclay, b. 2005

I also wish to recognize the children of my father's sister, Marie Irma Lorna Haggerty. My Aunt Lorna and her children have been close to me all my life. Lorna married Joseph Francis Haggerty in 1939. They had two children: Eleanor Doris, 1940–2003, and Joseph Francis Jr. (Joe), b. 1944. Eleanor married Ron Bernard Code, b. 1937, in 1966. They had one child, Christine Patricia, b. 1971, and one grandchild, Derek Phipps, b. 2001. Joe married Diane Presley Furman, b. 1946, in 1983. They have one child, Joseph Francis III, b. 1987. They also have three children from Diane's previous marriage (Matthew Furman, Lana Furman, and Shelia Furman Hiltabiddle), and four grandchildren.

Marie Irma Lorna (Aunt Lorna), 1908–1994
m. (1939) Joseph Francis Haggerty, b. 1906

They had two children:

Eleanor Doris, b. 1940
m. (1966) Ron Bernard Code, b. 1937

they have one child

Christine Patricia, b. 1971

Joseph Francis Jr., b. 1944
m. (1983) Diane Presley Furman, b. 1946

they have four children

Matthew Furman, b. 1968; Lana Furman, b. 1971
Sheila Furman Hiltabiddle, b. 1973
Joseph Francis Haggerty III, b. 1987

Meet the Labauve Family

I know exactly why my father was drawn to San Francisco after he left his home in Louisiana. Within days of arriving in Palo Alto in 1932, he headed north to settle in the city by the Bay. It was more than curiosity; instinct pulled him up there. San Francisco was the bayou-country of the West. Its Fisherman's Wharf overflowed with crab, shrimp, and oysters like the ones Dad left behind in Louisiana. In Chinatown, he found streets lined with open-air fruit and vegetable stalls, an Asian version of the French Market in New Orleans. Cafés in North Beach served coffee made from beans roasted deeply enough to please even Dad, who was an avowed coffee aficionado and used to the brew being French-roasted, French-dripped, and sometimes chicory-infused.

Although my father's love affair with San Francisco began the day he arrived in town, he never forgot his Cajun roots. He instilled the importance of our ancestry in all four of his children. We were raised on stories about generations of our Cajun relatives and descriptions of Home Place, the farm that belonged to our Cajun family for more than 120 years. We heard tales of my father's tedious job of collecting crawfish from the bayou as a child, and of his work helping on the farm. Above all, we were enthralled by mouth-watering images of the food created in their Cajun kitchen.

Dad spoke of bowls of crab and sausage gumbo eaten on a blanket beneath the shade-offering pecan trees, Grandma Olympe's famous chicken étouffée for Sunday dinners, jambalaya rich with meat from the ducks that the eccentric uncles hunted (when they weren't in jail), and homemade vanilla ice cream churned beneath the jasmine-trellised porch on hot summer days. These were but a few of the enticements that sold us on Cajun food.

At home, in our San Francisco kitchen, we loved to spend time with our father and aunt, and with our Cajun grandparents when they visited. We were fascinated by the stories about food, cooking, and the people of Home Place. Cajun cooking techniques and ingredients were as important to us as our family and holiday traditions.

It was expected that my three siblings and I would stand by the stove, watching and learning how to blend roux to the correct nutty fragrance and chocolate color, drip the perfect pot of French roast coffee, and learn to take the prawns out of the boiling water the second they turned pink. Our father, aunt, and grandparents taught my generation the making of crawfish étouffée; rice dressing flecked with andouille; shrimp anything—always the adored shrimp; fricassees with gravies that transformed plain chicken or seafood into delicious entrées; and the proper roasting of pecans that filled the air with an almost burned, yet spicy and comforting aroma. These and dozens of other culinary practices and tricks were simply part of our everyday kitchen and dinner table experiences. The passage of the culinary heritage that began hundreds of years ago in France, and came down through Acadia to the Louisiana bayous, was the watering of our roots.

The recipes in this book are filled with history. Once in Cajun country, our ancestors' Acadian techniques and methods of cookery had to be adapted to the many unusual and sometimes strange foods that were available in their new homeland. Some recipes were developed to make use of a seasonal overabundance of pecans, okra, eggplant, tomatoes, and shellfish, for nothing was wasted in a Cajun kitchen: leftover rice or cornbread became dressing; extra bread was turned into bread pudding; the morning coffee that wasn't finished showed up in gravy, barbecue sauce, or bread. Many dishes were devised to stretch a small amount of food to feed a lot of people, such as jambalaya, which uses a pot full of rice, seasoning vegetables (onion, celery, bell pepper, and sometimes garlic, green onions, and parsley), and bits of whatever sausage, fish, or meat were on hand. Whatever the Cajuns made, the taste was memorable.

By the spring of 1992, my sisters and I, having heard it all and feeling a part of it all, wanted to experience native Cajun food and life for ourselves. So we traveled to Louisiana to trace our Cajun roots, to see the remains of Home Place, and to get in touch with all the things that had been a part of our father's life on the family farm.

Once there, I instantly fell in love: in love with the mysterious bayou behind Great-Uncle Adolphe's store; with the pecan trees that provided the nuts sent to us in California each winter; with the sweet, sensuous fragrance of gardenia and jasmine that once had perfumed the garden and house; with the gracious and warm people living on and near Home Place; and with the outstanding Cajun cuisine—familiar, yes, but somehow more authentic in the land of our ancestors.

Home Place was the farm our great-grandfather, Theodore Stephen Labauve, built as the wedding home for himself and his bride (our great-grandmother Marie Clara Prevost). This was home to their children and grandchildren, and the gathering place for dozens of nieces, nephews, cousins, and neighbors who came to know that farm as Home Place. I, too, felt immediately at home as I walked among the groves of now barren pecan and fig trees, through the old barns, cookhouse, honey house, and the store.

It was with awe that I stood in the Cajun kitchen I had been hearing about all my life. Seeing a slight sparkle under a dilapidated cabinet, I reached down and uncovered a small old olive oil jar. Knowing it had once been used in cooking by one of our ancestors, it seemed that the search for our culinary heritage had brought us right to the center of where it all began.

This dirt-encrusted jar was embossed with olive branches and the words "bon oil." Looking at the tiny bit of amber-colored liquid still clinging to the bottom of the jar, I felt a direct connection to the ancestor who had last used it. She had most certainly shared my love of cooking, and had once lifted the jar off the shelf to start a meal. What was she preparing to make as she carried this jar of oil to the cookhouse—an étouffée? Some gumbo? Who had been present to share the meal—Great-Grandma Clara? Great-Aunt Irma? My hands were shaking as I held this precious find that truly tied me to these people and their culinary skills, to one of the last meals they made in the farmhouse kitchen. This little forgotten jar was waiting in the deserted farmhouse for more than forty years to bridge the gap between my Cajun ancestors and me.

I knew then that I was part of that once lively kitchen; that I belonged there even though I was a bit late in arriving. Even more intense was the knowledge that I was part of those food lovers who had laboriously and happily prepared three meals a day in that very room, for generation after generation of Labauves.

Standing in the deserted kitchen, I felt intensely drawn to my Cajun roots, to the food I had been taking for granted all my life, and to the joy with which my fellow Cajuns prepared that food. I was so moved that I wanted to bring these people and their recipes to life in order to preserve their memory, their love of food, and their traditional, outstanding cooking. I knew the way to capture it all was in a book containing their recipes and stories. *In a Cajun Kitchen* is that book.

Glossary

Boudin: a fresh sausage with pork, rice, and seasonings, served warm and eaten by cutting one end off and squeezing the sausage out of the casing, as the filling is not firm enough to stand on its own, and the casing is too tough to eat. Boudin is a very popular snack, appetizer, or lunch dish.

Boulettes are made from meat or seafood, vegetables, and a binder of cooked rice, bread crumbs, or cornbread. They are formed into meatballs about 2½ inches across and either deep-fried, or browned and served in gravy (and then called meatball stew).

Chaurice is a flavorful sausage similar to the Spanish sausage chorizo.

Chicory: some Cajuns say that chicory in coffee is strictly for their New Orleans neighbors, and others swear it's not coffee without the slight bitterness of added chicory (the ground dried root of the chicory plant). My grandparents sometimes purchased coffee with chicory, and sometimes bought beans and roasted them at home. Either way, they made their coffee so strong that you could smell it through the entire house.

Corn flour, also known as fish fry, is made from cornmeal that is finely ground to the texture of flour (commercial fish fry is seasoned).

Courtbouillon (pronounced COO-be-yon) is a thick fish soup (or thin fish stew), sometimes started with a roux. It is served with bread rather than rice and seems to be a favorite of many Cajun people; it is the only dish for which my grandmother had two recipes.

Coush-coush is an old-fashioned dish, a cornbread batter cooked in a skillet with a small amount of fat until the bottom is crispy, then stirred and cooked until that bottom layer is crispy, and so on until all the batter is cooked and you have a pan full of crisp pieces of what is essentially fried cornbread. It is wonderful served hot, with cane syrup or jam, and a bit of milk or half-and-half drizzled on top.

Étouffée (pronounced A-2-fay, meaning smothered) is the cooking of a vegetable, poultry, fish, or meat without a roux, in a covered pot where it braises (is smothered in its own juices).

Filé powder is made by grinding the dried leaves of the sassafras tree. It is both a thickener and a seasoning that the Choctaw Indians taught the Cajuns how to use. My family had a sassafras tree and made their own filé powder.

Fricassee, or stew, contains meat, poultry, or seafood, the holy trinity of onion, celery, and bell pepper, and dark roux; it is served over rice.

Gumbo can be described as a thin stew or a thick soup, with a roux base and usually two or more types of meat, seafood, or poultry. It is served with rice and is thickened by the roux and either okra (okra gumbo) or filé powder (filé gumbo), and sometimes both. Some Cajuns say that since gumbo means okra in the African language, it is not a true gumbo without okra. Others disagree, but the bottom line is not to add filé (if you are using it) until serving time, preferably to individual portions, as it will become stringy or ropey if heated. We always make gumbo with roux, usually add okra, and have filé at the table for those who choose to sprinkle it on the gumbo (actually on the rice before the gumbo is ladled on top, for better mixing).

Holy trinity refers to the combination of onion, celery, and bell pepper that is the base of most savory dishes, along with roux (to which the holy trinity is added). Garlic is sometimes included with the holy trinity, and green onions and parsley are usually added to a dish during the last few minutes of cooking, or sprinkled on top at serving time.

Hush puppies are made from a thick cornbread mixture that is fried until crispy and golden brown on the outside. They may be served sweet, with some sugar in the mixture and cinnamon and sugar sprinkled over them, or as a savory dish with green onions, garlic, and spices in the batter.

Jambalaya is a rice-based dish with one or several main ingredients. Vegetables are browned, a seasoning meat is added (such as ham or sausage) along with the main ingredient(s), and then rice, parsley, stock, and spices are put in and cooked together until the rice is done. Jambalaya may also be prepared with cooked rice, making it an ideal way to use up leftovers by adding a bit of extra chicken or seafood, plus cooked seasoning vegetables, spices, and some stock to the rice.

LAGNIAPPE **Each recipe is followed by a lagniappe, which in southwest Louisiana means something extra, a thank-you or a bonus. My great-uncle would give adults who purchased something in his store one of the prized dried shrimp from the wooden barrel, and children would receive a piece of candy. Lagniappe, pronounced "lan-yap," in this book is extra information (about an ingredient, cooking method, or tool) relating to the recipe.**

Remoulade sauce is technically a New Orleans or Creole sauce, but it was very popular with my grandmother. I am including her handwritten recipe for Sauce Remoulade in this book. Hers is mayonnaise-based, with green onions and seasonings, and is usually served with seafood (but it's good with almost anything!). Remoulade can also be made like thick vinaigrette, with paprika, onion, celery, and parsley added, then used to dress shellfish or vegetables.

Rice dressings appear on the Cajun table almost as often as plain rice. The rice can be combined with vegetables, meat, poultry, or seafood. In the case of "dirty rice," organ meats are cooked with the holy trinity, then added to cooked rice (frozen dressing mix is available for purchase in Acadiana).

Roux: Fat and flour are cooked together until light brown (for a blond roux), medium brown (for a peanut butter roux), or dark brown (for a chocolate roux). More on roux on pages 11–13.

Sauce Piquante is an intensely seasoned, spicy stew with a roux base and tomatoes, served over rice. It is usually made from just one main ingredient. While chicken is possibly the best-known sauce piquante dish, it is also a popular way to prepare wild animals, as the strong flavors in the sauce mask the gamy taste of venison, alligator, rabbit, turtle, and frog.

Cajun Cookery

Joseph Pischoff and Olympe Labauve,
Lake Charles, Louisiana, 1920

A Love Affair with Food

Cajun Country is the southwest section of Louisiana, unique unto itself. The northern part of the state is considered to belong to the large region considered the American South and has much in common with the adjacent states of Mississippi, Arkansas, and Texas. Southwest Louisiana, on the other hand, is not thought of as being part of "the South," but geographically below it.

Acadiana, a combination of the words Acadia and Louisiana, is an area comprising twenty-two parishes (counties) in Southwest Louisiana. This area is predominately populated by Cajun people who are, technically, descendents of the Acadians expelled from Acadia, now known as Nova Scotia, in 1755. While their new home in Acadiana was familiar in terms of being an agrarian setting already populated by Catholic, French-speaking people, the Cajuns had to adjust to the unknown terrain of swamps, bayous, and prairies that presented exotic forms of meat, game, fish, produce, and grains.

The Cajuns applied their French cooking techniques to these new ingredients, with a result that is recognized and respected as one of the great regional cuisines of America, as well as one of the world's most unique cuisines. There are versions of Cajun dishes on restaurant menus across the country, from upscale to hip and trendy to fast-food establishments. Unfortunately, many of these restaurants misrepresent Cajun food by using their standard menu items and carelessly overspicing them, making the food unbearably hot, then calling it "Cajun." Cajun food and culture has little to do with the mass media hype of the past twenty years that presents Cajun cookery as fiery hot, and Cajun people as hot-pepper-eating, beer-swilling caricatures of themselves. Pepper and spices are merely one element of Cajun cookery, and not the most important one at that.

Cajuns in Southwest Louisiana have steadfastly adhered to the preservation of their habits, traditions, and beliefs in terms of lifestyle, language, and cooking. They became noticed by society during the oil boom, which brought many outlanders (non-Cajuns) into the area. These new residents began to discover the food-oriented, talented Cajun cooks whose lives and socializing revolve, to a large extent, around the preparation, sharing, and enjoyment of food. The word began to spread.

Cajun vs. Creole

Although Cajuns are descendents of French Acadians who were expelled from Acadia in

1755, many people were brought directly from France to South Louisiana when the Spanish were trying to populate the area. My seventh great-grandfather, Louis Noël Labauve, was one of the first settlers in Acadia, yet another branch of the Labauve family came directly from France and settled in the prairie area of South Louisiana. Many Acadiana residents whose ancestors were not from Acadia consider themselves to be Cajuns because they have lived in Cajun Country and followed a Cajun lifestyle for generations.

Whether technically Cajun or not, Cajun homes and kitchens are always open—open and ready to stretch the jambalaya by adding more rice, sausage or, perhaps, leftover meat from the previous night. It would be unfathomable for me not to offer food, or at least a beverage and snack, to anyone visiting our home. Southern hospitality is a way of life, not just an expression. My Cajun father carried this further than my mother would have liked, inviting anyone and everyone who stopped by our house from late afternoon on to have dinner with us. He greeted the men picking up the weekly garbage with a cup of coffee, and several of our friends in high school knew that the best time to come over was about six P.M. One of my brother's friends had dinner with us almost every Friday night all through high school, after realizing that if Grandpa Pischoff wasn't cooking Cajun food that night, Mom would be frying shrimp or catfish. This hospitality is typical of Cajun people.

The Cajun method of cooking had European origins, but had to be tailored to the foods in Louisiana. Like their Acadian ancestors, these French folks starting a new life accepted the challenge of the natural and abundant food resources available in their new homeland. The Cajun love of food and instinct for preparing it superbly gave birth to a new cuisine from the bounty of the water (crawfish, shrimp, crab, turtle, frog, catfish, trout, flounder, and alligator); sky (duck, pigeon, dove, grouse, turkey, and quail); land (beef, pork, possum, rabbit, raccoon, squirrel, and deer); and earth (okra, green onions, sweet bell peppers, greens, berries, beans, pumpkin, squash, watermelon, cherries, peaches, Muscadine grapes, pecans, rice, sweet potatoes, and corn).

Cajun food is the robust food of country people, not developed by chefs but by talented cooks who took the time to work out recipes that adapted their knowledge of cooking to the local ingredients. The food is always well seasoned and sometimes, but not necessarily, spicy. It is simple food, usually with roux as the base for savory dishes, and without the refinement of delicate butter or cream-enriched sauces.

The majority of Cajun dishes are one-pot meals, cooked for a long time until rich, thick gravies are naturally formed by the merging of the vegetables with the juices in the dish. While this merging of ingredients imparts a wonderful flavor and texture, the original reason for the slow cooking is that the housewife had to put dinner on to cook and leave it unsupervised while she was attending to the children, garden, livestock, weaving, soap making, and her many other duties.

What Is Cajun Cooking?

Cajun cooking has flavors that are intense but not necessarily hot. It uses ingredients that are readily available to most people (although substitutions may be necessary in the case of game and some shellfish).

A simplified description of any Cajun dish based on roux is to make the roux, add the holy trinity and cook for a few minutes, add the main ingredients and seasonings and cook for a few minutes, then add the liquid and cook for a long time over low heat. For a seafood dish, the fish is added at the end of the cooking process so it is not overcooked.

The holy trinity of Cajun cooking (the combination of onion, celery, and bell pepper) will be found in almost all savory Cajun dishes, sometimes accompanied by fresh garlic or garlic powder, and often finished with sliced green onions and chopped fresh parsley sprinkled on top of the dish just before serving.

Gumbo usually starts with a roux, and since the African word for gumbo is okra, it generally contains okra (though some Cajuns will argue this point). We always had filé powder at the table when we were having gumbo; as heat will make the filé stringy, it is added to individual servings just before eating. Roux, okra, and filé are all thickeners as well as flavoring elements.

Traditional, long-cooked Cajun dishes cannot be found on the grocer's shelf and are not usually seen on restaurant menus outside of Louisiana. Some Cajuns insist that the only real Cajun cooking is found in a Cajun home.

Garlic powder and onion powder are used in batters and on the outside of foods to be fried, as fresh chopped onions or garlic would burn at the high temperature needed for frying.

Stocks are dark and highly flavored.

Meats are seasoned before cooking.

In the past, flour was used mainly for roux and for occasional desserts or French bread, as wheat doesn't grow well in South Louisiana and wheat flour was therefore imported. Corn was the main grain for bread and cereal and is used in many delicious, inventive ways, including Lemon Cornmeal Pie, both savory and sweet Hush Puppies, Bacon Cornmeal Cakes, Coush-Coush, Breakfast Cornbread with Sausage and Apples, and Cornbread-Andouille Dressing. All these recipes are in this book.

Francis Bodin, a lifelong neighbor of our Louisiana family and of Home Place, told me that hot pepper sauce is an important seasoning in that area of South Louisiana, and each family has their own secret recipe, which they don't usually share. He did reveal that his family makes their hot pepper sauce with vinegar, salt, and chiles; the chiles could be just one type, or several chiles mixed together. This is actually a homemade version of the Tabasco sauce that has been made on Avery Island by the McIlhenny family since 1868.

Boneless, skinless chicken breasts aren't ordinarily used in traditional Cajun cooking, as dark meat and meat on the bones are more flavorful. Stews and soups are almost always cooked with a cut-up chicken, leaving the bones in and skin on. My dad did sometimes cook with boneless, skinless chicken breasts. A few persnickety kids (not me!) didn't like the skin and bones floating in their gumbo or stew, so dad would make two batches of whatever dish he was preparing: one for the fussy kids using the white meat, and one with the legs, thighs, and wings for the "real Cajun gumbo or stew." What Cajuns want from their food is flavor, and if that means loose skin and bones in a soup or stew, it isn't even an issue—flavor won't be sacrificed for convenience or aesthetics.

Green onions and parsley are usually sprinkled on, or stirred into, savory dishes just before serving. We have always used curly parsley, although flat-leaf parsley is currently in favor, as some people feel it has more flavor. I don't agree. To me, curly parsley has more flavor and a better texture than the flat-leaf (Italian) variety. I don't remember my grandparents or Dad ever using flat-leaf parsley.

Cajuns don't worry if the sauce slathered on food is messy, or if the crab in the soup is unshelled. They have no problem with removing shells from prawns or crawfish at the table, or eating fried chicken with their fingers. Food is meant to be savored, and if the best way to enjoy something is to cook it in the shell or on the bone, then bring it to the table that way and use your fingers to eat it.

Cajuns are very thrifty people. Leftover bread becomes bread pudding or dressing; extra rice is used with gumbo or jambalaya, or made into rice pudding; vegetable scraps and poultry, meat, or fish carcasses give flavor to stock; and fat from pork, chicken, and duck is rendered and saved to be used in a variety of ways. Even leftover coffee is used in gravy, barbecue sauce, or bread. (See Sources, page 267, for how to order Crazy Charley's Barbecue Sauce—the best I've ever tasted, a century-old recipe developed so the leftover coffee wouldn't be thrown out.)

Shortcuts are rare in traditional Cajun cookery, since long cooking gives the dishes their characteristic flavor. Meats and vegetables are usually cooked until the vegetables begin to break down and form their own thick base. A light roux takes at least ten minutes, and a dark roux takes at least thirty minutes, and up to an hour, depending on the thickness of the pan used and the heat under it—rushing it simply will not give the same result.

A Cajun meal usually has a main dish, rice (or cornbread), and whatever vegetable is in season.

As the recipes in this book are authentic, lard and salt pork are sometimes used. The reader may substitute oil, and the recipe will still work and be delicious, though not quite the same. Some people who are watching their diets feel it's better to have a small portion of the "real thing" rather than compromise the recipe. A small portion of something wonderful may be more satisfying than a large portion of a reduced fat or reduced sugar version of the same dish.

Basics

There are three types of Cajun cooking as I see it: traditional (as in this book); shortcut Cajun cooking that came about when prepared foods such as canned soups and sauces and roux in a jar became readily available; and contemporary celebrity chef recipes that are creative and wonderful but are not necessarily the traditional recipes that are presented here.

The Cajuns are adaptive people who were spread out in different terrains from the beginning of their settling in Louisiana. Some lived near the Gulf and had access to a large assortment of fish, while others lived in the prairie areas and relied more on chicken, pork, beef, and wild animals such as squirrel, rabbit, and duck. So even among Cajun people, the dishes varied according to what was available. The people on the prairies had cattle, and were able to get milk and cream, and thus butter, while other areas didn't have an environment that was conducive to raising cattle, and milk wasn't used in their cookery. The Cajuns who had cows would enjoy cream and butter but did not necessarily extend the use of milk into making cheese, sour cream, or other dairy products. Milk wasn't incorporated into soups, chowders, or sauces, and a glass of milk was not a common drink. Dad always enjoyed a glass of buttermilk but continued to be disappointed that the commercially produced buttermilk didn't compare to the liquid that was left after he used to churn the butter.

In Cajun cooking, most dishes that are not desserts or baked items have two distinct elements: 1) you make a roux, and 2) you add the holy trinity of celery, onion, and bell pepper (and sometimes garlic). It is important in this style of preparing food that the flavor of the main ingredient predominate. No single seasoning should stand out, but all elements should enhance the dish as a whole. While chiles are sometimes used, they are intended to bring out the goodness of the other ingredients, never to overpower a dish with heat.

The belief that Cajun food is always hot is unfortunate, as it deters many people from enjoying one of the world's most flavorful cuisines. A recipe cannot become Cajun by being sprinkled with peppery spices, or with mild spices, or "Cajun blend" spices, for that matter.

Traditional Cajun cooking uses ground red cayenne, black and white pepper, and chiles as its main sources of heat, with hot pepper sauce added when vinegar is a desired element. We always had black pepper, white pepper, cayenne pepper, and Tabasco sauce on the table and at the stove. They were the source of spiciness.

Another misconception is that blackened food is Cajun food. The high-heat frying of food that is coated with spices, when properly cooked, produces a wonderful tender interior with a beautiful dark, crispy crust. However, it is not a traditional Cajun dish. This process requires specific techniques that are often not adhered to by chefs in restaurants, who are harried or untrained in blackening food. This results in an overcooked or even burnt product that, like the overspicing, gives Cajun food a bad name.

Cajuns season their savory dishes more with vegetables than with herbs and spices, almost always using the holy trinity. Green bell pepper, celery, parsley, green onions, onions, and garlic are found in most savory dishes, along with salt and pepper, cayenne pepper, and perhaps thyme and bay leaves. Cajuns love to stuff vegetables and other foods—roasts with seasoned slivers of garlic;

stuffed eggplant, bell peppers, mirliton, and tomatoes; stuffed crabs; even crawfish-stuffed crawfish heads.

Cajuns used to rely on the environment for their food the way people now rely on their local market for food. Yet, even with reliance on markets in this busy and changing culture, Cajun people are still very much connected to the land. Hunting and fishing were, and still are, an important part of Cajun culture and life, and most Cajun men regularly hunt for wild game and poultry, and fish for freshwater fish as well as gathering their own crawfish, crabs, and shrimp. Early in the twentieth century, my Cajun relatives in Louisiana sometimes purchased canned tomato juice, wheat flour, lard, coffee beans, and dried shrimp from the store, and occasionally, canned cherries, evaporated milk, cocoa powder, and flavored gelatin for special desserts. I don't see evidence of any other purchased items from the recipes that have been handed down to me; everything else they grew, raised, gathered, or hunted.

What's in a Cajun Pantry?

The Cajun pantry contains surprisingly few things that are not found in everyone's pantry. I realized this several years ago when I was at a writers' colony that is equipped with a kitchen, so that food writers can test the recipes that are an integral part of their work. I was preparing to test several recipes and began to make out my shopping list:

Salt, black pepper, oil, lard, rice, and flour were in the cupboard, and it quickly became apparent that the remainder of what I needed consisted of a large amount of only a few items:

Onion, celery, bell pepper, garlic, green onions, parsley, bay leaves, thyme, stock, cayenne pepper, chicken for Chicken Fricassee.

Green onions, parsley, thyme, bay leaves stock, white pepper, crawfish, for Crawfish Stew.

Onion, celery, bell pepper, garlic, green onions, parsley, stock, thyme, tomato paste, bay leaves, cayenne pepper, ham, for Ham and Shrimp Jambalaya.

Garlic, bay leaves, thyme, black pepper, turnips, duck for Braised Duck.

Andouille Sausage: A flavorful dried, smoked pork sausage used more as a flavoring ingredient (in gumbo, jambalaya, etc.) than by itself, although sliced andouille makes a good appetizer or snack. Substitute any spicy smoked sausage (see Sources, page 267). Can keep in freezer.

Beans: dried red beans and white beans are staples in a Cajun kitchen, along with a few cans of beans for emergencies. We also always have black-eyed peas.

Cane syrup is a dark, flavorful syrup made from sugarcane by Steen's, in Abbeville, Louisiana—sugarcane country. You can order Steen's syrup (see Sources, page

267), but for something similar in a pinch, you may substitute 3 parts dark corn syrup to 1 part molasses.

Cornmeal is dried, ground corn that is available in white or yellow cornmeal, which are interchangeable, the only differences being the color and the fact that yellow cornmeal has a bit more flavor.

Dried shrimp are very much a part of our family cooking. Great-Uncle Adolphe ran a country store that always had a huge barrel full of large dried shrimp, so it figured in many of our dishes. (See Sources, page 267, for ordering from the same company my great-uncle ordered from in the 1930s, Blum & Bergeron.)

Fats:

Corn oil for frying and roux (vegetable or peanut oil may also be used).

Butter, vegetable shortening, or lard for baked goods and desserts.

For those of you who scoff at using lard, please note that per tablespoon lard has less saturated fat than butter (5 g in lard; 7 g in butter); less cholesterol than butter (10 mg in lard; 30 mg in butter); less sodium than butter (0 mg in lard; 90 mg in butter). To present the whole picture, 1 tablespoon of lard has 20 more calories than butter and 2 grams more total fat—but lard is lower in saturated fat, which is the type of fat to avoid. Additionally, lard offers more flavor when frying, and fabulous texture in baked goods.

Flour: All-purpose white flour is the only type needed.

Grits are made from ground hominy, which is corn that has been dried, and from which the hull and germ have been removed, either mechanically or by soaking in lime or lye. The difference between cornmeal and grits is that cornmeal is finely ground and grits are coarsely ground. *Instant grits* are very finely ground and not recommended; *quick grits* are more coarsely ground than instant and are the only type available in many markets. With apologies to my southern cousins who prefer slow-cooking grits, the quick varieties are used in the dishes in this book to make the ingredients accessible to all readers. *Old-fashioned grits* and *stone-ground grits* are for the grits connoisseur. They take up to an hour to cook, as the germ of the corn has not been removed; they have more flavor and texture.

Herbs and spices, dried: basil, bay leaves, black pepper, celery seed, crushed red pepper, cumin, dried mustard, filé powder, garlic powder, onion powder, marjoram, oregano, paprika, poultry seasoning, cayenne (red) pepper, rosemary, salt, thyme, white pepper. (By using cumin, dried mustard, marjoram, poultry seasoning, and rosemary you can make all the seasoning blends at the end of this chapter, saving the cost of purchasing expensive seasoning blends at the market.)

Hot sauce: We've always used McIlhenny Tabasco sauce. Grandpa Pischoff used to go duck hunting with E. A. "Ned" McIlhenny (the great-uncle of Paul MacIlhenny, the president and CEO of McIhenny Company). Perhaps that was why only McIlhenny Tabasco sauce made its way to our table, but I don't think Grandpa even knew there was another brand.

Mustard: Use a stone-ground mustard, Cajun or Creole preferred. Creole mustard has whole seeds that are marinated in wine before the mustard is made.

Oysters in a jar are acceptable substitutes when fresh, unshelled oysters aren't available. They are sold in the fresh seafood section of the market. Check the date, as oysters should be as fresh as possible. Small oysters are much preferred to medium or large oysters for cooking, as they don't have to be cut up. Your seafood vendor should be able to order fresh oysters in a jar, if they don't carry them.

Produce: In addition to produce items already mentioned, okra and corn freeze reasonably well, so when they are out of season, keep a supply in the freezer. Whole okra is better after freezing than sliced okra, and corn both on and off the cob is good to have around in case you get the urge for a crawfish or shrimp boil with corn on the cob.

Rice: Some Cajuns like long-grain rice, as the grains stay a bit more separate, but many use medium-grain rice. Short-grain rice is preferred by some for jambalaya as the grains are stickier, but I think short-grain rice makes a heavy jambalaya. Whichever you choose, keep lots of it on hand if you plan to cook Cajun—most Cajuns eat rice at least once a day.

Seafood boil for crab, shrimp, or crawfish comes packaged and is sold in the spice section of the market. You may also use the recipe for Shrimp Boil in this book (see page 130) and save money by making your own simple blend.

Shellfish: I beg the indulgence of those people residing in South Louisiana or on the Pacific, Atlantic, or Gulf coasts who are fortunate enough to have easy access to shellfish. I know y'all would never use frozen crab, shrimp, or crawfish, but many people around the country don't have access to your wonderful fresh seafood. So I offer the possibility of keeping frozen crabmeat, crawfish tail meat, and shrimp on hand (not the very small shrimp, though, as they always seem freezer burned). The key is to buy from a reputable source that carefully ships the shellfish—whether fresh or frozen—packed with ice (see Sources, page 267).

Crab: There are sources for crabmeat that is canned almost immediately after it is caught and, while it is not as good as fresh, it is very good quality. It's usually sold in 1-pound cans and has a refrigerator shelf life of several months. Blue crabs are the specialty of Louisiana and may be ordered.

Crawfish: Crawfish tail meat is packed in 1-pound bags for the freezer and includes the "butter" or fat that is an important part of the flavor. Whole crawfish, either live or frozen, are also available. I suggest avoiding crawfish from Asia, as the flavor is not the same as that from our own crawfish state, Louisiana.

Shrimp: Shrimp is readily available without special ordering from Louisiana. Shrimp is sold by the number per pound: 40/50 per pound; 21/30 per pound; 16/20 per pound, and so on. Prawn is a Yankee word and not used in Louisiana, where there are small shrimp, medium shrimp, and large shrimp.

Smoked ham is used as a flavoring ingredient as well as a supplemental ingredient in dishes such as jambalaya. It keeps a long time in the refrigerator, and you can keep it in the freezer if necessary, but the texture will suffer.

Stock (broth): If you don't make your own stocks (stock is sold as "broth" in the market), purchase good-quality canned or paste broth to have on hand. If you can't find low-sodium broth, use caution in adding salt to the dish until you taste it, as purchased broth can be very salty.

Tasso: Intensely flavored smoked pork (or sometimes beef), used as a seasoning. There is no close substitute, but smoked ham and increased seasonings in a recipe may be used for a similar result. Can keep in freezer.

Tomato paste: A concentrate used for thickening and flavoring.

Tomatoes: One of the few canned staples used in Cajun cooking. Out of season tomatoes don't have much flavor, so if you don't can your own tomatoes, a good-quality canned variety is preferable to the out-of-season "fresh" tomatoes sold in the market.

Basics of Everyday Cajun Cooking

I could tell you how to make roux in a couple of sentences, or I could write a book about it. I'll try to stay somewhere in between, but first some facts.

Roux is such an important element of Cajun cooking that when anyone asks a Cajun for a nondessert recipe it almost always begins with, "first you make a roux."

In brief, roux is a blend of fat and flour, cooked over low heat until it gets to a degree of brown (from blond to peanut butter to chocolate). The darker the roux, the more intense the flavor, the longer it takes to cook, and the less thickening power it has. Since a dark roux has less thickening power than a light or medium roux, if both a thick gravy *and* a dark roux are desired, start with 4 parts flour to 3 parts oil.

Traditionally, lard was used to make roux for two reasons: first, nothing is wasted in a Cajun kitchen, and lard was considered a perfectly good food that was left after a pig was prepared for the winter meals. Why discard one fat and use another? Second, lard adds a wonderful flavor to both savory and sweet foods. (See page 9 for the nutritional comparison of lard and butter. Lard is lower in both saturated fat and cholesterol.)

The majority of people seem to use half fat (whether oil or lard) and half flour. My family uses more flour in most recipes, because we like thicker gravies (sauces are French; gravies are Cajun). Butter is not used for roux, as it would burn during the long time it takes to brown the flour to a dark color. Butter and flour are the base of French sauces, while oil (or lard) and flour are the base of Cajun gravies.

Fat drippings (from roasted meat and poultry and from frying bacon) were strained and saved in a covered can in a cool place or in the refrigerator. This was considered a food, and one that lent a particular character to whatever dishes were made from it including roux, sauces, and almost any savory dish that needed fat for cooking and flavor. Each Cajun woman's cooking was distinctive in relation to the type of fats she used and saved, which is the core of what gave a unique flavor to her recipes.

Since roux takes from 20 minutes to 1 hour to cook, stirring constantly, many people make up a large batch of roux and keep it in the refrigerator or freezer. If you make roux ahead, these are the proportions you will end up with:

3 cups oil + 3 cups flour = 3⅔ cups roux
1 cup oil + 1 cup flour = 1 cup plus 3 tablespoons roux

If a recipe calls for a roux made with ½ cup oil and ½ cup flour, use ½ cup of prepared roux (stir before using), or the amount of flour called for in the recipe.

When asked how long it takes to make a roux, a Cajun has one of two answers: as long as it takes to drink a six-pack of beer, or, as long as it takes to brew and drink a pot of coffee. While these answers are humorous, they are not helpful. Cooks vary greatly in their estimate of how long to cook a roux, but my guideline is:

Cast iron pan	Non–cast iron pan	for a:
20 minutes	30 minutes	blond-colored roux
30 minutes	45 minutes	peanut butter roux
45 minutes	60 minutes	chocolate roux

There are variables such as how hot your pan is when you start, and the heat throughout the cooking process. The cooking heat in turn depends not just on the numbered setting of the dial, but the accuracy of the burner and the thickness of your pan. I suggest using a cast iron skillet, or your heaviest skillet, and timing how long it takes you to make a light, medium, and dark roux, then use that same pan each time, thereby knowing in future just how long it will take you to make a roux in your pan and on your stovetop.

The majority of savory dishes start with a roux: gumbos, fricassees, stews, courtbouillon, and sauce piquante. Vegetables can be sautéed in roux (to bring out the flavor and add thickness), before being added to a soup or stew. Only an étouffée is cooked without a roux, although as in all Cajun dishes, some people will disagree about étouffée and say they use a roux when making it. By definition, étouffée is made without a roux and the food is "smothered in its own juices."

Roux

This recipe for roux gives tips on what to look for as the roux progresses through the cooking stages. Refer to this, if desired, when making the roux within individual recipes. Heating the pan for 2 minutes, then heating the oil for 2 minutes, is key to the roux darkening in the prescribed amount of time. Note: If you are not using a heavy skillet or Dutch oven, you may need to start the roux over medium-low heat. ***Makes about 1 cup roux***

¾ cup corn oil or lard
1 cup all-purpose flour

Heat a heavy Dutch oven or large skillet (preferably cast iron) over medium heat for about 2 minutes. Add the oil and heat for 2 minutes. Add the flour all at once and whisk or stir constantly to combine the oil and flour. When combined, **reduce heat to low** and stir or whisk constantly until roux is desired color:

Cast iron pan	Non–cast iron pan	for a:
10 minutes	20 minutes	blond-colored roux (light)
20 minutes	30 minutes	peanut butter roux (medium)
30 minutes	40 minutes	chocolate roux (dark)

When the roux reaches the desired color, immediately transfer to a large plastic or glass (not steel) bowl to stop the cooking process, stirring until the roux cools down. Be very careful as the roux is very, very hot.

LAGNIAPPE Here is what to look for when cooking the roux:

After a few minutes the roux may become foamy, and stay that way for several minutes. After about 10 minutes the roux will become darker and have a nutlike fragrance. After about 20 minutes, watch extra carefully, as the roux begins to cook faster and can burn at this point; adjust the heat lower if necessary.

Roux cannot be rushed. Turning the heat higher than suggested above will just burn the roux, and you will have dark brown specks of burned roux that will make it scorched and inedible.

In spite of all the above information, making roux is not really difficult if you are armed with the facts. The main thing to remember is to keep the heat low and stir constantly.

The darker the roux the more flavor, but the less thickening power.

I like to use a metal spatula to stir the roux, as it covers so much more surface on the bottom of the pan than a spoon.

Seasoning Blends

These are not really a part of traditional Cajun cooking, as specific spices and herbs are added to each individual recipe while that particular dish is being prepared and cooked. Yet, commercial blends of spices and/or herbs have become popular in the past few decades and can be convenient. There are times when I'm grilling a piece of fish, frying a pork or lamb chop, roasting some beef, barbecuing a chicken, or preparing a salad or vegetables when I want to grab an all-in-one seasoning, either bland or spicy, rather than pulling half a dozen jars out of the spice rack.

So I developed two seasoning salts (mild and spicy), and four seasoning blends containing herbs and spices to complement poultry, seafood, beef and game, and pork and lamb. The recipes are easily made for a fraction of the cost of purchasing similar seasoning salts and seasoning blends at the market.

Be sure to purchase herbs and spices in small quantities so they are replenished periodically, as they lose their flavor after a few months. If you only have an old jar of an herb you need to use, then use a bit extra to compensate for lost flavor. Rub dried herbs between your fingertips, or briefly crush with a mortar and pestle, to release more flavor.

Everyday Seasoning Salt

When I realized that so many of our family recipes called for the ingredients in the list below, I decided to make up this seasoning salt so I didn't have to get out all five of the spices when I was in the middle of cooking. It's good sprinkled on salads, vegetables, or almost any savory dish. I think of it as "fast food" seasoning, because it's the only spice I need when I'm in a hurry. Any herbs may be added to a dish along with the seasoning salt. Do be aware that it is a salt, with seasoning, so don't overdo or you will oversalt your dish. ***Makes about 2½ cups***

1½ cups salt
½ cup onion powder
⅓ cup garlic powder
2 tablespoons white pepper
1 tablespoon celery seed

Combine all ingredients and store in an airtight container in a cool dark place for up to 6 months.

LAGNIAPPE This is an everyday seasoning that goes with almost everything savory—no spices or herbs to slant it toward one type of food or another. I use this so often I make it up in large batches. It's important to store seasoning salts and spice blends in an airtight container, as moisture can make them harden into a clump. If this happens the mixture is still good, you just have to scrape or grate it to break it up. As with all the seasoning and spice blends in this book, you may reduce the amount of pepper if you prefer a milder flavor.

Rice

There are many different ways that Cajuns, and non-Cajuns for that matter, cook rice, and most of those methods are more complicated than necessary, in my opinion. Various procedures involve having the water up to the first joint of your index finger (but what if a person has very long fingernails?); boiling rice and water and getting them to the same level (the timing of this will vary, however, depending on whether the saucepan is small and high, or flat and round); and the ultimate time-wasting method to this cook, who doesn't take any unnecessary steps in the kitchen, is to partly cook the rice, remove it from the pan, then transfer it to a strainer over a pot of boiling water to steam until it is done.

My tried and true way of cooking rice seems to turn out just right every time, and it is the easiest method possible. My grandfather taught me to cook it this way, so I don't claim any credit for its success, but try it for yourself.

Grandpa made rice almost every day of his life, and always made it according to this method. He liked long-grain rice, as the grains stayed more separate, but many Cajuns like medium-grain rice; both cook in the same amount of time.

Makes about 3 cups

1 cup rice
1¾ cups water
¼ teaspoon salt

Place the rice, water, and salt in a medium saucepan, stir, and put a tight-fitting lid on the pan.

Place over high heat and bring to a boil (when it comes to a boil, you will see steam begin to escape, and the lid will rattle a bit—don't lift the lid). Immediately turn the heat down to the lowest setting, and set the timer for 15 minutes. *Do not remove the lid from the pan at any point.*

After 15 minutes, remove the rice from the heat, remove the lid, and gently stir. If it's still a bit too moist put it back on the heat, covered, for another 2 minutes. Rice will stay warm in the covered pan, off the hot burner, for about 20 minutes.

LAGNIAPPE **Brown and wild rice take longer than 15 to 17 minutes to cook; check package directions for time, and cook as above for the suggested length of cooking time and water for each particular variety.**

Seasoning Blend for Beef and Game

Beef wasn't eaten as much on our farm at Home Place as chicken, fish, and game were, though they did have cattle grazing in the orchard. My ancestors consumed beef often enough that there were several beef recipes passed down to me. The most frequent game seems to have been venison, and mallard and teal ducks. Mallards are larger and fattier than teals, but both are very flavorful. Turtle, frog, squirrel, and rabbit are also frequently found on the Cajun dinner table, but I didn't inherit any recipes for these foods. The bold spices in this blend, such as dry mustard and filé powder, stand up to the strong flavors of beef and game.
Makes about 1½ cups

3 tablespoons salt
2 tablespoons white pepper
2 tablespoons dry mustard
2 tablespoons onion powder
1½ tablespoons garlic powder
1 tablespoon black pepper
1 tablespoon paprika
1 tablespoon dried oregano
2 teaspoons dried basil
1½ teaspoons filé powder
½ teaspoon cayenne pepper

Combine all ingredients and store in an airtight container in a cool dark place for up to 6 months.

LAGNIAPPE **Although mallard ducks are now farm raised in some areas, they are very expensive at the supermarket—at least at my markets. If you don't have a hunter in your family, try an Asian market for ducks, as they are a common food in Asian cooking and so are priced much more reasonably than ducks sold elsewhere. As with all the seasoning and spice blends in this book, you may reduce the amount of pepper if you prefer a milder flavor.**

Seasoning Blend for Pork and Lamb

Lamb is a young sheep that is less than a year old. At this age it is tender and mild in flavor, as opposed to mutton, which is older and can be tough and strong in flavor. My Irish mother served lamb at least once a week, but Dad didn't like to eat it unless it was loaded with slivers of garlic and rubbed with the following seasonings.

Makes about 1 cup

6 tablespoons onion powder
2 tablespoons black pepper
2 tablespoons celery seed
2 tablespoons dried thyme
2 tablespoons salt
1 tablespoon garlic powder
1 tablespoon dried rosemary
1 teaspoon cayenne pepper

Combine all the ingredients and store in an airtight container in a cool dark place for up to 6 months.

LAGNIAPPE **This makes a great dry rub on the outside of a roast. If you use this mainly for lamb, you might want to substitute 2 tablespoons dried mint for the dried thyme. Mint is one of the few herbs that comes very close to the flavor of the fresh version, once it is added to a dish and reconstituted. As with all the seasoning and spice blends in this book, you may reduce the amount of pepper if you prefer a milder flavor.**

Seasoning Blend for Poultry

Chicken and turkey were the primary forms of poultry enjoyed at Home Place, other than ducks, for which I suggest the beef and game seasoning blend. When roasting a chicken or turkey, we always put some of this seasoning inside the bird and between the skin and the breast meat, as well as liberally coating the outside of the bird with the blend. It gives a wonderful color to the skin, in addition to the flavor it imparts to the flesh. ***Makes about 1⅓ cups***

½ cup salt
⅓ cup paprika
¼ cup onion powder
2 tablespoons garlic powder
2 tablespoons dried marjoram
2 tablespoons dried basil
2 teaspoons poultry seasoning
1 teaspoon black pepper
1 teaspoon white pepper
½ teaspoon cayenne pepper

Combine all the ingredients and store in an airtight container in a cool dark place for up to 6 months.

LAGNIAPPE **You can adjust the seasoning blend according to the other dishes you usually serve with poultry: for example, if oregano and rosemary are the herbs most often used in your side dishes, you may substitute them for the marjoram and basil. Other seasonings may be used along with the spice blends: if lemon or orange are components in the rest of the meal, add some lemon or orange zest to the seasoning blend, and place lemon or orange slices in the cavity of the bird. As with all the seasoning and spice blends in this book, you may reduce the amount of pepper if you prefer a milder flavor.**

Seasoning Blend for Seafood

A light dusting with this seasoning blend and a quick sauté in a frying pan is all you need for a fast and delicious fish dinner. Grandpa Pischoff would sometimes add these same spices to flour (although he didn't make up a seasoning blend ahead of time), then dip the fish in the seasoned flour before frying. For a quick dip or sauce, add a bit of this blend to mayonnaise, melted butter, or olive oil. ***Makes about 1 cup***

½ cup garlic powder
¼ cup salt
2 tablespoons black pepper
1 tablespoon cayenne pepper
2 teaspoons white pepper
2 teaspoons dried marjoram
2 teaspoons dried thyme
2 teaspoons dry mustard

Combine all the ingredients and store in an airtight container in a cool dark place for up to 6 months.

LAGNIAPPE **This seasoning blend may be sprinkled on fish before cooking but should not sit for more than 20 minutes for delicate fillets or 40 minutes for thick, firm fish, as the spices will overpower the flavor of the fish if left on too long. Whether with a dry rub like this one, or a liquid marinade, fish should be kept covered and under refrigeration while marinating. As with all the seasoning and spice blends in this book, you may reduce the amount of pepper if you prefer a milder flavor.**

Spicy Seasoning Salt

Salt and black, white, and cayenne pepper were used in abundance by Grandpa Pischoff whenever his daughter-in-law wasn't in the kitchen. She did not like food that was very spicy, and believed that Grandpa shouldn't have salt or lots of pepper (perhaps she was right—he died when he was ninety-three years of age; maybe it was the salt and spices that did him in). ***Makes about 1½ cups***

1 cup salt
3 tablespoons garlic powder
3 tablespoons paprika
2 tablespoons onion powder
1½ tablespoons dried basil
1½ tablespoons dried oregano
2 teaspoons black pepper
2 teaspoons cayenne pepper
1 teaspoon ground cumin
1 teaspoon white pepper
1 teaspoon crushed red pepper

Combine all ingredients and store in an airtight container in a cool dark place for up to 6 months.

LAGNIAPPE **This seasoning salt gives a real kick to anything it touches. If you don't like spicy food use it sparingly, though using just a bit of it will add a wonderful flavor without adding too much heat. Do be aware that it is a salt, with seasoning—so don't overdo or you will oversalt your dish. As with all the seasoning and spice blends in this book, you may reduce the amount of pepper if you prefer a milder flavor.**

Gumbo and Soup

Rhea, Darrell, and Lorna Pischoff,
Lake Charles, Louisiana, 1920

Great-Grandma Marie Clara: Life on a Cajun Farm and the Beginning of Home Place

It was spring of 1875, and the Ashton farm was stunningly beautiful. Handsome young Theodore Stephen Labauve had cultivated the property and built a farmhouse in anticipation of finding a wife. As was common at that time, he was to meet his future bride, Clara Prevost, at a dance. It may have been a **fais do do** *(a dance in a community hall), or a* **bal de maison** *(a dance held in a private house), and certainly it was held near the Prevost home on the banks of the Bayou Teche.*

Clara's great-great-grandfather, François Prevost, was considered the "Father of the modern town of New Iberia," according to the Acadian historian Glenn Conrad. However, the Prevosts had moved to Charenton by the time Clara was born, and she and her twelve siblings were raised there by their parents, Joseph Alcée Prevost and Marie Rodrigues Prevost. The family owned a plantation where, before the Civil War, the male family members worked the land alongside their slaves. The Prevost slaves chose to stay with the family after being freed.

When Clara turned thirteen, she became eligible for courtship. Sometimes a young girl's father whitewashed the chimney of the family home to let the community know he had a daughter of marriageable age. With the Prevost family, however, courtship began at a dance. It was time for Clara to do some serious looking: nearing the age of eighteen she was on her way to becoming **une vieille fille** *(an old maid). Clara and her younger sister Josephine were escorted to dances by their brother Anatole, with the younger children attending as a family group. These were social occasions enjoyed by young and old alike, even though a major purpose was to provide a meeting place for young men and women who had thoughts of finding a spouse.*

Balls or dances were held frequently, almost every Saturday night, and often didn't end until early Sunday morning. Cajuns have always loved music and dancing, and local musical talent was plentiful. Children, grandparents, and everyone in between participated in the festivities, which were announced by a messenger on horseback who went from farm to farm, fired a gun, and declared, **"bal ce soir chez,"** inviting all members of the household to the dance or ball.

We do know from ball gowns found in a trunk in her attic that our great-grandmother Clara had attended more than one ball during her courting years. As a little girl, my sister Lorna braved the side entryway of the Ashton farmhouse, which was full of noisy, pecking chickens, and tiptoed up the short, steep staircase to the attic. The attic and its contents were supposed to be strictly off limits to children.

Once upstairs she spied, and gingerly opened, a massive trunk, pulling out a dress that seemed straight from **Gone with the Wind**. She describes the dress as "an unbelievably beautiful, jade green, watermarked silk taffeta gown with a billowing skirt and fine, fine netting used as flounces on the sleeves. The netting edges were finished with tiny sparkling green beads." She also pulled out a black taffeta dress with a higher cut neckline and a similar full floor-length skirt but it could not compete with the exquisite green ball gown. The trunk was deep, and if there were other treasures to be found there we will never know, because, frightened by her own disobedience, Lorna pushed the dresses back into the trunk, closed the lid, and ran downstairs.

The dance at which our great-grandparents met was in 1874. During their courtship Theodore and Clara were not left alone, even on the front porch swing, until he officially visited the family home and asked her father for her hand in marriage. This ritual traditionally was carried out on Thursday nights. I have a note written in May 1875 by Alcée Prevost, Clara's father, which states, "Any concerned party legally authorized to celebrate marriages in the parish of St. Mary, is hereby licensed and authorized to celebrate a marriage between Theodore Stephen Labauve and Marie Clara Prevost, and join them together as husband and wife agreeably to the laws of this state." Theodore brought the note down to the Franklin Courthouse to obtain the marriage license, and set the wheels in motion.

Clara was given a ring, the two fathers negotiated the dowry, the marriage contract was written up, and the engagement was announced at Sunday Mass for three consecutive weeks. Theodore then was allowed to call on his bride-to-be and take her to dances and on walks, though they were never allowed out of the sight of a chaperone. Clara's brother Anatole was the usual chaperone, as their parents were busy with the farm and the other children. Her brother was Clara's favored choice, according to her granddaughter, our Aunt Lorna, as "Great-Uncle Anatole was a bit more lenient as a chaperone than Grandpa Theodore or Grandma Clara would have been. However, as brothers were also quite protective in that day, lenient probably meant turning a blind eye to hand-holding, but not much more."

The marriage license was issued in May 1875. On Sunday, June 6, 1875, the marriage took place at Immaculate Heart Church in Charenton. The way the story has been handed down, Theodore arrived at the home of the bride accompanied by his family and neighbors. Clara appeared in a traditional white gown with fresh flowers adorning her hair, and knelt with her husband-to-be while her father gave them a blessing and talked to them about married life.

Her father escorted Clara to the church in a buggy, followed by a procession of guests in buggies or on foot as bells rang out proclaiming the joyous occasion. Clara's mother stayed home from the wedding as was usual at that time. A wedding was said to be a sad occasion for the mother of the bride. However, I suspect that part of the reason the bride's mother traditionally stayed home from the wedding had more to do with the fact that she was about to entertain dozens of people with a lavish feast. Following the ceremony the newly married couple left the church for the wedding party in the lead buggy, with guests trailing behind. It was the custom for the bride to ride to the wedding with her father, and ride home with her new husband.

While all the details of Clara's wedding feast were not handed down, wedding receptions were always lavish occasions, and Clara's family would have put forth the very best they could offer. A summer wedding feast typically consisted of gumbo, crawfish étouffée, fried chicken, boudin and andouille sausages, maque choux or other corn dishes, fresh tomatoes, and homemade breads. A bounty of sweets was offered in addition to the groom's cake (usually chocolate), and wedding cake (always white). This would all have been set up outside under the shade of the moss-draped oaks and flowering magnolia trees that graced the Prevost plantation. Relatives and neighbors would have provided some of the food, which helped with the cost as well as the logistics of cooking enough food to provide a banquet for a large group.

It was related that toasts were drunk to the bride and groom, and the cake was cut and passed around on platters, reserving some slices to send to those who were not able to attend the reception. The **"bal de noces"** (wedding ball) began with a wedding march, during which the newlyweds walked around in a circle, leading the wedding party. The couple then shared their first dance together as husband and wife, which started the dancing that was enjoyed for hours. It was considered polite for the bride to dance with everyone present—men and women, old and young.

Following a wedding reception, a couple often stayed with the bride's parents or at a neighbor's house for several days, during which time food and beverages were brought to them. However, since Theodore and Clara had their own lovely farm to go home to, they went there after the wedding ball. We don't know if there was a **charivari** (a gathering of friends and relatives under the couple's bedroom window, who would make tremendous noise until the newlyweds invited everyone inside for food and coffee), but stories of charivaris were handed down as being part of a wedding, so it is likely that Theodore and Clara were "honored" with one. As thoughtless as the idea may sound in this day and age, it was actually considered a compliment to the young couple, and a testament to wishing them a happy future.

The Newlyweds Move to Their New Home

T.S. and Clara were given gifts of a practical nature to help them set up their new life on the farm, Home Place, in Ashton. Some of the gifts Aunt Lorna remembers hearing about included live chickens, quilts and blankets, and used cast iron skillets and pots—especially valued as they were already well seasoned.

When Theodore brought his young bride of eighteen years of age to Home Place after the wedding, Clara must have been thrilled to walk under the arbor draped with graceful wisteria, through an aisle of sixteen fragrant gardenia bushes, and past the fenced garden at the right of the house, resplendent with vegetables and herbs. An 18-inch-thick bed of violets and other colorful flowers surrounded the vegetable garden, beyond which were blueberry bushes, peach, plum, cherry, apple, pear, fig, grapefruit, tangerine, lime, kumquat, and pecan trees.

A bayou meandering through the farm would provide thousands of crawfish dinners for the family over the next century. In the fall, when things got dry, crabs would come crawling up from the brackish water of the bayou. The beach at nearby Cypremort Point was a haven for blue crabs, oysters, redfish, shrimp, and flounder that Theodore would "catch" at night, using a pitchfork and the aid of a lantern. He said he could see the flounder's red eyes in the clear water. In his older years, Theodore and Clara's son, Theodore Adolphus (Great-Uncle Adolphe), remembered the property from his childhood in the 1880s: "I am still living where Mama and Papa used to be and where the little birds would come and go, and where the watermelon and the pecans and sugarcanes would grow, and the crawfish run about, and the lovely sea tide would come and go by the cypress trees."

When I asked Dad to describe Home Place as it was in his childhood, he said that "It was more like something in a well-written book than a real place. The bayou dissected the property and offered us an abundance of crawfish. There were wild ducks, rabbits, and other game to hunt. There were dozens of fruit trees and pecan trees, as well as bean fields and sugarcane. Arbors with trailing vines of wisteria seemed to be everywhere. It was heaven."

Home Place was a classic Cajun farmhouse raised off the ground by brick pillars. Its single wall construction used wide, wide cypress planks, only five of which, laid vertically, comprised the entire front wall of the home. There were stairs leading up to the open front porch that had an overhang roof, lush with a trellis of fragrant jasmine, where free time and meals would be enjoyed during warm months for generations to come. Inside were four bedrooms, a living room, and a hall entryway that separated the main part of the house from the indoor kitchen. Since taxes were figured on the number of inside walls, there were no built-in closets.

The hall entryway was always being invaded by chickens. These chickens provided eggs, and when the hens were no longer producing or the roosters stopped fathering chicks, they became main ingredients for gumbo. There were three hen houses, but as chickens were allowed to run free for one week before being consumed, there were always some flying about, noisily squawking, pecking, and intimidating the children. My older sister, Lorna, remembers tossing feed to the chickens in the yard when she was a small child.

She also still has a vivid picture of our grandmother doing what had to be done if chicken was on the menu. "Grandma Olympe held the chicken against her body with one hand. She had her other hand on its neck. For some reason, she was looking long and steadily only at me, with her black penetrating eyes. Unsmiling. I was standing maybe fifteen feet away, then—snap."

There was an outdoor cookhouse, both for safety and for comfort during the summer months, so heating the oven and stove wouldn't make the house unbearably hot. The many outbuildings included barns to shelter the cattle when they weren't grazing in the fields, sheds and storage buildings, a nursery or hot house, and a honey house where the bees were kept. There was a huge syrup pot used to make syrup from the sugarcane grown on the farm. The outhouse was large, and even had a porch and a very good roof, although the structure was eventually replaced with a modern "two-seater," built by my Great-Uncle Adolphe.

Theodore and Clara had a huge, handsome bedroom set, described to me by my aunt as "beautifully defined wood, of a deep, rich color. The four tall, carved posts of the bed supported an awning of crushed red velvet. The wardrobe was huge and went all the way to the ceiling." I don't know how they acquired the magnificent furniture with which the house was decorated, but I believe that it was a combination of furniture that

Clara's half brother, Solange, purchased during his trips to France and, at least in the case of the bed, furniture brought over from France when one of the ancestors immigrated—probably one of Clara's ancestors who came directly to Louisiana from France. The bed was most likely part of Clara's dowry.

Two sons were born to Theodore and Clara between 1877 and 1879. The first son, Adolphe, was healthy from birth, but sadly, little Joseph died before he reached the age of one. Five girls, Irma, Victoria, Olympe, Oréline, and Alice, followed between 1880 and 1890, my Grandma Olympe being the fifth of the seven children.

The Labauves lived a happy, family-centered life as has always been typical of Cajun people. They lived off the land and were almost completely self-sufficient, with bountiful fruit trees, berry bushes, and a garden where they grew almost every type of vegetable. They raised sheep for wool; cows for milk, cream, and butter; and pork and poultry for the table. Fish, shellfish, and wild game were plentiful and ready to be caught, gathered, or shot for dinner. They were surrounded by relatives who lived on nearby plantations. Many cousins, aunts, uncles, and grandparents were just a buggy ride away and an important part of their lives, especially on Sundays, the traditional day to spend with family.

A piece of land between the Ashton farm and the adjacent Bodin farm was set aside for a school, and a two-room schoolhouse was built. Education was very important to Theodore, and he insisted that all his children attend the Bodin School. He passed on a love of reading and education that would serve his offspring well throughout their lives. My Grandma Olympe grew up to teach at the Bodin School.

The family grew enough cotton for their own needs. Clara had a spinning wheel and loom in the attic, and produced material that she used for clothing, sheets, mosquito nets, blankets, and curtains. She was also an avid gardener and was adept at raising chickens. According to a letter her husband wrote to their son, Theodore Adolphus, in 1906 while he was away furthering his education, "Your mother takes great pride in her vast vegetable and flower gardens and her chickens. She had very hard luck and has lost most of her chickens. Twenty—thirty died in 6 hours. We used a wheel barrow to take them out of the yard." (He didn't say why the chickens were lost.)

Along with caring for the gardens and livestock, Clara's favorite occupation was cooking, and her children were often at her side watching her cook and helping her prepare meals, as were her grandchildren during their frequent visits to the farm. Preparing food could be a social activity, but was also an intimate time that family members shared together. Cajun children typically learned how to cook. It wasn't a rule, it was just their way of life for children to be a part *of the daily goings-on in what was the main room of the house.*

A big, long wooden table was the center of the kitchen and the center of family activity. A table that would only accommodate the members of the family would have been too small, as guests were always welcome in a Cajun home and visiting was a major focus of their existence. Likewise, cooking and meals were an important part of visiting. My dad remembered, "There always seemed to be something in a big iron pot on the back of the stove. Whether it was left from the previous meal, or being prepared for an upcoming meal I don't know. But Grandmother Clara could always produce a bowl of food for a visitor, or a hungry child. During summer months, this iron pot of food would be simmering away in the outdoor cookhouse, not the indoor kitchen."

My father and aunt spent a great deal of time in their grandparents' kitchen, and spoke fondly of a big sideboard loaded with family pictures, white enamel plates with dark blue rims, and pitchers of water from the well for both drinking and cooking. There were big barrels of flour, cornmeal, and cane syrup, and a huge can of lard. Flour was probably the only purchased item among those listed above, as wheat would not grow well in the area. A woodstove was used for indoor cooking, and there were wooden cupboards with screen fronts, and numerous black cast iron pots that hung on the walls.

Dad and Aunt Lorna described the kitchen as warm and inviting, a place where they always felt wanted, a bustling center of cooking, visiting, laughing, and good-natured arguing among their grandmother, mother, and four aunts over who was the best candidate to make the gumbo, étouffée, or bread pudding. According to Dad, "The meals and conversation lasted until it was time to clean up and get ready for bed. As youngsters we knew we were part of something that mattered tremendously. We were part of a clan that was so strongly bonded with love, and fun, and delight in meals—we never doubted that we were extremely important in the scheme of life."

Theodore and Clara raised their seven kids on the peaceful farm, welcomed their grandchildren and great-grandchildren there, and died where they had lived together happily for fifty-eight years.

According to my Aunt Lorna, "Kieau was a black man, the son of slaves who had worked with his parents on a Labauve plantation prior to and after the Civil War, when he was given his freedom. He and Grandpa Theodore were raised as companions, and worked together most of their lives. Grandpa Theodore was an only child, and he and Kieau were like brothers. In their later years, Kieau would come to Home Place every day to spend the day with my grandfather."

Aunt Lorna continued, "Grandpa was a

very intelligent man. He was a funny old guy. He was tall and he had the typical southern goatee. Until my grandfather died, he and Kieau remained buddies. Grandpa would sit on a little bench on the back porch and Kieau would sit on the porch with his feet hanging off. They would talk for hours. When it was time for supper, Grandma would ask what Grandpa wanted to eat. The answer was always the same, rain or shine, cold or unbearably hot: gumbo."

It was never too hot for gumbo, and there's nothing more Cajun than a bowl of steaming gumbo, brimming with chicken, seafood, or sausage. No doubt the gumbo varied from day to day, depending on what had been just caught, shot, or gathered. Dad said that he and my Aunt Lorna were sent down to the bayou to gather crawfish if there was nothing else for the gumbo, at least during the January through June crawfish season. They used net baskets with either raw liver or chicken to lure the crawfish. Between dried shrimp, cured ham, smoked tasso and sausage, and the bounty from the fishermen and hunters in the family and the neighborhood, there was always something good to grace the gumbo bowl.

Aunt Lorna recalls that "Grandma would set the dining room table and call to Grandpa Theodore. He would come in and fill a heaping plate for Kieau, and ask him to sit at the table, but Kieau would always sit on a stool near the corner of the room. They continued their talks while they ate. They talked about everything, the old days, the Bible, wars and everything. Time and again, each summer, weekend, or holiday, Grandpa would tell about his Acadian ancestors and their search for religious freedom. He sat on his porch reading his Bible every day, before the noon meal. Even when I was in my twenties, and living in Lafayette, every Christmas I would go over to my Grandpa Theodore's house and bring presents. I would bring a pair of JCPenney overalls for Kieau; he would wear them the whole year." Kieau lived on for many years after his lifelong friend, Theodore, passed away in 1933 from complications of heart disease. Theodore was eighty-three years old.

Great-Grandma Clara was to live another thirteen years. My older sister, Lorna, went to Home Place many times as a little girl, and remembers meeting our Great-Grandmother Clara. It was three years before Clara died, on the last visit Lorna made to the farm until she, our other sister, Bonnie, and I visited there almost fifty years later. Lorna recounts the story: "I think of myself as being about seven years old. I was alone in the old farmhouse, or so I thought. I remember standing in front of a door to a room I had never been in before. It was in the front of the house, past the area with the staircase. Perhaps I never went there because the staircase area was also an entry and chickens used to get in, roost, and put up a scary squawk if you came near. I opened a door. A tiny *old woman sat in a rocking chair next to a huge four-poster bed. I was frightened, but then immediately calm. She smiled and I remember feeling, knowing, that she loved children. In my child's mind, she was 107 years old, which is something I believed into adulthood until I was told that Clara died at the age of eighty-nine. I walked in and touched her hand and she smiled again. She was blind and frail and made me feel very wanted."*

Clara had been deaf and nearly blind for many years. Her daughters who lived in the area, Alice, Irma, and Olympe, took turns helping to take care of their mother at the farm. Solange, Clara's half brother, lived at the house for a while to help with the care of his sister. He was there with her when she died of old age in 1946, at the age of eighty-nine years, with hardly a gray hair on her head. Aunt Lorna wrote in her notes regarding her Grandmother Clara's dark hair, "Now I know—I remember her dark hair, as dark as mine today at 86 years of age. I inherited it from her! My mother's hair also stayed dark."

After the death of Clara, my grandparents, Olympe and Joseph Pischoff, moved from Lafayette back to the farm. But their stay ended in 1954 when Grandma died. Great-Uncle Adolphe and Great-Aunt Irma both lived on the property, Adolphe in a room off his store and Irma in the old honey house. Great-Aunt Alice lived at nearby Four Corners, in her store. The other two daughters lived in other parts of the state, and Home Place began the steady deterioration caused by neglect. It would be almost forty years before three of Clara's great-granddaughters, my two sisters and I, would visit Home Place and become thoroughly enchanted by it, even in the sadly dilapidated state in which we found the old house.

Chicken and Andouille Sausage Gumbo

I remember Grandma and Grandpa standing at the stove together, staring into the big pot of gumbo, adding spices, vegetables, chicken, and big fat slices of sausage. Wordlessly, they watched, and knew when to add the next ingredients, as they cooked in unison, creating a simple soup with the precision of conducting a symphony—an incredibly aromatic symphony.

Serves 8 as an entrée

- 2 pounds boneless, skinless chicken breasts, cut into ½-inch cubes
- 1 teaspoon salt
- 1 teaspoon paprika
- ½ teaspoon black pepper
- ¼ teaspoon cayenne pepper
- ½ cup corn oil
- ½ cup all-purpose flour
- 1½ cups chopped onion
- 1½ cups chopped celery
- 1 cup chopped green bell pepper
- 2 quarts warm chicken stock
- ¼ teaspoon Tabasco® sauce
- 1 pound andouille sausage, sliced 1 inch thick
- 1½ pounds fresh okra or 20 ounces frozen okra, (defrosted) sliced
- 2 cups raw rice
- 1½ tablespoons filé powder
- 1 cup chopped fresh parsley

Season the chicken cubes with the salt, paprika, and black and cayenne pepper; set aside.

Heat the oil in a large heavy pot or Dutch oven over medium heat. Add the flour and cook for 20 to 30 minutes, stirring constantly, to make a medium roux (see page 14).

Add the onion, celery, and bell pepper and cook for 5 minutes, stirring frequently. Add the seasoned chicken cubes and cook for 5 minutes, stirring constantly (and reducing the heat, if necessary, to prevent burning).

Add the stock and bring to a boil, stirring constantly. Add the Tabasco and sausage; reduce the heat to low and cover the pot. Simmer for 1 hour, stirring occasionally. Add the okra and simmer for 30 minutes. (Begin cooking the rice when you add the okra.)

Remove the pot from the heat and stir in the filé just before dishing it up. Serve in soup bowls, with a mound of rice in the center of each portion, and parsley sprinkled on top.

LAGNIAPPE **Gumbo always starts with roux, usually contains okra, and sometimes filé (which shouldn't be heated) is added. All three are thickeners, as well as flavoring elements.**

Crab and Shrimp Gumbo

In the fall, when things got dry, crabs would come crawling up out of the brackish water in the bayou. Grandpa would go to Cypremort Point for a sack of shrimp, and Grandma would make this crab and shrimp gumbo which, Dad always said, was the best gumbo in the world. **Serves 8 as an entrée**

- 1 cup corn oil
- 1 cup all-purpose flour
- 1½ cups chopped onion
- 1½ cups chopped green bell pepper
- 1 cup chopped celery
- 1 teaspoon salt
- 1 teaspoon paprika
- ½ teaspoon black pepper
- ½ teaspoon cayenne pepper
- 5 cups water
- ½ teaspoon Tabasco sauce
- 1½ pounds fresh okra or 20 ounces frozen (defrosted), sliced
- 1 pound crabmeat
- 1 pound shrimp, peeled and deveined (see Lagniappe)
- 2 cups raw rice
- 1 cup chopped fresh parsley

Heat the oil in a large heavy pot or Dutch oven over medium heat. Add the flour and cook for 30 to 40 minutes, stirring constantly, to make a dark roux (see page 14).

Add the onion, bell pepper, celery, salt, paprika, and black and cayenne pepper and cook over medium heat, stirring frequently, for 10 minutes.

Add the water and bring to a boil, stirring constantly until blended and smooth. Add the Tabasco; reduce the heat, cover, and simmer for 30 minutes, stirring often. Add the okra and simmer for 15 minutes. Add the crab and shrimp, reduce the heat to the lowest setting, and cook for 15 minutes longer. (Begin cooking the rice when you add the okra.)

Serve in soup bowls, with a mound of rice in the center of each portion, and parsley sprinkled on top.

LAGNIAPPE **The black vein along the back of the shrimp is the intestinal tract and is usually removed, although this isn't imperative. To devein shrimp, make a shallow slit down the back, exposing the vein; the vein may then be removed with a knife, or by rinsing briefly under running water. There are tools that simultaneously peel and devein shrimp.**

Crab Soup with Lemon

My grandfather thought lemons belonged in or with almost every dish: mayonnaise, salad dressings, sauces, wedges to squeeze over shellfish, zest in bread and cake batters and, as below, cut in paper-thin slices for garnishing. When he lived with us in California he loved our huge Meyer lemon trees and found even more uses for that almost sweet variety. ***Serves 6 as an entrée***

- 8 tablespoons (1 stick) butter
- ½ cup all-purpose flour
- 1 cup chopped onion
- ½ cup chopped celery
- 2 cloves garlic, minced
- ½ teaspoon fresh thyme or ¼ teaspoon dried thyme
- 6 cups fish or chicken stock
- 2 tablespoons fresh lemon juice
- 2 teaspoons lemon zest
- 1 teaspoon salt
- ½ teaspoon white pepper
- 2 pounds fresh crabmeat
- ¾ cup chopped fresh parsley
- 6 very thin slices lemon for garnish

Melt the butter in a large heavy pot or Dutch oven over medium heat. Add the flour and cook for 10 to 20 minutes, stirring constantly, to make a light roux (see page 14). Add the onion, celery, garlic, and thyme and cook for about 10 minutes.

Raise the heat to high, add the stock, lemon juice, lemon zest, salt, and pepper and bring to a boil. Reduce the heat and gently boil for about 3 minutes, stirring constantly, until thickened a bit.

Stir in the crab and parsley, reduce the heat, and simmer gently for 5 minutes, covered.

Serve in soup bowls; float a lemon slice on top of each serving.

LAGNIAPPE **Crab boils combine a favorite food and a favorite pastime—crab and partying. These events find people gathered around a table covered with newspapers, enjoying a messy meal of freshly boiled crab, potatoes, and corn. Live crabs are the best for crab boils: purchase them, immediately place in a cooler, cover with ice, and allow to sit for 1 hour. The cold will calm the crabs down, thus making them easier to cook when you are ready.**

Crawfish Bisque

When my great-grandparents got married and moved to the farm, Great-Grandma Clara was said to have been thrilled with the bayou on the property, full of crawfish. The season was almost over, and she cooked crawfish every night during the first month of their marriage. ***Serves 8 as a soup***

- 1 cup corn oil
- 1 cup all-purpose flour
- 1 tablespoon tomato paste
- 1½ cups chopped onion
- 1 cup chopped celery
- 1 cup chopped green bell pepper
- 3 cloves garlic, minced
- 1 teaspoon dried thyme
- 2 bay leaves
- One 14-ounce can diced tomatoes, undrained
- 4 cups water
- 2 cups raw rice
- 1 pound crawfish tail meat
- 1¼ teaspoons salt
- 1 teaspoon white pepper
- 8 whole crawfish for garnish (optional)
- ½ cup sliced green onions
- ½ cup chopped fresh parsley

Heat the oil in a large heavy pot or Dutch oven over medium heat. Add the flour and cook for 30 to 40 minutes, stirring constantly, to make a dark roux (see page 14).

Add the tomato paste, onion, celery, bell pepper, garlic, and thyme and cook over medium heat for 10 minutes. Add the bay leaves and tomatoes with their liquid and cook for 5 minutes.

Add the water and bring to a boil, stirring to blend. Reduce the heat to medium-low and simmer, covered, for 30 minutes, stirring occasionally. (Begin cooking the rice when you start simmering the bisque.) Add the crawfish tail meat, salt, and pepper. Reduce the heat to low and simmer gently for 10 minutes. Serve with a scoop of rice in the center of each serving, topped with a whole crawfish, if desired. Sprinkle the bisque with green onions and parsley.

LAGNIAPPE **If crawfish are unavailable, shrimp or crab may be substituted for a different but still delicious bisque. See Sources (page 267) for ordering fresh crawfish from Louisiana.**

Crawfish Soup with Corn

Crawfish season is eagerly awaited each winter, and this soup is way up there on our list of treasured crawfish dishes. We order fresh crawfish from Louisiana, shipped overnight, to have as a special meal on the day we decorate our Christmas tree. Fresh corn is not in season when the first crawfish appear, so my grandmother developed this soup using frozen corn, enhanced by cream-style corn that she felt gave the creaminess of the fresh variety.

Serves 6 as an entrée

- ½ cup corn oil
- ½ cup all-purpose flour
- 1½ cups chopped onion
- 1½ cups chopped celery
- 1 cup chopped green bell pepper
- 3 cloves garlic, minced
- 2 cups fresh or frozen corn
- One 16-ounce can cream-style corn
- 4 cups fish or chicken stock
- 1 teaspoon salt
- ½ teaspoon white pepper
- ½ teaspoon cayenne pepper
- 2 pounds crawfish tail meat
- 1 cup sliced green onion tops

Heat the oil in a large heavy pot or Dutch oven over medium heat. Add the flour and cook for 20 to 30 minutes, stirring constantly, to make a medium roux (see page 14).

Add the onion, celery, bell pepper, and garlic and cook, stirring often, for 15 minutes.

Add the remaining ingredients, except the crawfish and green onions. Bring to a boil, reduce the heat, cover, and simmer for 30 minutes, stirring occasionally.

Add the crawfish, reduce the heat to low, and gently simmer for 10 minutes, covered, to blend flavors and heat through.

Sprinkle each serving with green onion tops.

LAGNIAPPE **Crawfish season in Louisiana is December through June.**

8 to 10 pounds live crawfish equals 1 pound or 3 cups tail meat.

2 pounds live crawfish equals ¼ pound or ¾ cup tail meat.

There are 100 to 150 crawfish tails in 1 pound tail meat.

Creamy Oyster Soup

Oyster lovers fancy them on the half shell, unadorned, except for accompaniments. However, this is such a creamy, sensuous soup that even purists enjoy it. It is simple and delicate. The goodness of the oysters should shine through, so no strong ingredients are added, and no garnishes are needed. ***Serves 6 as a soup***

- 4 tablespoons (½ stick) butter
- ½ cup chopped onion
- ½ cup chopped celery
- 2 tablespoons all-purpose flour
- 4 cups (32 ounces) oysters and their liquid, fresh or jarred (32 to 48 fresh, shucked; or three 10-ounce jars; or four 8-ounce jars; see Lagniappe)
- 2 cups cream
- ½ cup sliced green onion tops
- ½ cup chopped fresh parsley
- ¼ teaspoon salt
- ¼ teaspoon white pepper

Melt the butter in a large heavy pot or Dutch oven over medium heat. Sauté the onion and celery for 5 minutes.

Add the flour, reduce the heat to medium-low, and cook for 5 minutes, stirring constantly.

Add the oysters and their liquid, bring to a gentle simmer, and simmer for 5 minutes.

Add the remaining ingredients and simmer just until heated through.

LAGNIAPPE Oysters are ideally purchased live, in the shell. Only those with tightly closed shells, or shells that close when the oyster is tapped, should be chosen, as open, or partly open shells indicate dead oysters. Since oysters aren't always in season, a jar alternative is given; jarred oysters being preferable to canned.

One dozen large fresh oysters and their liquid equals approximately 1 pint, or 2 cups, or 16 ounces oysters, *or*

one and a half 10-ounce jars of oysters labeled "medium," *or*

two 8-ounce jars of oysters labeled "extra small"

The above yield in cups or ounces from fresh oysters is approximate, as yield depends on their size; oysters vary from small to large (16 to 24 per pound).

Dried Shrimp Gumbo

Drying shrimp was a method of preserving the product before canning and freezing became the norm. However, my Cajun relatives favored the dishes they made with dried shrimp so much that they used it even when fresh were available. My Great-Uncle T.A. Labauve ran a country store in Ashton, Louisiana, where he kept a barrel full of large, fragrant, dried shrimp for people to purchase by the pound; he didn't stock the more common small shrimp. Serves 6 as a soup

- 1½ cups (about 4 ounces) dried shrimp
- ¼ cup lard or corn oil
- ¼ cup all-purpose flour
- 1½ cups chopped onion
- 1 cup chopped green bell pepper
- 3 cloves garlic, minced
- 6 green onions, white part only, sliced
- ½ cup chopped fresh parsley
- ¾ teaspoon salt
- ½ teaspoon white pepper
- ¼ teaspoon cayenne pepper
- ½ pound thinly sliced fresh or frozen okra
- 3 bay leaves
- 1 cup raw rice

Place the shrimp in a bowl and cover with 3 cups water; soak for at least 30 minutes. Drain, reserving the liquid. Add enough water to the reserved liquid to equal 5 cups.

Melt the lard in a large heavy pot or Dutch oven over medium heat. Add the flour and cook for 20 to 30 minutes, stirring constantly, to make a medium roux (see page 14).

Add the onion and bell pepper and cook for 5 minutes. Add the drained shrimp, garlic, green onions, parsley, salt, white and cayenne pepper, and okra and cook for 5 minutes, stirring often.

Add the 5 cups reserved shrimp-water and the bay leaves. Bring to a boil, reduce the heat, and simmer for 1 hour, covered. (Begin cooking the rice after the gumbo has cooked for about 30 minutes.)

LAGNIAPPE One pound dried shrimp, after soaking, will yield 4 pounds reconstituted shrimp. They may be mail ordered (see Sources, page 267), purchased at specialty markets, or found in Asian or Hispanic markets, as they are popular in both cuisines.

Duck and Andouille Sausage Gumbo

My grandfather loved to go duck hunting, and would come back with gunny sacks full of ducks, which he shared with neighbors. This gumbo was one of Grandma's favorites, and has become one of ours over the years. Dad carried on the hunting tradition, and for years his Christmas gift from Mom was another annual membership in a duck hunting club.

Note that you will need ½ cup dark roux. ***Serves 6 as an entrée***

- 1 duck (4 to 5 pounds), cut into serving pieces
- 1½ teaspoons salt
- 1 teaspoon black pepper
- ½ teaspoon cayenne pepper
- ¼ cup corn oil
- ½ cup dark roux made with ½ cup oil and ½ cup flour (see page 14)
- 1½ cups chopped onion
- 1 cup chopped carrot
- 3 cloves garlic, minced
- 4 cups water
- 1½ pounds andouille sausage, sliced
- 1 cup raw rice
- ¾ cup sliced green onions
- Filé powder

Remove any large pieces of fat from the duck. Season with salt, pepper, and cayenne. Heat the oil in a large heavy pot or Dutch oven over medium-high heat and brown the duck pieces on all sides, removing pieces as they are browned. Pour off the fat, reduce the heat to medium-low, add the roux, and stir until smooth.

Add the onion, carrot, and garlic and cook for 5 minutes, stirring frequently.

Add the water and bring to a boil, stirring to combine the roux into the liquid. Add the duck pieces and sausage to the pot and bring to a boil. Reduce the heat and simmer, covered, for 2 hours. (Begin cooking the rice about 30 minutes before the gumbo is done.)

Stir green onions into the gumbo, and serve the gumbo over rice, passing the filé powder at the table to be added just before eating.

LAGNIAPPE Southwest Louisiana, or Cajun Country, is hunting country and especially known for its plentiful mallard and teal ducks. Wild ducks have a darker flesh than their domesticated cousins and, not surprisingly, a gamier, nuttier flavor. The gamy taste of duck, and other game birds and game animals, is toned down by the addition of a carrot.

Filé Gumbo with Chicken and Oysters

My father adored the Gulf oysters from his home state of Louisiana, and never stopped missing them. No other oysters would do. As children, we would always hold our breath when a restaurant menu listed oysters, as we knew the inevitable conversation that was about to ensue. "Are these from the Gulf?" our father would ask. "No, sir, they're from the East Coast." "Oh, never mind then," Dad would say. "I'm from Louisiana and no oysters can top those from the Gulf." I suppose the taste of the water, the diet of the oysters, and the freshness were all factors in making the Gulf oysters so wonderful, but I also think that they just reminded Dad of home. They probably would have been his oysters of choice even if they weren't the best.

While the ingredient list is long, this gumbo is simple to prepare, as almost everything goes in one pot and the chicken doesn't need to be browned.

Serves 4 as an entrée, 8 as a soup

8 chicken thighs (about 2 pounds)
6 cups chicken stock
½ teaspoon plus an additional ½ teaspoon salt
1 cup onion plus 2 cups chopped onion
½ cup chopped celery
½ cup chopped green bell pepper
¼ cup chopped fresh parsley
2 bay leaves
½ teaspoon white pepper
1 cup raw rice
8 tablespoons (1 stick) butter
½ cup all-purpose flour
⅛ teaspoon black pepper
⅛ teaspoon cayenne pepper
16 ounces (2 cups) oysters and their liquid, fresh or jarred (see Lagniappe, page 39)
1 tablespoon filé powder

Place the chicken and the chicken stock in a large heavy pot or Dutch oven, and add ½ teaspoon of the salt, 1 cup of the onion, the celery, bell pepper, parsley, bay leaves, and white pepper. Bring to a boil, cover, and simmer over low heat for 45 minutes, stirring often. (Begin cooking the rice after the chicken has cooked for 30 minutes.)

Melt the butter in a heavy skillet over medium heat; add the flour and cook for 5 minutes, stirring constantly. Add the remaining 2 cups onion, the remaining ½ teaspoon salt, and the black and cayenne pepper and cook for 5 minutes, stirring often. Add the oysters and their liquid with the contents of the skillet to the pot of gumbo. Bring to a boil, stirring to combine the roux into the stock. Reduce the heat and gently simmer for 5 minutes, uncovered.

Remove the gumbo from the heat. Mix the filé powder with about ½ cup liquid from the gumbo. Return the mixture to the pot and stir to blend. Serve with a scoop of rice in the center of each serving of gumbo.

LAGNIAPPE **This gumbo doesn't start out with the usual roux. Instead, a butter-flour roux is made and added at the end to thicken the liquid. A butter roux is not typical in Cajun cooking; it is a hangover from classic French cooking, but goes so well with the combination of chicken and oysters that we use it here.**

Gumbo Z'herbes

Grandpa used to make a meatless version of this gumbo during Lent and a seafood version on Friday nights, and when the Catholic Church lifted the ban against eating meat on Fridays, in the early 1960s, he began to add andouille sausage. ***Serves 8 as a soup***

- 1 pound spinach
- 1 pound collard greens
- 1 pound mustard greens
- 1 large bunch watercress
- 1 large bunch parsley
- 4 quarts water
- 1 pound Andouille sausage, coarsely chopped (optional)
- 2 pounds potatoes, peeled and coarsely chopped
- ½ cup corn oil
- ½ cup all-purpose flour
- 2 cups chopped onion
- 1 teaspoon salt
- ½ teaspoon dried thyme
- ½ teaspoon black pepper
- ¼ teaspoon cayenne pepper
- 2 cups raw rice
- 4 teaspoons filé powder

Wash and trim the greens, discarding tough stems, and coarsely chop.

Bring the water to a boil in a large pot. Add the sausage, if using, and simmer for 15 minutes ; add the greens and potatoes and simmer for 5 minutes. Remove from the heat while making the roux.

Heat the oil in a heavy skillet over medium heat. Add the flour and cook for 20 to 30 minutes, stirring constantly, to make a medium roux (see page 14). Add the onion and seasonings to the roux and cook for 5 minutes, stirring constantly.

Bring the greens mixture to a boil, add the roux-onion mixture and, when the roux is dissolved into the liquid, reduce the heat to a simmer. Cover and simmer for 1½ hours. (Begin cooking the rice after the gumbo has simmered for about 1 hour.) Dish up the rice into soup bowls, sprinkle with filé powder, and ladle the gumbo on top.

LAGNIAPPE **Tradition maintains that for every type of green used in Gumbo Z'herbes, a new friend will appear during the following year. Often, eleven or more greens are used, but, again according to tradition, always an odd number. Any greens may be used.**

Lorna's Chicken Gumbo

I don't know why Aunt Lorna used half corn oil and half olive oil in this dish, but I present the recipe as she wrote it. I do know that olive oil was used by my grandmother and great-grandmother to moisturize their skin and hair, as well as for cooking. ***Serves 8 as a soup***

- 2 tablespoons corn oil
- 2 tablespoons olive oil
- 1 chicken (about 4 pounds), cut into serving pieces
- 1 teaspoon salt
- ½ teaspoon black pepper
- ¼ teaspoon cayenne pepper
- ¼ cup all-purpose flour
- 1½ cups chopped onion
- ½ cup chopped celery
- ½ cup chopped green bell pepper
- 2 cloves garlic, minced
- 2 bay leaves
- 1 teaspoon dried thyme
- 2 cups chopped tomatoes, fresh or canned, undrained
- 2 cups warm water
- 2 cups raw rice
- 2 tablespoons chopped fresh parsley
- 2 cups fresh or frozen (defrosted) okra, sliced ½ inch thick

Heat the corn and olive oil in a large heavy pot or Dutch oven over medium-high heat. Pat the chicken dry, season with salt and black and cayenne pepper, and brown on all sides, in a single layer, removing the pieces to a dish as they are browned.

Add the flour to the oil remaining in the pot; reduce the heat to medium-low, and stir constantly for 5 minutes, incorporating crusty bits on the bottom into the flour.

Add the onion, celery, bell pepper, and garlic and cook, stirring frequently, for 5 minutes. Add the bay leaves, thyme, tomatoes, water, and chicken and accumulated juices, and bring to a boil. Reduce the heat and simmer, covered, for 45 minutes. (Begin cooking the rice after the chicken has been cooking for about 15 minutes.)

Add the parsley and okra and simmer for 15 minutes; serve over rice.

LAGNIAPPE **The word gumbo is a derivative of the Bantu (an African language) word for okra; the original word was *ochinggombo*, and was shortened by the slaves to gumbo.**

Mama's Easy Chicken Gumbo Filé

This was my great-grandmother's idea of fast food. It is quickly made, since the chicken doesn't need to be browned. Her version of chicken gumbo, handwritten on an old, yellowed index card, is presented here much as she wrote the recipe, the only change being the addition of exact measurements. Through testing, I've realized that to her "pot spoon" meant about 1½ tablespoons. She didn't specify amounts; rather she called for a "cut-up chicken" and "a few onion tops (green)." However, for the benefit of my readers, I have determined the amounts necessary, so there is no guesswork.

Serves 6 as a soup

1 cup corn oil
1 cup all-purpose flour
1½ cups chopped onion
1 teaspoon salt
½ teaspoon black pepper
¼ teaspoon cayenne pepper
6 cups water
1 large chicken, cut into serving pieces
1 cup raw rice
⅔ cup sliced green onion tops
¼ cup chopped fresh parsley
Filé powder

Heat the oil in a large heavy pot or Dutch oven over medium heat. Add the flour and cook for 20 to 30 minutes, stirring constantly, to make a medium roux (see page 14).

Add the onion and spices and cook for 10 minutes, stirring often to coat the onion with roux.

Add the water and bring to a boil, stirring to incorporate the roux into the water. Add the chicken, bring back to a boil, reduce the heat, and simmer, covered, for 1½ hours. (Begin cooking the rice after the chicken has cooked for 1 hour.)

Serve the gumbo on top of the rice in soup bowls, with the green onion tops, parsley, and filé powder added by each person, as desired.

LAGNIAPPE **Gumbo is generally made using seafood or poultry, with meat (usually andouille sausage, ham, or tasso) added as a seasoning element but not as the main ingredient.**

Mama's Okra Gumbo with Round Steak

No amounts were specified in this old, stained recipe from my great-grandmother, but I've tested and tested to determine the exact amounts so I could, hopefully, produce the results she had in her original version of this gumbo. It is a bit unusual for a gumbo in that beef is the main ingredient, and it doesn't use a roux (although the okra thickens the gumbo sufficiently). Rice is not indicated as an accompaniment, which could be because it went hand-in-hand with gumbo and to Great-Grandma it didn't need mentioning. **Serves 6 as an entrée**

- 2 tablespoons plus ¼ cup corn oil (2 tablespoons is used first)
- 1 pound fresh okra or 20 ounces frozen (defrosted) okra, sliced
- ¼ cup all-purpose flour
- 1½ cups chopped onion
- 2 pounds round steak, cut into ¾-inch cubes
- 3 cups chopped tomatoes, fresh or canned, undrained
- 1 teaspoon salt
- ½ teaspoon black pepper
- ⅛ teaspoon cayenne pepper
- 2 cups warm water
- 1 cup raw rice

Heat the 2 tablespoons oil in a large heavy pot or Dutch oven over medium heat. Reduce the heat to low and sauté the okra for 15 minutes, stirring occasionally. Set aside.

Heat the ¼ cup oil in a large heavy skillet over medium heat. Add the flour and cook for 20 to 30 minutes, stirring constantly, to make a medium roux (see page 14). Add the onion and cook for 5 minutes, stirring often. Pat the steak cubes dry, raise the heat to medium-high, and add the steak to the skillet. Cook for 10 minutes, stirring often to brown the meat evenly.

Add the contents of the skillet to the okra in the large pot, including any crispy bits on the bottom of the skillet, along with the tomatoes, spices, and water. Bring to a boil, reduce the heat, and gently simmer for 1½ hours, covered. (Begin cooking the rice after the gumbo has cooked for about 1 hour.)

LAGNIAPPE Cooking okra separately helps to get rid of the slippery texture. It also browns the okra, adding more flavor from the natural sugars being caramelized. Okra is generally found in seafood gumbos, but since gumbo isn't usually made from beef, this invention of Grandma's probably happened because she had extra beef and lots of okra.

Onion Soup

Onion soup was served when there wasn't much in the cupboard for dinner. There were always onions in the garden, or in storage in the barn. Cajuns know the value of lengthy, slow cooking and this soup is rich from the onions being cooked for a long time in butter. Serves 6 as a soup

- 3 tablespoons butter
- 3 tablespoons corn oil
- 4 cups coarsely chopped onion
- ½ teaspoon salt
- ¼ teaspoon white pepper
- 1 tablespoon sugar
- ½ cup plus 2 tablespoons white wine
- ½ cup all-purpose flour
- 9 cups beef stock
- ½ teaspoon fresh thyme or ¼ teaspoon dried thyme

Heat the butter and oil together in a large heavy pot or Dutch oven set over medium heat. Add the onion, salt, and pepper and cook for 15 minutes, stirring occasionally.

Sprinkle the onion with the sugar and cook 10 minutes longer, stirring occasionally.

Add the ½ cup wine and cook until the liquid is almost evaporated, about 10 minutes.

Sprinkle the flour over the onion and cook for 2 minutes, stirring constantly.

Add the stock and thyme; bring to a boil, stirring to blend the flour completely into the stock. Reduce the heat and simmer for 15 minutes, uncovered, stirring occasionally. Stir in the 2 tablespoons wine and serve.

LAGNIAPPE **Onions are among the three most important vegetables in Cajun cookery. Onion, celery, and bell pepper are known as the holy trinity of Cajun cooking and are the foundation of most savory dishes (along with roux). They are known as "seasoning vegetables," meaning they are intended to break down through long cooking and season the food, not act as a vegetable component within a dish. The next in line of importance are green onions and parsley. This duo is sprinkled on top of the majority of stews, gumbos, and other savory dishes after cooking and, occasionally, added during cooking. The entire green onion is used in cooking, but some cooks use only the green onion tops to sprinkle on finished dishes, along with parsley. We almost always use the whole green onion; I've never been able to figure out what people do with all those hundreds of green onion bottoms.**

Seafood Soup

My Cajun grandparents arrived each fall to stay through the holidays. This soup was the first meal they prepared, usually the day after their arrival. I think they wanted an excuse to go down to Fisherman's Wharf, where they could choose from the large variety of fresh seafood. This soup must be served with lots of good bread to sop up the broth.

Serves 8 as a soup

2 tablespoons corn oil
1 cup chopped onion
1 cup chopped celery
½ cup chopped green bell pepper
2 pounds boneless, skinless fish fillets*
1 teaspoon fresh thyme or ½ teaspoon dried thyme
½ teaspoon salt
¼ teaspoon white pepper
⅛ teaspoon cayenne pepper
1 pound potatoes, peeled and cut into 1-inch cubes
One 14-ounce can diced tomatoes, undrained
6 cups fish stock or 3 cups chicken stock, 2 cups water, 1 cup clam juice
2 dozen shrimp
1 pound crabmeat

*Use whatever fish looks fresh at the market. However, a relatively firm fish is more desirable than thin fillets, and salmon is a bit too high in oil and flavor for this dish.

Heat the oil in a large heavy pot or Dutch oven over medium heat. Layer the onion, celery, bell pepper, and then fish in the pot, in that order. Sprinkle with thyme and the spices. Add the potatoes, then tomatoes.

Pour the fish stock over the top and bring to a boil. Reduce the heat, cover, and gently simmer for 1 hour. Add the shrimp and cook for 2 to 5 minutes, just until opaque; add the crabmeat, cover, and cook over low heat 5 minutes longer. Serve in large soup bowls.

LAGNIAPPE Every culture adjacent to water seems to have its own version of seafood soup. Bouillabaisse is a popular seafood soup from Provence. In San Francisco, the Italian immigrant fishermen are credited with creating cioppino, which is a perfect partner for our famed sourdough French bread. And, yes, San Franciscans love their sourdough French bread as much as the tourists do.

Shrimp, Okra, and Andouille Sausage Gumbo

No one could ever make this gumbo quite as well as Grandpa did. I tried numerous times, but couldn't figure out why it had such a rich tomato flavor without any apparent tomatoes or tomato sauce. Then I tried adding tomato paste, and I think that was his secret. ***Serves 8 as a soup***

- 1 cup corn oil
- 1 cup all-purpose flour
- 2 cups chopped onion
- 1 cup chopped celery
- 4 cloves garlic, minced
- 1 pound fresh okra or 20 ounces frozen okra (defrosted), sliced
- 12 ounces andouille sausage, sliced
- One 6-ounce can tomato paste
- 2 bay leaves
- 1 teaspoon salt
- 2 quarts water
- 2 cups raw rice
- 1½ pounds small shrimp

Heat the oil in a large heavy pot or Dutch oven over medium heat. Add the flour and cook for 30 to 40 minutes, stirring constantly, to make a dark roux (see page 14).

Add the onion, celery, and garlic to the roux and stir to coat them. Cook for 5 minutes, then add the okra and cook for 5 minutes, again stirring to coat the vegetables with the roux. Add the sausage, tomato paste, bay leaves, salt, and water; stir, and simmer, covered, for 2 hours. (Begin cooking the rice after the gumbo has cooked for about 1 hour and 30 minutes.)

Add the shrimp to the gumbo after 2 hours cooking time has elapsed, and cook for 5 minutes longer. Serve with a scoop of rice in the center of each serving of gumbo.

LAGNIAPPE Many years ago when I began to study various ethnic cuisines, I was surprised to find that stock was the liquid added to most stews, soups, and vegetables rather than just plain water, as in Cajun cooking. One reason that the main ingredients stand out in Cajun dishes is that water doesn't compete with other flavors, as stock sometimes does.

Split Pea Soup

Dad always doubled this recipe and made a huge batch of split pea soup in the cast iron Dutch oven. I can still envision the smooth green soup bubbling away in the old black pot. It's easy and quick to make, but so comforting and hearty. It's also inexpensive, and one of the first recipes all of us brought with us when we left home—a great cheap meal for college students, or a young couple just starting out. ***Serves 8 as a soup***

- 1 pound (2 cups) dried split peas
- 1 ham hock or ham bone (about 1 pound)
- 1½ cups chopped onion
- 1 cup chopped celery
- 1 cup chopped carrot
- 1 cup chopped unpeeled potatoes
- 3 cloves garlic, minced
- 1 teaspoon salt
- ½ teaspoon white pepper
- 8 cups water
- Optional garnishes: croutons, fresh chopped parsley, sliced green onions, crumbled bacon

Place all the ingredients in a large soup pot. Bring to a boil; reduce the heat and simmer, partially covered, for 1½ hours, stirring occasionally. Remove the ham hock and cut the meat into small pieces; return the meat to the soup. Serve with garnishes, if desired.

LAGNIAPPE Dried or split peas are a smooth variety with a lot of starch, different from both fresh peas (which have a higher sugar content) and the thin, crisp peas (also known as Chinese or snow peas). Split peas are high in protein and fiber.

Vegetable-Beef and Corn Soup

Packed with beef and vegetables, and thick from the corn, this probably started out as a way to make use of beef bones and the bounty from the garden when corn and tomatoes were in season. It evolved into a family tradition with the addition of cream-style corn, one of the only canned products (other than canned tomatoes and tuna) that my family uses. Alternatives to fresh tomatoes and corn are given so the soup may be enjoyed year round. ***Serves 12 as a soup***

- 3 to 4 pounds soup bones (beef, veal, or a combination)
- 4 cups water
- 1 pound boneless lean beef, cut into ¾-inch cubes
- 1 teaspoon salt
- ½ teaspoon black pepper
- ½ teaspoon dried basil
- ½ teaspoon dried thyme
- ⅛ teaspoon cayenne pepper
- 2 cups chopped onion
- 2 cups chopped celery
- 2 cups chopped carrot
- 2 cups chopped green cabbage
- 4 cups chopped fresh tomatoes or 4 cups canned diced tomatoes, undrained (about 32 ounces)
- 2½ cups fresh corn or 20 ounces frozen corn
- One 14½-ounce can cream-style corn

Preheat the oven to 375°F. Place the soup bones on a baking tray and bake for 30 minutes. Add the bones and any browned bits on the tray to a large heavy pot or Dutch oven. Add the water, bring to a boil, and boil gently for 1 hour, covered.

Lift the bones out of the water and cool a bit. Remove any meat from the bones and return the meat to the soup pot.

Add the beef, salt, black pepper, basil, thyme, and cayenne pepper and bring to a boil. Boil gently for 1 hour, covered. Add the onion, celery, carrot, cabbage, and tomatoes, bring to a boil, reduce the heat, and simmer for 30 minutes, covered. Add the fresh and canned corn and simmer 15 minutes longer.

LAGNIAPPE **Corn was extremely important in Louisiana. Wheat was not suited to the hot, humid climate, and wheat flour was only available in urban markets, where it was expensive. Corn, native to Louisiana, became the main grain and was used for bread and cereals, as well as featured in soups, salads, and as a popular vegetable dish called maque choux.**

White Bean Soup

Dishes with white beans seemed somewhat bland to me until I tasted this soup, a favorite of my grandparents. It's very simple, with little more than beans and ham, but the mild white beans and smoked ham flavors are made for each other. We often had this as a light meal, made festive with bowls of garnishes so diners could personalize their own bowls of soup.

It is not necessary to soak beans. Soaking does cut the cooking time, but only by a few minutes. This is the way Grandpa taught me how to make these beans, however, so I'm including the soaking step. If you choose, skip that step and plan on about 15 minutes more cooking time. *Serves 8 as a soup*

1 pound white beans
2 quarts chicken stock
1 pound ham, coarsely chopped
1½ cups chopped onion
1½ cups chopped celery
1 cup chopped green bell pepper
1 teaspoon white pepper
Salt (optional)
Optional garnishes: black pepper, chopped ham, green onions, parsley

Place the beans in a bowl, cover with water, and soak overnight. Drain and pick out any stones or bad beans. Transfer the beans to a large heavy pot or Dutch oven and add the remaining ingredients, except salt and optional garnishes. Bring to a boil, reduce the heat, and simmer, covered, for 1½ hours, or until the beans are tender. Taste and add salt, if needed.

Serve with small bowls of the garnishes to pass at the table, if desired.

LAGNIAPPE Beans are very popular in Cajun country. My family loves black-eyed peas (which they call black-eyed Susans) as well as red beans, and white beans. Traditionally, red beans and rice used to be served on Monday, as that was the day to do the wash and the beans could cook unattended while laundry was being done. These days it's served just because it tastes good and is still a time-saver, whether Monday is wash day or not. Red beans (*or* white beans) and rice could be called the original Cajun fast food—while they cook for a long time, they are very quick to prepare.

Poultry

Great-Uncle Leon

The Great-Great Uncles: Murder, Music, and Mallards

My father and Aunt Lorna had so many great-aunts and great-uncles they couldn't remember all their names. There were thirteen Prevost children, including their grandmother, who was the oldest. Visiting back and forth was the way people spent their time back then, and not more than a few days went by without one of the great-aunts or great-uncles showing up to say hello and share a cup of coffee or a meal. Back then, dropping in on someone in this manner was considered a compliment to the family, not an intrusion.

An afternoon visit called for everything to stop and coffee to be served. There was a ritual with coffee, and the good pot and cups would be used. Sugar would be offered along with any snacks or sweets that were on hand, though the coffee itself took center stage. Everyone would sit down at the big table in the kitchen, and then someone would invariably say, as if it were a brand-new idea, "Well, would y'all like some coffee?" Never mind that "y'all" had been drinking it since dawn. Of course the guest—whether family, friend, or neighbor—would be expected to stay for dinner, and Grandma would unobtrusively add more sausage to the gumbo.

Sunday evenings were reserved for visiting. Whether you went to the homes of relatives or friends, or expected them to visit you, Sunday evening visits were an absolute. It was the time for relaxing, storytelling and, of course, preparing and sharing food. These evening visits were called **veillées,** *and often found the men in one room discussing the business of farming. The adult women generally chose to gather together privately in another room, as they offered each other a great deal of friendship and support in a time when life was constant hard work and could be very lonely. The children were put to bed early, unsupervised, thrilled to be allowed to giggle and tell stories way past their usual bedtime.*

The most noteworthy of Dad and Aunt Lorna's great-aunts and great-uncles, in terms of their repeated appearances in family stories, were Great-Uncles Edward and Leon. They were twelve and fifteen years younger than Great-Grandma Clara, and as she was settled down as a bride when her brothers were six and three, she probably had little interest in their shenanigans as they grew into adulthood. They were, however, frequent visitors to Clara and Theodore's house and always welcome at Home Place, even though they were sometimes scalawags when away from the family.

Aunt Lorna, somewhat reluctantly, related the true facts: "My Aunt Alice said they were charming and thoughtful, but heavy drinkers. They were always at the races or parties. She was very fond of them and they were sweet to her. She called them rascals and was amused by what she called their antics."

However, the brothers' "antics" were the reason the family eventually lost the remainder of the wealth that had not been depleted during the Civil War. The final blow to the financial status of the Prevost family came when resources were exhausted to save Edward from hanging. Dad remembered, "Edward had been in New Orleans and bet five hundred dollars on a horse race with an Italian fellow, the two of them betting on competing horses. An argument ensued which, according to the old southern Culture of Honor, demanded a duel. Edward shot the man and killed him. The family bankrupted the plantation to buy Edward's life (duels were illegal by that time). He went to jail but was released within a year."

Family members looked upon Edward with affection, despite his problems with the law. He was referred to as a "bon vivant," and considered to be a likable man who was talented with a fiddle. Great-Aunt Alice, his niece, used to say "Edward could make a fiddle sing." The Prevost family was artistic and had a great deal of musical talent. Aunt Lorna wrote of her Great-Uncle Edward, "When I was a little girl, I'd sit with Aunt Alice in her store, and Uncle Edward would sit on the outside steps playing his fiddle. It sounded like liquid gold to me."

Edward and Leon were excellent hunters. They taught Dad, their great-nephew, how to shoot. They would go snipe hunting together. They were also excellent duck hunters. Dad recalls, "Edward never missed. He and his brother Leon used to get a case of shells each, take a large wagon, and hunt ducks. They would come back with the wagon loaded to the top with ducks, and then give their bounty away to neighbors, with the caution to add a carrot when cooking the ducks, as it would help remove the strong wild taste from the meat." Edward's cooking tip works well for any wild game.

Edward was somewhat of a vagabond, and the subject of many letters that passed between family members. They often noted whether Edward was in town on a visit to Home Place, or away on one of his many excursions. His lifestyle took a toll on him, however, and he died of an ulcer in 1928, at the age of fifty-nine. As most of the Prevost family lived well into their eighties, they felt cheated by Edward's early death and greatly missed this never-married son, brother, and uncle.

Leon also had scrapes with the law. In 1919 the Prevost land was given as bond when Leon was charged with two attempts to kill with a gun. Both attempts were on the Prevost property, the same day at different times. Since Leon was such a great shot, we suspect that his gun use was intended to threaten rather than to hurt or kill. If he could accurately shoot dozens of small ducks in flight, it seems that he should have been able to shoot a full-grown man a few yards away if that had actually been his intent.

We know that Leon was married, as his wife, Bertha, on the same day Leon was charged with two attempts to kill with a gun, was charged with "attacking and cutting with a razor." Now whether she was attacking Leon, or attacking the person at whom Leon was shooting is unknown. It seems likely that either someone was threatening the couple or their property, or there was a domestic dispute of monumental proportions between Leon and Bertha. Though not all the Prevost brothers were infamous. . . .

Of all her siblings, Great-Grandma Clara was closest to her half-brother, Solange. In fact, he was the sibling who stayed by Clara's side when she was on her deathbed. Her grandson, my father, recollected, "He was her mulatto half-brother, but the will of their father, Alcée Prevost, did not distinguish between his white children and Solange, just as the children did not distinguish between the aunts and uncles who were the children of their Grandfather and Grandmother Prevost, and Uncle Solange, who was the child of their Grandfather Prevost and his mistress."

Aunt Lorna remembers Solange as "extremely handsome, a tall mulatto. He was gorgeous, with blue-green eyes." He carried the family name of Prevost, and took a different path in life from his half brothers, Edward and Leon. He was married to a woman who was quite beautiful. They traveled to France (he was the only one among his siblings to go abroad), where they purchased and brought back fabulous antiques, including a Louis XIV bedroom set. His niece, my Great-Aunt Alice, bought the Louis XIV bedroom set from Solange for $450, intending it to be part of her trousseau.

Many of the antiques Solange brought back from Europe were at Home Place, and a few were with his niece Alice. Sadly, when Alice died, leaving her home vacant, and when Great-Uncle Adolphe died and there was no one watching over Home Place, all the furniture was stolen from the two homes; the houses were stripped to the bare walls. The thieves did not even leave items of sentimental value such as family photos or my grandmother's cast iron skillets.

Boneless Chicken Fricassee

Grandma Olympe devised this recipe with boneless chicken, in order to use up the chicken breasts. Most of the family members have always liked the dark meat better, as it has much more flavor, so the legs, thighs, or wings were usually first choice for stew-type dishes, and for fried chicken. Grandma said that it was a treat for her mother to serve a dish of this type, as the boneless pieces of chicken allowed her to enjoy her own meal without having to cut the chicken off the bone for six little children before she could eat.

Serves 6

- ¼ cup corn oil
- ⅓ cup all-purpose flour
- 2 cups chopped onion
- 3 cups hot water
- 2 pounds boneless, skinless chicken breasts, cut into 1-inch cubes
- 4 cloves garlic, minced
- 1 cup sliced green onions
- 2 bay leaves
- 1 teaspoon dried thyme
- 1 teaspoon salt
- ¼ teaspoon white pepper
- 3 cups cooked rice (about 1 cup raw)

Heat the oil in a large heavy pot or Dutch oven over medium heat for 2 minutes. Add the flour and cook, stirring constantly, for 20 to 30 minutes, to make a medium roux (see page 14).

Add the onion and cook for 5 minutes, stirring often. Add the hot water and bring to a boil, stirring to incorporate the water into the roux; reduce the heat and simmer for 5 minutes.

Add the remaining ingredients, except the rice, to the pot. Bring back to a boil, reduce the heat, stir to incorporate all the ingredients, and simmer, covered, for 30 minutes. Serve with rice.

LAGNIAPPE **I found a letter from a vendor to Great-Uncle Adolphe, written in 1921, which regretfully stated that the vendor could not sell any eggs to my uncle as they were scarce, but that he had live spring chickens for sale at $.17 per pound; hens at $.15 per pound; Muly ducks at $.16 per pound; and French ducks were selling from $.45 to $.50 each, depending on their size.**

Buttermilk-Fried Chicken Legs

Chicken legs are our favorite for picnics, as they don't need any utensils, have a lot of meat in a compact little cylinder, and are easy to pack. We can now purchase a package of chicken legs, but Grandma had to cut up a whole chicken when she wanted specific pieces. After she got an icebox in the 1920s, she was able to serve dark meat one day, while soaking the breast meat in buttermilk, or vice versa, for the next day. She thereby had more freedom and versatility in her cooking, as she no longer had to use the whole bird each time she cooked chicken in order to avoid leftovers before refrigeration. ***Serves 4 to 6***

3½ to 4 pounds chicken legs (14 to 16 drumsticks)
2 cups buttermilk
2 tablespoons Tabasco sauce
1 tablespoon salt
1 tablespoon plus 1 tablespoon black pepper, divided
2 cups all-purpose flour
1½ teaspoons cayenne pepper
Corn oil for frying (about 3 cups)

Place the chicken in a bowl and toss with the buttermilk, Tabasco, salt, and 1 tablespoon of the black pepper. Cover, refrigerate, and marinate for at least 1 hour and up to 24 hours.

Remove the chicken from the buttermilk and let excess buttermilk drip off.

Combine the flour, additional 1 tablespoon black pepper, and the cayenne. Shake the chicken legs in the seasoned flour and place on a rack while waiting for the oil to heat.

Place the oil in a Dutch oven or large saucepan (about 6 quarts in size) and heat the oil to 365° to 375°F, using a deep-fry or candy thermometer to check the temperature.

Give the chicken another light toss in the flour, shaking off the excess. Place the chicken in the hot oil, frying about 5 legs at a time without crowding. Cook the chicken for 5 to 6 minutes on each side (10 to 12 minutes total), depending on the size of the legs and the heat of the oil. Keep a close watch on the temperature, trying to maintain 350° to 365°F. Remove the chicken as it is done and place on a clean rack to drain until all the chicken is fried.

LAGNIAPPE Deep-frying vs. pan-frying: in deep-frying, the food is completely immersed in the oil, while in pan-frying the food is placed in enough oil to cover the bottom and sides of the food, necessitating that the food be turned over to fry the top. Three cups of oil will give a depth of ½ inch in a 10-inch skillet and is sufficient to pan-fry.

Chicken Étouffée

Chickens were plentiful on Cajun farms, and a morning decision to have étouffée or gumbo for the noon meal occurred more often than Aunt Lorna would have liked. She dreaded the words "let's have some chicken for lunch," as she had the unappealing task of wringing the chicken's neck, although Grandfather Theodore would help her de-feather it.

Serves 8

- ½ cup corn oil
- 1 chicken (about 4 pounds), cut into 12 pieces (see Lagniappe)
- 2 teaspoons salt
- 2 teaspoons black pepper
- 1 teaspoon cayenne pepper
- 1 pound andouille sausage, cut into ½-inch slices
- 3 cups chopped onion
- 2 cups chopped green bell pepper
- 2 cups chopped celery
- 2 teaspoons garlic powder
- ½ cup water
- ⅔ cup sliced green onions
- ⅓ cup chopped fresh parsley
- 4 cups cooked rice (about 1⅓ cups raw)

Heat the oil in a large heavy skillet or Dutch oven over medium-high heat. Pat the chicken dry with paper towels. Combine the salt and black and cayenne pepper and sprinkle over the chicken.

Brown the chicken pieces (in two batches) for about 3 minutes per side, removing the chicken from the skillet as the pieces are browned. Turn up the heat for 2 to 3 minutes when adding the second batch of chicken to return the heat to medium-high.

Pour the oil into a measuring cup and return about ¼ cup to the pan (there is no need to clean the pan first). Turn the heat back to medium-high. When the oil is hot, add the sausage, onion, bell pepper, celery, and garlic powder and cook until the onion is soft, about 15 minutes.

Return the chicken to the skillet, add the water, spoon the sausage-vegetable mixture over the chicken, cover, and simmer for 40 minutes over medium-low heat. Sprinkle with the green onions and parsley and serve over rice.

LAGNIAPPE To get 12 pieces, cut each breast into 4 pieces, each wing in 2 (discarding the tips or saving them for stock), and separate the legs from the thighs. You will have 4 breast pieces, 4 wings, 2 legs, and 2 thighs. The back may be saved for stock.

Chicken Fricassee

Chicken fricassee was the best dish our dad made. After we all grew up and left home, we would come back for a visit and invariably start sniffing as we got out of our cars, hoping that chicken fricassee was waiting in the big oval pot that covered two burners on the stove. It was always his welcoming dinner when we came home for the holidays.

Serves 6

- 1/3 cup corn oil
- 1/3 cup all-purpose flour
- 1 1/2 cups thinly sliced onion
- 1 cup chopped celery
- 1 cup chopped green bell pepper
- 1 chicken (about 4 pounds), cut into 12 pieces (see Lagniappe, page 62)
- 3 cups hot water
- 1 teaspoon salt
- 1/2 teaspoon black pepper
- 1/2 teaspoon white pepper
- 3 cups cooked rice (about 1 cup raw)

Heat the oil in a large heavy pot or Dutch oven over medium heat. Add the flour and cook, stirring constantly, for 30 to 40 minutes to make a dark roux (see page 14).

Add the onion, celery, and bell pepper, raise the heat to medium-high, and cook for 10 minutes. Place the chicken pieces skin side down on the bottom of the pot, moving the vegetables on top of the chicken as the pieces are placed in the pot. Brown the chicken for 5 minutes.

Add the water and seasonings and bring to a boil. Reduce the heat and simmer, covered, over medium-low heat for 1 hour and 30 minutes, or until the chicken is tender but not falling off the bone. Serve over rice.

LAGNIAPPE **This may be served right away, but I like to make it the day before and cool and refrigerate it. As with many stew-type dishes, this is even better after sitting for a day. It also gives the fat the chance to rise to the surface when refrigerated, and it can be lifted off if desired.**

Chicken Jambalaya

One of many Cajun controversies is whether jambalaya should have tomatoes in it. A restaurateur I know once had a group from Lafayette in her restaurant, Café New Orleans, in Old Town Sacramento, California. The guests loved the jambalaya but picked out any evidence of tomato before they would eat it. Our family puts tomato in almost all of our jambalaya recipes; it's just the way we've always made it.
Serves 6

3 strips thick bacon, coarsely chopped
½ cup chopped onion
½ cup chopped celery
½ cup chopped green bell pepper
Two 14-ounce cans diced tomatoes, drained
2 cups chicken stock
1 cup raw rice
3 cups coarsely chopped cooked chicken
1 teaspoon salt
½ teaspoon white pepper
2 bay leaves
3 tablespoons sliced green onions

Cook the bacon in a heavy skillet or Dutch oven until it is crisp. Remove the bacon (leaving the drippings), crumble, and set aside.

Set the heat at medium-high, add the onion, celery, and bell pepper to the drippings, and cook until the vegetables are translucent and browned, about 10 minutes, stirring often.

Add remaining ingredients, except green onions, and bring to a boil, stirring to combine the ingredients.

Reduce the heat to low, cover, and cook for 1 hour, stirring every 15 minutes. (Keep the heat adjusted so the jambalaya is cooking just under a simmer; add a bit of water, if necessary, to keep it from sticking.)

Remove the bay leaves and serve sprinkled with the crumbled bacon and green onions.

LAGNIAPPE A half pound of thick bacon equals 9 pieces, and yields ½ cup strained drippings.

To cook bacon without having to keep a close eye on it, cook it in a heavy skillet for about 30 minutes over medium heat. It cooks slowly but ends up crispy. For bacon that is especially crusty, dip it in flour before cooking it; the flour forms a thin crust as the bacon cooks. Any leftover poultry, fish, or meat could be used in place of the chicken as a delicious way to turn leftovers into a prized dish.

Chicken Maque Choux

Maque choux was one of Aunt Lorna's most loved dishes, but she could never seem to get it exactly the way her mother made it. We had some great meals, however, while she was trying. Though maque choux is usually just a vegetable dish, this recipe includes chicken, for a complete meal. Serves 6

- 6 large ears corn
- 1 tablespoon salt
- 1 teaspoon black pepper
- ½ teaspoon cayenne pepper
- 1 chicken (about 4 pounds), cut in 12 pieces (see Lagniappe, page 62)
- ½ cup corn oil
- 1 cup chopped green bell pepper
- 1 cup chopped fresh or canned tomatoes
- ¾ cup sliced green onions

Place the stem end of the corn on a cutting board. Holding the tip, cut vertically down the ear to remove the corn from the cob. Cut again vertically down the cob to get the liquid or "milk" from the cob. Set aside.

Combine the salt and black and cayenne pepper and sprinkle over the chicken.

Heat the oil in a heavy pot or Dutch oven over medium-high heat.

Brown the chicken pieces, a few at a time, about 5 minutes on each side, removing them to a platter as they are browned.

Pour the oil into a measuring cup, and return about ¼ cup of the oil to the skillet (there's no need to clean the pan first). Reduce the heat to medium, add the corn, bell pepper, and tomatoes and stir to combine. Add the chicken and any accumulated juices, and spoon the vegetables over the chicken. Cover and cook for 45 minutes, stirring every 15 minutes to prevent sticking, and to redistribute the vegetables and chicken. Sprinkle with the green onions before serving.

LAGNIAPPE **Six large ears of corn will yield about 6 cups of corn. You could use frozen corn for this, but as this dish was probably developed to make use of wonderful, sweet fresh corn it somewhat defeats the purpose to use a frozen version of the vegetable.**

Chicken Pecan Salad

This dish uses two ingredients we can't get enough of: chicken and pecans. It's a dish we often take on picnics because it is so versatile: it makes a great hors d'oeuvre spread on Crispy Cayenne French Toasts (page 146) or bread; a hearty sandwich filling; stuffing for fresh tomatoes; or a topping for fresh, crisp salad greens. The pecans and celery give it an appealing crunch. This is our standard dish when we have leftover chicken. Grandpa made it even better by toasting the pecans before adding them to the salad, as it gave them a deeper, nuttier flavor. Serves 6

- 4 cups cooked white meat chicken, cut into ½-inch cubes (about 2 pounds raw)
- 1 cup chopped celery
- 1 cup sliced green onions
- ¾ cup mayonnaise
- ½ cup chopped pecans
- ½ cup chopped fresh parsley
- 1 teaspoon salt
- ½ teaspoon white pepper
- ¼ teaspoon cayenne pepper

Combine all the ingredients and use as an appetizer, a sandwich filling, or a stuffing for tomatoes; or serve on lettuce leaves.

LAGNIAPPE **When poaching or baking a whole chicken for chicken salad, or any dish requiring boneless chicken, one 5-pound chicken will yield about 2¼ pounds of boneless, skinless chicken meat. Of course, it's easier (though more expensive) to purchase 2 pounds of boneless, skinless chicken to cook; even easier than that, however, is to purchase roasted chicken from the deli.**

Chicken Pie

This is one of our frequent uses for leftover chicken stew, or leftover chicken with gravy. Chicken fricassee, étouffée, any stew-type dish, or even jambalaya encased in pie crusts disguises last night's dinner as something new. Dad loved using leftovers creatively, and with this pie in his repertoire we were able to steer him away from saving bits of this and bits of that and mixing it all together into what was always different, but invariably a horrible concoction he called "icebox stew."

Serves 6

2 pie crusts, purchased or homemade (page 263)

5 cups boneless leftover chicken stew, fricassee, étouffée, sauce piquante, chicken and gravy, or jambalaya (if leftovers don't measure 5 cups, add cooked vegetables and/or potatoes to equal 5 cups of filling for pie)

2 tablespoons cold butter, cut into pieces

Preheat the oven to 400°F.

Fit one pie crust onto the bottom of a pie plate, and fill with the chicken stew. Dot with the butter.

Place the top crust on the pie, fold the edges underneath the edges of the bottom crust, and crimp with fingers or a fork to decorate and hold in place. Cut a few slits in the top of the crust.

Bake for 40 minutes. Let sit for a few minutes, then cut.

LAGNIAPPE **This can also be made with beef or seafood stew and is a great way to turn the ubiquitous leftover turkey, gravy, and vegetables from Thanksgiving into an appealing dish.**

Chicken Sauce Piquante

This is the hottest dish that my grandparents made, and probably their favorite. The amount of pepper in this, their version, is not excessive. It is spicy but not painfully hot. Grandma and Grandpa generally made dishes that were loaded with flavor, but not hot enough to burn your tongue; many Cajuns add a lot more pepper than you will find here.
Serves 6

⅓ cup corn oil, or more if needed
2 pounds boneless, skinless chicken breasts, cut into 1-inch cubes
½ cup all-purpose flour
1 cup chopped onion
1 cup chopped celery
½ cup chopped green bell pepper
2 cloves garlic, minced
1 teaspoon dried thyme
1 teaspoon salt
1 teaspoon black pepper
½ teaspoon cayenne pepper
¼ teaspoon Tabasco sauce
¼ teaspoon sugar
One 6-ounce can tomato paste
One 14-ounce can diced tomatoes, undrained
2 cups chicken stock
2 bay leaves
3 cups cooked rice (about 1 cup raw)
1 cup sliced green onions
½ cup chopped fresh parsley

Heat the oil in a large heavy pot or Dutch oven over medium-high heat for 2 minutes. Add the chicken and cook for 5 minutes, stirring constantly. Remove the chicken from the pot with a slotted spoon, cool, and refrigerate.

Pour the oil from the pot into a measuring cup, and add enough additional oil to equal $\frac{1}{3}$ cup total (there's no need to clean the pot). Return the oil to the pot, reduce the heat to medium, and heat for 2 minutes, scraping the bottom of the pot to incorporate crispy bits on the bottom into the oil. Add the flour to the oil and cook, stirring constantly, for 5 minutes.

Add the onion, celery, and bell pepper and cook for 5 minutes, stirring often. Add the garlic, seasonings, Tabasco, and sugar and cook for 5 minutes. Add the tomato paste, tomatoes, chicken stock, and bay leaves; stir to combine, and bring to a boil.

Reduce the heat to medium-low, cover, and simmer gently for 1 hour, stirring occasionally (stir every few minutes toward the end, and reduce the heat if necessary, as the sauce may scorch as it thickens). Add the chicken cubes and any accumulated juice from the chicken, and cook for an additional 20 minutes, covered, stirring occasionally. Serve over rice sprinkled with green onions and parsley.

LAGNIAPPE **Sauce Piquante is one of the oldest and most loved of all Cajun dishes. It always has a roux, tomatoes, and plenty of pepper, and may be made with any poultry, meat, or seafood. It is a popular way to cook game, as the intense flavor in the sauce will counterbalance the hearty flavor of game such as squirrel, rabbit, turtle, frog, alligator, or duck.**

Chicken Pie with Shrimp

Chickens were always a big part of Home Place. They were raised for the family's consumption, but also raised to sell—both eggs and chickens. My grandparents had endless ways of preparing chicken: smoked, stuffed, used as stuffing, stewed, barbecued, roasted, made into pies, salad, gumbo, fricassee, jambalaya, maque choux and, of course, fried. Serves 6

- ¼ cup corn oil
- ⅓ cup all-purpose flour
- 1 cup chopped onion
- ½ cup celery
- ¼ cup chopped green bell pepper
- 2 cups cooked chicken, cut into ½-inch cubes
- ½ pound raw shrimp, peeled and deveined
- 1 cup chicken stock
- 1 teaspoon salt
- ½ teaspoon white pepper
- ¼ teaspoon cayenne pepper
- 2 pie crusts, purchased or homemade (page 263)
- 2 tablespoons cold butter, cut into pieces

Preheat the oven to 350°F.

Heat the oil in a large heavy skillet over medium heat for 2 minutes. Add the flour and cook for 20 to 30 minutes, stirring constantly, to make a medium roux (see page 14).

Add the onion, celery, and bell pepper and cook for 10 minutes, stirring often.

Add the chicken, shrimp, stock, and seasonings and bring to a boil. Immediately reduce the heat to low and cook gently for 3 minutes, stirring often, until the shrimp begin to turn pink.

Remove from the heat. Fit one pie crust onto the bottom of a pie plate, and fill with the chicken-shrimp mixture. Dot with the butter. Place the top crust on the pie, fold the edges underneath the edges of the bottom crust, and crimp with fingers or a fork to decorate and hold in place. Cut a few slits in the top of the crust.

Bake for 1 hour and 15 minutes, or until golden brown.

LAGNIAPPE **Shrimp may be deveined by running the pointed end of a beer-type can opener down the center of the back. This intestinal tube doesn't have to be removed, but usually is for aesthetics, and because it may contain sand.**

Daddy's Cajun Chicken Wings

We could eat these every day. The fact that they take only minutes to prepare is just a bonus. Chicken wings were Dad's favorite and he never, never, got enough of them. The serving size listed below is for normal people; not "chicken wing" people. I've seen three people eat the entire batch as an appetizer.

Makes 40 pieces; serve 4 as an entrée, 10 as an appetizer

2 tablespoons plus ½ cup corn oil
20 chicken wings (about 4 pounds)
8 tablespoons (1 stick) butter
¼ cup Tabasco sauce
1 tablespoon salt
2 teaspoons black pepper
1 teaspoon white pepper

Grease a large baking sheet(s) with the 2 tablespoons oil (see Lagniappe).

Discard the wing tips (or save for stock), and cut the wings at the joint into two pieces.

Heat the remaining ingredients with the ½ cup corn oil in a small saucepan until the butter melts to make the marinade.

Place the chicken wing pieces in a large bowl, add the marinade, and toss to coat the chicken evenly. Marinate for 30 minutes at room temperature or longer in the refrigerator (the chicken may be marinated in the refrigerator for several hours). Stir a few times while marinating to evenly coat the wings with sauce.

Preheat the oven to 400°F.

Transfer the wings to the greased baking sheet(s) and place in the oven. Cook for 30 minutes, then pour off excess liquid, leaving some liquid on the baking sheet. Loosen the wings with a metal spatula and turn, repositioning the browned wings with those less browned so they all cook evenly. Cook 20 minutes longer.

LAGNIAPPE **If you don't have a baking sheet large enough to hold the wings in a single layer without crowding them, bake the wings in two batches, with 1 tablespoon oil on each sheet. (If the wings are baked on two sheets with one under the other, the lower one will tend to steam rather than get crisp and browned.) If you like your wings very crisp and browned, spread them out on the baking sheets with lots of room around each one.**

Fried Chicken, Aunt Lorna's Way

There's absolutely no doubt—fried chicken is the number one favorite food of most Cajuns in our family. My birthday dinner is always the same—rich, unbalanced, and wonderful: fried chicken, mashed potatoes, gravy, corn, biscuits with butter and honey, and green beans. I really look forward, with guilty pleasure, to that yearly birthday feast. Serves 6

- 1 chicken (about 4 pounds), cut into 12 pieces (see Lagniappe, page 62)
- 2 cups buttermilk
- 2 teaspoons salt
- 1 teaspoon black pepper
- ½ teaspoon cayenne pepper
- 2 cups all-purpose flour
- 3 cups lard or corn oil

Gravy

- ¼ cup all-purpose flour
- ½ teaspoon salt
- ½ teaspoon black pepper
- ¼ teaspoon cayenne pepper (optional)
- 2 cups whole milk, or more if needed

Place the chicken pieces in a large bowl and toss with the buttermilk; cover and refrigerate for several hours or overnight. Remove the chicken and let the excess buttermilk drip off.

Mix the salt, pepper, and cayenne and sprinkle over both sides of the chicken.

Place the flour on a baking sheet and toss the chicken pieces in the flour, shaking off the excess and transferring the floured chicken pieces to a rack on a baking sheet.

Divide the oil between two skillets and heat over high heat for several minutes, until the oil is about 365°F.

As soon as the oil reaches 365°F, toss the chicken in the flour again, shaking off the excess, and place in the hot oil, skin side down, with thighs and legs in the center and breasts and wings around the sides.

Cook for 3 minutes, then turn the heat down to medium and turn the chicken over. Cook 5 minutes longer, reduce the heat to low, cover tightly, and cook over low heat for 15 minutes. Remove the lid, turn over once more, raise the heat to medium, and cook 5 minutes longer, uncovered.

Remove the chicken and keep warm by loosely covering with foil while making the gravy.

To make the gravy, remove all but about 1/4 cup oil from one of the skillets (leaving as many crispy bits as possible in the bottom). Turn the heat to medium-low and add the flour and the spices. Cook for 5 minutes, whisking constantly.

Add the milk, turn the heat to high, and bring to a boil, whisking constantly. Reduce the heat to low, and whisk for 3 minutes until the gravy is smooth (add a bit more milk if the gravy is too thick).

LAGNIAPPE **Buttermilk adds a bit of a tangy flavor to foods, as well as having a tenderizing effect. It helps to give baked goods a light texture. Traditionally, buttermilk was the liquid that remained after butter was churned, but due to a shortage of buttermilk in the mid-1900s, "cultured buttermilk" was developed by fermenting skim milk until it was thick and acidic. Cultured buttermilk is the form most commonly found in markets today, along with "Bulgarian buttermilk," which is thicker and more acidic and, thus, more tart.**

Grilled Duck Breasts

When Dad and Grandpa went on a duck hunting trip, it was always a mystery whether there would be enough ducks to invite neighbors over, or just the amount for everyone in the family to have a taste of the small bounty. I know that rare or medium-rare duck is the fashion now, but we always cooked a duck until it was about 180°F—still moist, and slightly pink only near the bone.

Serves 2 to 4 (see Lagniappe)

2 whole muscovy or teal duck breasts (about 1½ pounds total weight)
1 tablespoon Seasoning Blend for Beef and Game (page 18) or salt and pepper
1 tablespoon corn oil

Preheat the oven to 400°F.

Pat the duck breasts very dry with paper towels. Score the skin and fat of the duck breast in a crisscross pattern, taking care not to cut into the flesh. (Wild ducks do not have the thick layer of fat that domestic ducks do.)

Season all over with the seasoning blend, or season liberally with salt and pepper.

Heat the oil in a heavy ovenproof skillet over medium-high heat for 2 minutes. When hot, turn the heat down to medium, place the duck breasts in the skillet skin side down, and sear for 6 minutes. Turn over and sear for 2 minutes.

Turn skin side down again and place the skillet in the oven. Roast for 20 to 25 minutes, or until the meat thermometer measures about 175°F. Remove from the oven and allow to rest for 5 minutes (the temperature will rise to 180°F as the duck rests). To serve, carefully cut each duck breast away from the bone, in one piece, and slice at an angle.

LAGNIAPPE I'm not usually vague about serving amounts, but these two duck breasts, totaling 1½ pounds before cooking, yielded 14 ounces edible duck meat once they were cooked and the bones removed. This is about 3½ ounces edible duck meat per person for four people, or 7 ounces per person for two people. We find that the duck is rich and hearty enough that 3½ ounces per person is enough, and we serve four people with this recipe, but you may want to use this portion for two people.

Hot Sausage Po' Boys

I didn't realize that turkey was a part of the food on our family farm, until I saw a letter from my great-grandfather to his son, referring to turkey. My grandmother generally cut up the turkey rather than roasting it whole; she used the legs, thighs, wings, and back for stews or soups, then ground the white meat and dark meat from the carcass for sausages. Serves 6

Sausage

- 1 pound ground turkey (dark and white meat)
- ½ pound ground beef (not lean)
- ½ cup chopped onion
- ¼ cup chopped fresh parsley
- 2 cloves garlic, finely chopped
- 1 teaspoon salt
- ½ teaspoon crushed red pepper
- ½ teaspoon black pepper
- ½ teaspoon dried thyme
- ¼ teaspoon cayenne pepper
- ⅛ teaspoon ground allspice

- 3 tablespoons corn oil
- 1 large onion, halved lengthwise and sliced across
- 1 large green bell pepper, quartered lengthwise, seeded and sliced across
- ½ teaspoon salt
- 6 soft sandwich rolls
- Optional garnishes: tomatoes, lettuce, pickles

Mix all the sausage ingredients. Shape into 6 sausages about the length of the sandwich rolls, but flattened a bit so the center cooks.

Heat the oil in a large heavy skillet over medium-high heat. When the oil is hot, add the onion, bell pepper, and salt. Sauté for 5 minutes, stirring often, until the vegetables are tender but not soft; lift out of the pan with a slotted spoon.

Add the sausages to the pan and cook for 10 to 12 minutes, turning halfway through to cook evenly. (Gently cut into the center of one sausage to be sure it is done and not pink in the middle.) Don't overcook or the sausages will be dry.

Serve the sausages on rolls with the sautéed vegetables and desired garnishes.

LAGNIAPPE **Contrary to popular belief, many Cajun dishes are fairly low in fat, not because they were "reduced" in the amount of fat, but because they just don't contain a lot of it. This is one of those dishes, rich in flavor, but healthful.**

Old-Fashioned Chicken Stew

Chickens are versatile and adapt to slow or fast cooking, and the specific use depends on the age of the bird: younger chickens are fried, and older ones go into stew, gumbo, or fricassee. In spite of the three hen houses on Home Place, a few chickens were always loose, as chickens were allowed to run free for a week before they were eaten. **Serves 6**

- 4 tablespoons (½ stick) butter
- 1 chicken (about 4 pounds), cut into 12 pieces (see Lagniappe, page 62)
- 1½ cups chopped onion
- ¼ cup all-purpose flour
- 1 teaspoon salt
- ½ teaspoon pepper
- 4 cups water
- 1½ pounds unpeeled potatoes, cut into bite-size cubes
- ½ cup chopped fresh parsley

Heat the butter in a large heavy pot or Dutch oven over medium-high heat. Pat the chicken dry, and fry in butter, in a single layer, until browned, removing pieces to a platter as they are browned. Add the onion, reduce the heat to medium, and sauté the onion for 5 minutes. Add the flour, salt, and pepper and cook, stirring constantly, for 2 minutes.

Add the water and bring to a boil, scraping to incorporate the crust on the bottom into the liquid, and stirring until the sauce is smooth. Add the potatoes and chicken, with any accumulated juices, to the pot. Stir, reduce the heat to low, cover, and simmer for 1 hour. Sprinkle with parsley and serve.

LAGNIAPPE Two pounds of whole chicken breasts yields 1½ pounds boneless, skinless breasts. Most meat, poultry, and seafood have about a 25 percent loss after cooking. When roasting a whole chicken, plan on ¾ pound per person; thus, a 4½ pound chicken will feed six people.

Pepper-Roasted Chicken with Lemon Pan Drippings

Dad's cure for all ills was this roast chicken, with its tangy, lemony pan juices. ***Serves 4 to 6***

3 tablespoons olive oil
1 chicken (4 to 4½ pounds)
2 teaspoons salt
1 teaspoon black pepper
1 teaspoon dried thyme
½ teaspoon paprika
½ teaspoon white pepper
½ teaspoon cayenne pepper
4 cloves garlic, sliced
1½ cups chicken stock, or more if needed
2 tablespoons fresh lemon juice

Preheat the oven to 475°F.

Rub the olive oil over the outside of the chicken.

Combine the salt, black pepper, thyme, paprika, white pepper, and cayenne pepper and sprinkle on the outside of the chicken, using a bit to sprinkle inside the bird.

Insert the garlic slices under the skin of the chicken breast.

Place the chicken on a V-rack in a roasting pan, breast side down, and add stock to the bottom of the pan. Roast for 20 minutes. Turn the chicken breast side up, baste with any pan juices, return to the oven, and reduce the heat to 325°F.

Continue roasting for 30 minutes, then insert a thermometer into the thickest part of the breast meat, and then into the thickest part of the thigh meat; avoid touching the bone with the thermometer. The chicken has finished cooking when the temperature reaches about 160°F (it will rise to its ideal temperature of 165°F as it sits). Tip the chicken so its internal juices flow into the baking pan; if the juices are pink, cook the chicken 5 minutes longer.

Transfer the chicken to a platter, cover loosely with foil to keep warm, and allow to stand for 15 minutes before carving.

Pour the juices from the bottom of the pan into a small saucepan. Place in the freezer for 15 minutes while the chicken cools. Lift the fat off the pan juices with a spoon, add the lemon juice, and heat. Serve the juices with the chicken.

LAGNIAPPE **The amount of juices in the pan will depend on the amount of fat and juice in the chicken. You can always add more stock if the pan juices are cooking away too fast.**

Roast Teal Duck

Mallard and teal were the ducks Grandpa and Dad usually brought home, and we never knew until they got back if the duck (or ducks) would arrive in serving pieces or whole, how many there would be, or how big—or small—they would be. We had a few basic ways of cooking them, and would decide when we saw the ducks which method we would use, but this was the most common. Serves 4

- 1 teaspoon salt
- ½ teaspoon black pepper
- 4 teal or other small ducks (7 to 10 ounces each)
- 4 cloves garlic, sliced
- ¾ cup chopped onion
- ½ cup chopped green bell pepper
- ½ cup chopped carrot
- 2 tablespoons corn oil
- 4 baking potatoes (about 2 pounds), unpeeled, cut into eighths

Preheat the oven to 350°F.

Pat the ducks dry. Combine the salt and pepper and sprinkle evenly over the outside of the ducks.

Combine the vegetables, and insert into the cavities of the ducks.

Heat the oil in a heavy skillet over medium-high heat. When the oil is hot, brown the ducks on all sides (this will take 10 to 15 minutes).

Transfer the skillet to the oven and bake for 15 minutes. Add potatoes to the skillet, stir to coat with the fat, and bake 30 minutes longer. (A thermometer should measure 180°F when the duck is done. If the ducks are not the same size, they may need to be removed from the oven as they are done.) It's best to serve the ducks right away.

LAGNIAPPE Duck is wonderful with a hearty grain, like wild rice. Plan the cooking time so the rice is done at the same time the duck is ready. Flavorful greens, such as mustard greens, kale, or Swiss chard, are an ideal accompaniment to duck, as the strong flavors go well together, and the clean flavor of the greens is a balance to the richness of the duck.

Roasted Duck with Garlic and Turnips

All Cajun men seem to love hunting. Dad went hunting with his great-uncles, uncle, and father, then carried on the tradition by taking his son and nephews hunting. My cousin Joe loved the sport, but my brother, Linus, didn't care for hunting. We all, however, loved the results of the hunting excursions, especially this recipe for duck roasted with root vegetables. Serves 4

- 2 mallard or other ducks (about 1½ pounds each)
- 2 tablespoons corn oil
- 1 teaspoon salt
- ½ teaspoon black pepper
- ½ teaspoon cayenne pepper
- ½ teaspoon dried thyme
- 2 bay leaves
- 2 medium turnips (about 1½ pounds), cut into 1-inch cubes
- 2 medium carrots, cut into ½-inch cubes
- 8 whole cloves garlic, peeled

Preheat the oven to 350°F.

Cut a few slits in the duck skin and fat in several places on all sides of the bird using a sharp knife (do not cut into the flesh). (If using wild ducks, be aware that they may be lean and only need a few very shallow slits.)

Heat the oil in a large heavy Dutch oven over medium-high heat. Thoroughly brown the ducks on all sides. This will take about 15 minutes.

Spoon off some of the fat, leaving a thin layer of fat on the bottom of the pot. Sprinkle the ducks with salt, black and cayenne pepper, and thyme. Add the bay leaves to the pot and roast in the oven for 15 minutes.

Remove the pot from the oven and set the ducks on a plate. Add the turnips, carrots, and garlic to the pot and toss to coat with the fat. Place the ducks on top of the vegetables and roast for an additional 60 minutes. Ducks are done when a thermometer inserted into the thigh reads 180°F.

LAGNIAPPE **It is my experience that most duck hunters love the sport but have long ago lost their excitement over cooking the birds and, thus, usually have a freezer full of ducks. More than one hunter I know has gladly given me a few ducks in exchange for some gumbo, fricassee, or whatever I was planning to make.**

Turkey Jambalaya, Oven Style

We sometimes cut our Thanksgiving turkey in serving pieces and roast it, cooking the dark meat first, then adding the breast meat (which cooks in less time). As we usually carve in the kitchen, no one misses the whole bird at the table. When doing this, we reserve some of the breast meat uncooked to turn what would otherwise have been more leftover turkey into a flavorful jambalaya the next day.
Serves 6

- 3 slices bacon, coarsely chopped
- 1 cup chopped onion
- ¾ cup chopped celery
- ½ cup chopped green bell pepper
- 3 cloves garlic, minced
- 1 pound raw boneless, skinless turkey breast, cut into ½-inch cubes
- 3¾ cups chicken stock
- ½ cup plus ½ cup chopped fresh parsley
- 1 teaspoon salt
- ½ teaspoon black pepper
- ½ teaspoon dried thyme
- ¼ teaspoon cayenne pepper
- 2 bay leaves
- 1½ cups raw rice
- ½ cup sliced green onions

Preheat the oven to 350°F.

Cook the bacon in a large heavy pot or Dutch oven over medium heat, until the bacon fat is rendered and the bacon is crisp. Crumble the bacon and set it aside.

Add the onion, celery, bell pepper, and garlic and sauté for 10 minutes, stirring often. Add the turkey and cook 5 minutes longer, stirring often.

Add the stock, ½ cup of the parsley, salt, pepper, thyme, cayenne, and bay leaves and bring to a boil. Add the rice and stir to combine with the vegetables; cover and bake for 45 minutes.

Dish up and sprinkle with green onions, the additional ½ cup parsley, and the reserved bacon.

LAGNIAPPE **This method of cooking jambalaya is convenient when there is room in the oven and the burners are being used for stovetop cooking. As it needs no stirring, it can be put in the oven and forgotten until it is done.**

Meat

Olympe Labauve, 1918

Grandma Olympe and Her Magic Bag

The first time I saw my Cajun grandmother, I was very young.

Photos of her indicated an imposing presence. She was a thin woman, with angular features and dark hair—always in a bun. Her face was stern, yet my father spoke of her with tenderness. Not so my mother. When the impending visit was mentioned, Mom would clench her teeth and Dad would look at her and sigh. Evidently, a strong-willed French mother-in-law was an unfair match for a gentle Irish lady in her twenties. I had been anxious with anticipation ever since I heard that Grandma and Grandpa were coming from Louisiana to visit us in San Francisco.

I was standing by the living room window when Dad brought them from the train station. He opened the door and Grandma, all in black, walked directly across the room toward me, her eyes fixed on mine and her mouth set in determination. Without even speaking, she handed me a pair of beautiful black lace gloves, and I felt that she had kept them in her hands through the entire trip, just waiting to give them to me. She knew how to reach me, and I felt special that she cared enough to single me out. I was hers. The last time she and Grandpa had visited us in San Francisco I was only two, and I didn't remember her. She was determined to connect with her youngest grandchild, who was now old enough to have a relationship with her.

Even at my young age I could tell that my mother just put up with Grandma, and I wondered why my mom didn't like this elegant little woman. A clue came that first day when I overheard my grandmother tell my mother that "our family is descended from French royalty, but you are just a peasant." My mother didn't seem to like that. Mom didn't let me revel in my heightened status as half royalty, however, making it clear that the royalty was so far back that we were just as common as she. Though I never heard her tell that to Grandma Pischoff.

Another hint that my mother was less than enchanted with her mother-in-law was Grandma's immediate entry into the kitchen. While Mom was never thrilled about cooking, she had prepared a nice dinner for that night. In fact, she had fussed over it for days, probably knowing that anything she cooked would not be good enough. Right she was. With a wave of her hand, Grandma dismissed the *carefully seasoned crown roast of lamb, surrounded by potatoes and vegetables, waiting to go in the oven. "We don't eat roasted lamb, but we can make soup from it tomorrow," she proclaimed. "I'm going to make a real Cajun dinner."*

When Grandma began pulling strange items from her old flowered tapestry carpetbag, I was frozen with awe. She was thrilled that she still had an audience of one (everyone else had left the kitchen to go see how Mom was doing), and patiently explained each of the foods to me.

I had seen them all before, but Grandma gave me a personal introduction to each one and we had our own little taste test starting with tasso, a dried smoked pork that tasted very salty. Andouille, a sausage that was already familiar, had a wonderful spicy flavor when eaten all by itself. Crunchy fried pork skins, or cracklings, relegated potato chips to nothing but a bland memory. The powdery green substance called filé was a fixture on our dinner table, but on its own it was a bit like fine, dry dust, and it made my mouth pucker. I was not allowed to taste the red powdered cayenne pepper.

Grandma reverently unrolled a jar that had been wrapped in layers of cloth, still cold from being in the refrigerator on the train where the porter, apparently understanding the importance of roux, had kept it for her. I shivered as she said, in a most serious voice, "This is the basis of all good food; without it you can't cook anything." Wow. What was it? She finished removing the cloth and showed me some ugly brown stuff in a jar, with oil floating on top. It didn't look very good to me, but I wanted to pretend that I thought it did, so I asked if I could taste it.

"No child, it's not for tasting, it's for cooking."

"Oh," I said, but I wasn't impressed.

By that time, it was announced that Mom was going to take a nap before dinner, and everyone pretended gratitude toward my grandmother for stepping in to fix the meal. I still remember Dad pointedly saying to Grandma, "Mom, it won't be spicy. Right?" She nodded in agreement, looking none too pleased until she found some beef in the refrigerator that brightened up her spirits.

"Fricassee," she whispered to me, as if this new word was something she and I had been discussing for years. I never wondered why Grandma took over dinner that night. Somehow I knew it had been long planned, but I forgave her because I took to Grandma Pischoff the way I took to her magic bag of fascinating foods.

I'll never forget that meal, and how Grandma gathered her jar of roux and the meat she found in the refrigerator and deftly put them together into what I thought was probably the best thing I had ever tasted. What struck me, even at that age, was that she didn't use any of her secret foods from the carpetbag but, rather, the ordinary ingredients like salt and pepper that my mother used when she cooked. But it didn't remind me of anything my mother had ever made. And I probably shouldn't have shared that information with the rest of the family. When I tasted Grandma's fricassee of beef, I announced, "I didn't know anything could taste this good." My mother put down her fork and quietly said, "Terri, it's beef stew."

"Really? It doesn't taste like beef stew. You should get the recipe." This was so over-the-top that no one could keep from laughing, and it actually broke the tension. My grandmother spoke to my mother in a truly kind voice, lacking the patronizing tone she usually reserved for her, and said, "Mary, dear, would you like to learn how to make fricassee?" Mom was surprised enough to respond positively before she could think about her answer, and a cooking lesson was planned for the next day. I asked if I could watch the lesson and, in unison, Mom and Grandma said, "Yes!" No doubt thinking that I would be a buffer between them.

My pride in being singled out by Grandma to watch the cooking lesson is still with me. I knew I was her favorite—we just clicked. Not that my three older siblings seemed to care, as they were involved in more important things, like my brother listening to his Davy Crockett records while he wore the coonskin cap Grandma had given him, and my teenaged sisters talking on the phone and making plans to sneak out that evening.

We all went to bed early that night. I knew my grandparents must have been tired after their long train ride, but I was hoping they wouldn't sleep too late because I wanted to watch Mom's fricassee lesson.

My three older siblings laughed at me as I sat in the middle of the kitchen bright and early the next morning with one ear against the floor, hoping I could hear Grandma and Grandpa moving around in the guest room downstairs. My brother wondered why I wanted to spend the day watching someone cook, as he donned his aviator hat and stormed out of the house to meet Eddie Engler and jump out of trees. My sisters were putting on their gloves and hats and heading to Union Square to shop for clothes and have lunch at Blum's. They were instructed to bring a coffee crunch cake home with them. Mom wanted to show Grandma Pischoff that there were, indeed, things in California worth eating.

There was no noise coming from downstairs and I was instructed not to wake my grandparents "because they had a long, hard day yesterday," according to Dad. "Humph," murmured Mom, as she turned on her heel and went back to their bedroom. Dad fixed a big breakfast that included pain perdu (French toast) and scrambled eggs with andouille sausage and said, finally, that I could go downstairs and tell Grandma and Grandpa that breakfast was ready.

I felt shy, having become acquainted with them less than twenty-four hours before, but couldn't wait to see them. The door to their bedroom was open, and I peeked in. "Come in, child," they said, as if they had been waiting for me all night. They were putting on their shoes and I sat on the bench at the end of the bed. I didn't know what to say, and hoped they would start talking. They didn't say much, just smiled at me and I knew they really wanted me there, and that they loved me. I remember warmth and smiles, and no words seemed necessary.

I led them upstairs when they had their shoes on and were ready, and we sat down to breakfast, minus Mom and my siblings. The kids were absent, Dad explained, because it was Saturday, and they all had plans. I saw raised eyebrows on my grandparents' faces, wondering why the family wasn't eating breakfast together, but Dad assured them that everyone would be here for dinner.

"Including Mary?" queried my grandmother. "The fricassee we're going to make is mild enough for Irish people."

"Mom, I'm really glad you're here, but we've got to have a talk before you start the cooking lesson," announced Dad, with a somewhat defeated expression on his face. They went into the living room for what seemed like a long time. When they returned Grandma was very quiet, and proceeded to get things ready for the lesson.

"We'll wait for your mother before we start, but I'm glad you're going to watch. Since you are Cajun, you should learn how to cook like a Cajun."

"Half Cajun," my mother interjected, entering the kitchen, "and half Irish." Grandma gave her a sharp look, but she saw from my mother's facial expression that this particular point was non-negotiable. Very non-negotiable. She pursed her lips and turned to the stove.

"Shall we begin, Mary, dear?" It was the second and last time I heard my grandmother say anything in close to an affectionate tone to my mother, but the talk with Dad had been only moments before, and she did want to teach my mother and me how to make fricassee. Mom responded to my grandmother's momentary affection toward her and got out an apron for each of them. She saw my disappointed face and pulled out a third apron, gathering and tying it to fit my four-year-old frame. Pulling a stool over to the stove, Mom winked at me and said, "Let's get started."

This was the only dish Grandma ever taught Mom how to make, and one that Mom taught me several times afterward until I grasped the concept. Every time we made the dish together, Mom and I would go over the events of that visit and the day we learned to make fricassee. It is now as clear to me as if it had happened yesterday. Grandma began by saying the words I have heard thousands of times since that day, "First you make a roux." I whispered to Mom, "Oh, no! The ugly brown stuff in a jar." Fortunately, Grandma did not hear me.

"It has to be the first lesson. You can't cook anything properly unless you know how to make a roux." She heated a large, heavy cast iron pot until it was hot, then added some oil. She waited a bit, then added flour, and immediately began stirring. And stirring. And stirring.

"Remember, you must get the roux dark, dark, dark for meat, but you need a golden roux for seafood." It didn't occur to her that a four-year-old she'd just met, and an Irish lady who didn't really want to eat Cajun food, might not be interested in her light-roux-for-seafood and dark-roux-for-meat principle. Mom seemed to think it was more information than she needed, but I was interested, as Grandma knew I would be. She and I were on the same wavelength from the very beginning.

I was starting to have doubts about what was turning into a very long lesson, when the most amazing aroma began to fill the kitchen. It smelled like a combination of toasted nuts, roasted meat, and fried bread. I loved it. We watched as she stirred this mixture in the hot pot. The roux turned into a smooth, rich, dark-dark-dark brown and entered my senses to remain there forever. Thus began my lifelong love affair with Cajun cooking.

Beef Roast with Gravy

The vegetables in this recipe form a delicious sauce, as they break down after several hours of cooking and are then pureed. Even though Grandma used a potato masher rather than any electric appliance to puree the vegetables, she considered this to be an easy recipe. There's very little work involved here, even though the recipe looks long, but do ***note the 2- to 4-day marinating time.*** *Serves 8 to 10*

1 teaspoon plus 1 teaspoon salt
1 teaspoon plus 1 teaspoon black pepper
1½ teaspoons dried thyme
1½ teaspoons garlic powder
1 teaspoon cayenne pepper
¼ pound salt pork, cut into small cubes (about ½ inch)
1 boneless beef chuck, round, or rump roast (4 to 5 pounds)
½ cup red wine vinegar
½ cup water
¼ cup corn oil
4 cups coarsely chopped onion
4 cups coarsely chopped carrot
4 cups coarsely chopped turnip
1 cup beef stock
5 green onions, sliced
2 bay leaves
½ cup chopped fresh parsley

Mix 1 teaspoon of the salt, 1 teaspoon of the black pepper, the thyme, garlic powder, and cayenne in a large bowl and add the salt pork cubes; toss to coat the salt pork with seasonings. Make slits in the roast, enlarge the slits a bit with your finger, and insert the seasoned salt pork cubes into the slits, reserving any remaining seasoning in the bowl.

Add the vinegar and water to the seasoning in the bowl, and mix well. Add the meat and turn to coat on all sides. Tightly cover the bowl (or place the meat and juices in a 1-gallon zip bag), and place in the refrigerator for 2 to 4 days, turning each day. Remove the meat from the marinade and dry very well with paper towels.

Heat the oil in a large heavy pot or Dutch oven over medium heat. When the oil is hot, add the meat and brown well, about 3 minutes per side. Remove the meat to a platter.

Add the onion, carrot, and turnip to the hot oil. Cook the vegetables for 10 minutes, stirring often. Add the stock, green onions, bay leaves, and remaining salt and pepper to the pot and bring to a boil. Scrape the bottom of the pan to incorporate the crispy bits into the boiling stock.

Return the meat and any accumulated juices to the pot, reduce the heat to medium-low, cover, and simmer for 3 hours, stirring the vegetables and turning the meat over halfway through.

Remove the meat to a platter and puree the vegetables to make gravy, using a potato masher, blender, immersion blender, or food processor. Serve the sliced meat with the gravy, sprinkled with parsley.

LAGNIAPPE **An immersion blender is a small electric handheld blender with a rotary blade at one end. It is ideal for pureeing the vegetables, as you immerse the tall blender in the pot and don't need to transfer the food to another appliance to puree it. This inexpensive tool is also wonderful for turning any soup into a creamy, smooth soup; for making blended drinks right in the glass; and for whipping cream.**

Boudin Balls

We have never had a sausage stuffer to make this mixture into boudin sausages, so we form them into balls and fry them. These boudin balls are my grandchildren's favorite dish in this book (well . . . favorite along with the hush puppies and everything in the dessert chapter).

Makes about 30 balls; serves 6 as an entrée, 10 as an appetizer

2 pounds pork butt, cut into 1-inch cubes (don't trim fat from meat)
4 cups water
½ cup chopped onion
½ cup chopped celery
¼ cup chopped green bell pepper
2 cloves garlic, minced
2 teaspoons plus 2 teaspoons salt
1 teaspoon plus 1 teaspoon black pepper
½ teaspoon cayenne pepper
½ cup chopped fresh parsley
½ cup sliced green onions
3 cups cooked rice (about 1 cup raw)
¾ cup all-purpose flour
3 eggs, well beaten
1 cup plain dried bread crumbs
3 cups corn oil for frying (for a ½-inch depth in a 10-inch skillet)

Place the meat, water, onion, celery, bell pepper, garlic, 2 teaspoons of the salt, 1 teaspoon of the black pepper, and the cayenne in a medium saucepan. Bring to a boil, reduce the heat, and gently boil, uncovered, for 1 hour and 30 minutes until the meat is very tender.

Drain, reserving the broth. Place the meat, cooked vegetables, fresh parsley, and green onions in a meat grinder (a food processor may also be used) and grind together (or pulse about 20 times) until well mixed but not blended to a paste. Transfer to a large bowl.

Add rice to the pork mixture and gently stir to combine, adding the reserved broth 1 tablespoon at a time, until the mixture can be formed into balls but is still firm enough to hold its shape (I usually need 3 tablespoons broth). Taste, and add more seasoning if necessary. Using about 2 tablespoons meat mixture for each one, shape into balls.

Place the flour, eggs, and bread crumbs mixed with the remaining salt and pepper, in three separate dishes. Roll the balls in the flour, then the beaten egg, and then in the bread crumbs; place the balls on a rack to await frying.

Heat the oil in a large saucepan over high heat to 365 to 375°F. When the oil is hot, add the balls, 7 or 8 at a time, adjusting the heat up or down as necessary to maintain a temperature of 350 to 365°F, and transfer the balls to paper towels as you remove them from the oil; they will take 2 to 3 minutes to fry.

LAGNIAPPE **We keep these in the freezer uncooked for an instant meal or hors d'oeuvre. Let them defrost, pat dry, and proceed with frying.**

Braised Pork Roast

Pork has always been our favorite meat, and Grandma was a master at turning it into a crusty roast, tender shredded meat, crispy fried chops, or pork chops in tomato gravy. It is probably the most versatile meat, as it can be quick fried, long braised, or barbecued.
Serves 8

- 1 cup finely chopped onion
- 1 cup finely chopped celery
- ½ cup finely chopped green bell pepper
- 4 cloves garlic, finely chopped
- 1 teaspoon salt
- ½ teaspoon black pepper
- ¼ teaspoon cayenne pepper
- 4 pounds boneless pork shoulder or other non-lean cut
- ¼ cup corn oil
- ¼ cup all-purpose flour
- 1½ cups water
- 6 medium potatoes (about 2 pounds), unpeeled, quartered

Mix the onion, celery, bell pepper, garlic, salt, and black and cayenne pepper together to make a filling.

Cut a lengthwise pocket down the center of the roast, leaving 1 inch on each end, and going about two-thirds of the way into the roast (don't cut through to the opposite side). Gently open the pocket and insert as much of the filling as the pocket will hold without spilling out. Reserve all the leftover filling. Tie the roast to keep it together, and brush off any filling on the outside of the roast, as it may burn when the roast is browned.

Heat the oil in a large heavy pot or Dutch oven over medium-high heat for 2 minutes. Add the roast and brown on all sides; this will take 8 to 10 minutes.

Remove the roast from the pot, discard any burned filling that fell into the oil, and reduce the heat to medium-low. Add the flour and cook, stirring constantly, for 5 minutes. Add the reserved filling and cook, stirring often, for 5 minutes. Add the roast and water and bring to a boil. Reduce the heat to medium-low, cover, and simmer for 2 hours.

Add the potatoes and simmer 1 hour longer. Remove the roast and slice. For a thicker gravy, boil down the liquid in the pot for 5 to 10 minutes over medium-high heat. Serve the sliced pork with the potatoes and gravy.

LAGNIAPPE **Pigs are now slaughtered at six months, before they develop much fat. Even as recently as 1980, they had more than twice the amount of fat than they have now.**

Cajun Slow-Roasted Beef

Dad used to make this for Christmas Eve dinner when we were little, and it filled the entire house with a wonderful fragrance while we were wrapping gifts, enhancing the tree with even more popcorn strings, and waiting with eager anticipation for the evening ahead.

Note the 2- to 3-day marinating time, and 8-hour cooking time.

Serves 8 to 10

- 1 boneless beef chuck, round, or rump roast (4 to 5 pounds)
- 5 cloves garlic, sliced
- 4 teaspoons dried thyme
- 2½ teaspoons salt
- 1 to 2 teaspoons black pepper
- 2 teaspoons garlic powder
- ¼ to ½ teaspoon cayenne pepper
- ¼ cup corn oil
- ⅓ cup all-purpose flour
- 2 cups chopped onion
- 2 cups chopped celery
- 1 cup chopped green bell pepper

Cut small slits in the roast and tuck garlic slices into the slits.

Combine the thyme, salt, black pepper, garlic powder, and cayenne and divide the mixture in half, reserving half for the roux. Sprinkle half the herb-spice mixture evenly onto the roast, patting it onto the surface. Place in a large bowl and cover tightly (or place the meat and any juices in a 1-gallon zip bag), and refrigerate for 2 to 3 days.

Lift the meat from the bag, reserving any liquid, and pat the roast very dry with paper towels.

Heat the oil in a large heavy pot or Dutch oven over medium heat for 2 minutes. Add the flour and stir for 10 to 20 minutes to make a light roux (see page 14). Add the roast and brown for 3 minutes per side, stirring the roux each time you turn the roast, and reducing the heat if the roux is smoking or getting very dark. Measure the reserved juices from marinating the roast, and add enough water to equal ½ cup. Stir the liquid and reserved spice mixture into the roux (move the roast aside). Cover the pot, reduce the heat to very low, and cook for 4 hours at a bare simmer, occasionally stirring the gravy.

Add the onion, celery, and bell pepper and stir into the liquid. Turn the roast over; cover and cook for 4 hours longer. Spoon the gravy over the meat, and serve with either rice or grits.

LAGNIAPPE **Five pounds of boneless meat yields about 3 pounds of meat after cooking, with lots of liquid to turn leftovers into stew, soup, or meat pie.**

Canary Island Beef Steaks

One of my paternal great-great-grandmothers was Marie Rodrigues. She was descended from the Spanish colonists who migrated from the Canary Islands in 1778, ending up in Indian Bend, off the Bayou Teche, outside Charenton. I include this recipe, even though it is not actually Cajun, because it's an important part of our history (and a scrumptious dish!). Serves 6

- 4 tablespoons plus 4 tablespoons butter
- 3 pounds round steak, about 1 inch thick, cut into 6 pieces
- ¼ cup all-purpose flour
- 4 cloves garlic, minced
- 1 teaspoon salt
- 1 teaspoon black pepper
- 2 cups whole milk
- 2 tablespoons lemon juice

Melt 4 tablespoons of the butter in a large heavy pot or Dutch oven over medium-high heat. When the foam subsides, brown the steaks in batches, without crowding, for 3 minutes per side, removing the steaks as they are browned.

Pour out the butter and wipe the pan clean. Melt the remaining butter over medium heat, add the flour, and whisk constantly for 1 minute to incorporate the flour into the butter. Add the garlic, salt, and pepper, whisking to combine.

Add the milk, bring to a boil, and whisk until the milk is incorporated into the flour. Reduce the heat to medium-low, and return the meat to the pan, spooning the sauce over the meat. Cover and simmer gently for 2 hours, stirring to redistribute the meat and the sauce every half hour. Remove the steaks to a platter, whisk the lemon juice into the gravy, and serve the gravy over rice, alongside the steaks.

LAGNIAPPE On a trip to Louisiana in 2003, I made arrangements to attend the annual Crawfish Festival in St. Bernard Parish. The parish is the home of the Isleños Museum Complex, and the home of many people of Isleño ancestry, from the Canary Islands. I received a written confirmation of my proposed visit and was pleased that I would have the opportunity to interview an Isleña chief. The chief and I had a fascinating conversation about Isleño food, life, and culture. I was aware that she seemed startled each time I called her by her title of Chief, but never questioned her reaction, and she said nothing. It was only much later, referring to my background information, that I realized there had been a typographical error in the written communication. The gracious Isleña, whom I had been calling Chief all evening, was actually a chef.

Easy Steak in a Pot

Aunt Lorna said you could never have enough Worcestershire sauce, and she used it often. Even though it's not a Cajun ingredient, it does figure now and then in Cajun recipes. The Worcestershire adds a boost of flavor that helps make up for the meat and vegetables not being browned. This delicious recipe takes only minutes to prepare and finish up. **Serves 6**

1½ teaspoons salt
1 teaspoon black pepper
½ teaspoon cayenne pepper
1 round steak (about 3 pounds), about 1 inch thick
6 medium baking potatoes, quartered (about 2 pounds)
2 cups sliced onion
1 cup sliced green bell pepper
2 tablespoons Worcestershire sauce
6 tablespoons plus 2 tablespoons (1 stick) butter
3 tablespoons all-purpose flour

Preheat the oven to 300°F. Combine the salt and black and cayenne pepper.

Place the steak in a large heavy Dutch oven, and sprinkle with the salt-pepper mixture. Place the potatoes, onion, and bell pepper on top of the meat.

Mix ½ cup water and the Worcestershire sauce and pour over the meat and vegetables. Cut 6 tablespoons of the butter in pieces and distribute over the top of the meat and vegetables.

Cover and bake for 3 hours, periodically basting the meat and vegetables with the liquid. Remove the meat and vegetables to a platter with a slotted spoon.

Melt the remaining 2 tablespoons of butter in a small saucepan and add the flour, stirring to combine. Bring the liquid in the pot to a boil, add the butter-flour mixture, and whisk to incorporate into a smooth sauce. Reduce the heat to medium-low and cook for 5 minutes, whisking often. Serve the gravy with the meat and vegetables.

LAGNIAPPE **Worcestershire sauce was developed by the English in India, bottled by the English in Worcester, England, and is used around the world as a seasoning for meats, sauces, and soups, and as a condiment. It is, perhaps, most noted as a seasoning for Bloody Marys, the popular cocktail made from vodka and tomato juice. Worcestershire sauce is sweet, sour, and salty at the same time, from molasses, vinegar, and anchovies, among lesser-known ingredients such as tamarind.**

Fried Pork Chops

While 4 ounces of boneless meat is considered a serving, I must confess that whenever Grandpa made this family favorite many of us ate two chops—they're just so good! There is about a 25 percent shrinkage after the meat is cooked, so each chop is about 3 ounces when done. ***Serves 4 to 8***

- 8 boneless pork chops (about 2 pounds), ½ to ¾ inch thick
- 4 teaspoons salt
- 1 tablespoon black pepper
- 1 tablespoon garlic powder
- 1 teaspoon cayenne pepper
- ½ cup all-purpose flour
- 1 cup corn oil for frying (for a ⅛-inch depth in a 10-inch skillet)

Trim excess fat off chops, as desired.

Mix the spices and flour and coat both sides of the chops with the mixture, patting the seasoned flour onto the surfaces of the meat.

Heat the oil in a cast iron or other heavy skillet over medium-high heat for 5 minutes.

Add the chops without crowding—you will probably need to fry them in two batches. Fry 2 to 3 minutes per side, turning once. Remove them as soon as they are opaque all the way through; don't overcook or they will be dry. Drain on paper towels and serve.

LAGNIAPPE Grandma taught my sister, Lorna, the following rules for making gravy, depending on what is left in the pan after frying or roasting meat or poultry. Lorna, in turn, taught them to me:

> **For fat with brown crispy bits, add flour, make a roux, and add stock, water, or milk. This makes gravy for fried chicken or pork chops, after pouring off the excess oil, and roasted pork and beef.**
>
> **For lots of juice with just a small amount of fat on top, bring the liquid to a boil, and thicken with a flour–soft butter mixture (after roasting a chicken, for example).**
>
> **When making a gravy or sauce for chicken or pork, add a bit of cream at the end.**

Grillades

Dad only made this traditional breakfast dish on Christmas, and very special occasions. Serves 6

- **1 cup all-purpose flour**
- **2 teaspoons salt**
- **1½ teaspoons black pepper**
- **1 teaspoon white pepper**
- **½ teaspoon cayenne pepper**
- **2 pounds boneless pork, cut into 6 pieces (see Lagniappe)**
- **1 cup bacon drippings, lard, corn oil, or a combination**
- **2 cups chopped onion**
- **1 cup chopped green bell pepper**
- **1 cup chopped celery**
- **2 cloves garlic, minced**
- **1½ cups chicken stock**
- **1 cup sliced green onions**

Combine the flour, salt, and black, white, and cayenne pepper in a large bowl.

Toss the pieces of meat in the flour-spice mixture (reserve any extra mixture) and transfer to a cutting board. Using the textured side of a mallet, pound until doubled in size.

Heat ½ cup of the bacon drippings in a large heavy pot or Dutch oven over medium-high heat. Dip the meat in the reserved flour-spice mixture and quickly brown for about 1 minute on each side—you will need to do this in batches—removing slices of meat as they are browned.

Clean out the pan and heat the remaining ½ cup of drippings over medium heat. Add ½ cup of the reserved flour-spice mixture and cook for 15 minutes, stirring constantly.

Add the vegetables and cook for 5 minutes, stirring often.

Add the stock and bring to a boil, stirring constantly until the sauce is smooth. Return the meat to the pot, spoon gravy over each piece of meat, turn the heat to medium-low, and cook for 1 hour and 30 minutes, covered.

Dish up the grillades with a slotted spoon, and serve with grits, spooning the sauce over the grillades and grits. Sprinkle with green onions.

LAGNIAPPE **Thick pork chops are sometimes the easiest cut to find, and 3 thick boneless chops (about 1½ × 4 inches), cut horizontally, work beautifully here.**

Grandma Olympe's Fricassee of Beef

This is my ultimate comfort food. It is the one recipe my French grandmother taught my mother how to make, and it was Mom's best dish. I could always tell when this was on the menu, as Mom would start it early in the afternoon and by the time I came home from school you could smell the fricassee down the street. When no one was home, I would remove the large cover from the two-burner pot and dish up some of the gravy. Sliced French bread, a small bowl of gravy, and a quiet kitchen corner for dunking the bread in the rich, brown sauce was much more appealing to me than an ice cream cone or candy would have been. Serves 8

2 teaspoons salt
1 teaspoon black pepper
½ teaspoon white pepper
½ teaspoon garlic powder
¼ teaspoon cayenne pepper
4 pounds round steak, fat removed, cut into 1-inch cubes
1 cup corn oil
1 cup all-purpose flour
2 cups chopped onion
1½ cups chopped celery
1¼ cups chopped green bell pepper
1¾ cups water

Combine the salt, black and white pepper, garlic powder, and cayenne. Place the steak cubes in a large bowl and sprinkle with the seasonings, tossing to coat evenly; set aside.

Heat a large heavy pot or Dutch oven over medium heat for 2 minutes. Add the oil and heat for 2 minutes. Add the flour and stir constantly for 30 to 40 minutes to make a dark roux (see page 14).

Raise the heat to high and immediately add the beef cubes, a few at a time, constantly tossing with two long-handled kitchen spoons to evenly coat the beef cubes with the roux. As soon as the beef is coated with the roux, add the onion, celery, and bell pepper, and cook for 2 minutes, constantly tossing with the spoons.

Add the water, bring to a boil, and stir until the sauce is smooth. Reduce the heat to medium-low, cover, and gently simmer for 2½ hours, stirring occasionally. Serve with rice or grits (after sneaking some of the gravy, and dipping French bread in it).

LAGNIAPPE The long-cooked roux, and the browning of the meat and vegetables in the roux, give this fricassee a deep, rich flavor that can't be achieved by using shortcuts.

Holy trinity equivalents:

2 cups chopped onion = 2 medium onions

1½ cups chopped celery = 2 stalks celery

1¼ cups chopped green bell pepper = 1 large pepper

Madge's Pork Jambalaya

As I write this, my father's first cousin Madge is ninety-six years old, living in Abbeville, Louisiana, and just won two hundred dollars playing Bingo. There are two types of jambalaya: brown, with browned onions and meat, and red, which has tomatoes. Both usually have two main ingredients. Serves 4

- ¼ cup corn oil
- 1 pound boneless pork, cut into 1-inch cubes
- 1½ cups chopped onion
- 1 cup chopped green bell pepper
- 1 cup chopped celery
- 1 teaspoon salt
- ½ teaspoon white pepper
- ¼ teaspoon cayenne pepper
- 1 cup raw rice
- 2¼ cups water
- ½ cup sliced green onions
- ¼ cup chopped fresh parsley

Heat the oil in a large heavy pot or Dutch oven over medium-high heat. Brown the pork cubes until golden and crusty, about 10 minutes.

Reduce the heat to medium and add the vegetables and seasonings. Cook for 10 minutes, or until the vegetables are wilted, stirring often, and incorporating the crusty bits on the bottom of the pot into the vegetables.

Stir in the rice and water. Bring to a boil, reduce the heat to low, cover, and cook for 40 minutes, stirring occasionally, until the rice is tender. (Add warm water, ¼ cup at a time, if the water evaporates—I usually add ¼ cup water after about 30 minutes.) Garnish with green onions and parsley.

LAGNIAPPE **Pork was very important in Acadiana, as it was almost completely edible, with organs in *sauce de débris*, intestines as sausage casings, and skin for cracklings. It is said that the Cajuns use everything but the squeal when preparing a slaughtered pig.**

Mama's Stuffed Sweet Peppers with Ground Meat

I have Grandma's two-page, handwritten recipe for this dish, held together with a rusted straight pin. I work from a photocopy of the recipe as I want to preserve this seventy-year-old treasure. Grandma said to cook the meat "until it wants to start flying."

Serves 6

- **1 tomato**
- **1 tablespoon plus 1 teaspoon salt**
- **6 medium-large green bell peppers**
- **1 pound ground beef**
- **¼ cup hot water**
- **1 cup chopped onion**
- **3 cups cooked medium-grain rice (about 1 cup raw)**
- **½ teaspoon black pepper**
- **¼ teaspoon white pepper**

Remove the core from the tomato and cut it in half, across. Squeeze out the seeds and chop the tomato. Preheat the oven to 350°F.

Bring a large pot of water to a boil with the 1 tablespoon salt, and carefully drop the peppers into the boiling water. Bring it back to a boil, and boil the peppers for 5 minutes. Prepare the peppers by cutting around the stem on the top and removing the stem. With a spoon, remove as many of the seeds as possible (be careful not to cut into the bottoms or sides of the peppers).

Cook the ground beef in a large skillet over medium-high heat until it is browned, then add the hot water.

Cook the meat until the water evaporates, about 5 minutes, then add the tomato and onion and cook for 10 minutes, stirring often. Stir the cooked rice and remaining 1 tsp salt and black and white pepper into the meat mixture. Remove from the heat and stuff the peppers with the meat mixture.

Put the stuffed peppers into a baking pan that holds them snugly, and bake for 30 minutes.

LAGNIAPPE **In past days, it wasn't specified to use 85 percent or 95 percent lean ground beef, or ground sirloin, or ground round; they just used beef that was ground up with some fat. It was sometimes leaner in fat, sometimes higher in fat, and they didn't know until they started cooking the meat and saw how much fat was released whether they would need to adjust the recipe to compensate for a more-or-less-than-usual amount of fat.**

Meatball Stew

Since I started writing this book, I have come to know several Cajun cousins I had never met. Some were cousins I knew of but had never spoken to, and others were found online.

The Web is an amazing tool for genealogical research, and has put me in touch with relatives as close as second cousins whom I didn't know existed. This is one of the recipes my newfound cousin Bill Schmaltz shared with me from his collection of recipes.

Serves 6

- 1½ pounds ground beef
- 1 egg, beaten
- ½ cup dried unseasoned bread crumbs
- 1 teaspoon garlic powder
- 1 teaspoon salt
- ½ teaspoon black pepper
- ¼ teaspoon cayenne pepper
- ½ cup corn oil
- ¼ cup all-purpose flour
- 1½ cups chopped onion
- 1½ cups chopped celery
- 1 cup chopped green bell pepper
- 1½ cups water

Mix the ground beef, egg, bread crumbs, and seasonings in a large bowl. Form into 36 meatballs.

Heat the oil in a large heavy pot or Dutch oven over medium-high heat. Brown the meatballs in the hot oil for about 5 minutes, turning to brown evenly. You will need to do this in two batches, removing the meatballs to a platter as they are browned.

Pour the oil from the pot into a measuring cup, and return about ¼ cup oil to the pot. Add the flour, reduce the heat to medium, and stir constantly for 10 minutes.

Add the onion, celery, and bell pepper to the roux and cook for 10 minutes, or until the vegetables are wilted.

Add the water and bring to a boil, stirring to make a smooth sauce.

Return the meatballs to the pot, reduce the heat to low, and simmer for 1 hour. Serve over rice.

LAGNIAPPE Meatballs are often made with pork instead of beef, or with a combination of the two, or with seafood. We call them *boulettes* if they are fried and served without a gravy, and meatball stew if they are stewed in gravy (sometimes, but not always, fried first).

Pork Chop Étouffée

Étouffée is a method of cooking in which the food is cooked in a closed pot and smothered in its own juices. Typically, étouffée doesn't have a roux, and it usually contains one main meat, poultry, or seafood ingredient. Grandpa used this technique for vegetables as well as for chicken, pork, and seafood, and made étouffée with both okra and cabbage.

Note that the pork chops need to marinate overnight, or for up to three days. **Serves 6**

- 1 teaspoon salt
- 1 teaspoon black pepper
- ¼ teaspoon cayenne pepper
- 6 boneless pork chops (about 2 pounds total)
- 2 cups plus 2 cups chopped onion
- 1 cup distilled white vinegar
- ¼ cup corn oil
- 2 cups chopped celery
- 1 cup chopped green bell pepper
- 6 garlic cloves, minced
- ¾ cup water, or more if needed

Combine the salt, black pepper, and cayenne and sprinkle on both sides of the pork chops. Place the chops in a dish in a single layer, and cover with 2 cups of the chopped onion and the vinegar. Cover tightly and marinate overnight, or for up to 3 days.

Lift the chops out of the marinade, wipe off the onions, pat the chops dry, and discard the marinade. Heat the oil in a large heavy pot or Dutch oven over high heat. Brown the chops on both sides until golden (about 3 minutes per side); remove from the pan. (Brown in batches, if necessary, reducing the heat to medium-high if the chops are browning too fast.)

Add the celery, bell pepper, garlic, and remaining 2 cups onions, reduce the heat to medium, and cook for about 10 minutes, or until the vegetables are softened, scraping the bottom of the pan to release the browned, crispy bits into the vegetables.

Return the chops to the pan, add the water, and bring to a boil. Reduce the heat to a simmer, cover, and cook for 45 minutes, stirring occasionally. Add a bit more water, as needed, if the pork and vegetables are becoming dry.

LAGNIAPPE The vinegar in the recipe shows the bit of German influence found in Cajun cooking. The German Coast above New Orleans, on the Mississippi River, was settled in the mid-1700s.

Pork Chops in Tomato Gravy

This was one of the dishes Dad often requested on his birthday. He loved pork chops, and generally liked them fried and on the bone so he could enjoy the sweet meat next to the bone. However, he loved to spoon this thick tomato gravy over rice. This dish is rich enough that it could actually serve twelve people if each would be satisfied with one chop. Serves 6

12 boneless pork chops (about 3 pounds)
1½ teaspoons salt
1 teaspoon black pepper
¼ teaspoon cayenne pepper
½ cup corn oil
⅓ cup all-purpose flour
1 cup chopped onion
1 cup chopped celery
2 cups tomato juice
1 bay leaf
1 tablespoon tomato paste
1 tablespoon fresh lemon juice
1 teaspoon dried thyme
¼ teaspoon Tabasco sauce

Place the chops on a work surface. Combine the salt and pepper and lightly sprinkle both sides of the chops with the seasonings.

Heat the oil in a large heavy pot or Dutch oven over medium-high heat for 2 minutes. Add 6 of the 12 chops and brown for 2 minutes on each side. Remove the chops to a platter, and repeat with the remaining 6 chops.

Add the flour to the pot, reduce the heat to medium-low, and cook for 3 minutes, incorporating crispy bits on the bottom of the pan into the flour by stirring constantly.

Add the onion and celery and cook for 3 minutes, stirring constantly. Add the remaining ingredients, bring to a boil, stir, and add the chops and accumulated liquid to the pot.

Spoon the sauce over the chops, reduce the heat to medium-low, and simmer for 1 hour and 30 minutes, covered, redistributing the sauce and chops every half hour. Serve with rice or other starch of choice to sop up the wonderful, creamy gravy.

LAGNIAPPE **Dad said they used to fill empty tomato juice cans with water and kerosene and set the legs of the kitchen table in them. Ants wouldn't crawl across the kerosene-water, but would crawl across plain water—and right on up to the table.**

Beignets (left), page 141; and Sweet Hush Puppies (right), page 154

Crawfish Stew, page 122

Duck and Andouille Sausage Gumbo, page 41

Fresh Peach Shortcake, page 254

Mustard Greens with Turnips, page 179

Pork Chop Étouffée, page 103

Shrimp Boil with Potatoes and Corn, page 130

Pecan Praline Bites (top right), page 261; Coconut Pralines (middle left), page 252; and Pecan Brittle (bottom right), page 259

Quick Sausage Jambalaya

After he had his first heart attack, Dad was told not to eat sausage. His first words upon hearing this were "Oh, no, I won't be able to eat any of my favorite dishes." I wanted him to stick with his prescribed way of eating, so I "reinvented" many of Dad's special recipes, with surprisingly few changes needed. Oil instead of lard or salt pork for cooking was the biggest change, but this jambalaya recipe only needed the substitution of chicken andouille for pork andouille to make it conform to Dad's new way of eating, proving that you can enjoy wonderful Cajun dishes even on a restricted eating plan!

Serves 8

¼ cup corn oil
1 cup chopped onion
1 cup chopped celery
1 cup chopped green bell pepper
2 cloves garlic, minced
1½ pounds andouille or other smoked sausage, coarsely chopped
Two 14-ounce cans diced tomatoes, drained (or 2 cups fresh tomatoes, seeded and diced)
3 cups chicken stock
1 teaspoon dried thyme
½ teaspoon salt
¼ teaspoon black pepper
2 cups raw rice
½ cup chopped fresh parsley

Heat the oil in a large heavy pot or Dutch oven over medium-high heat.

Add the onion, celery, and bell pepper and cook for 10 minutes, stirring occasionally. Add the garlic and sausage and cook for 5 minutes, stirring occasionally.

Add the tomatoes, stock, and seasonings and bring to a rolling boil. Add the rice, stir, and reduce the heat to medium-low. Cover and cook for 10 minutes, then stir and reduce the heat to low. Cover and cook until the rice is tender, about 25 minutes longer.

Stir, and sprinkle each serving with parsley.

LAGNIAPPE Sometimes a quick meal is needed, without making a roux or allowing for a 2-hour cooking time. Most jambalayas have two main ingredients, but this one is designed to make use of leftovers. Cooked meat, chicken, shellfish, or any combination (about 1½ pounds, or 3 to 4 cups) may be used instead of sausage; if using cooked shellfish, add it when the jambalaya is done, then let it sit, covered, for 5 minutes to heat the shellfish.

Cayenne-Roasted Pork Muffaletta

This type of sandwich is a favorite of both Cajuns and their city cousins. Great-Uncle Adolphe discovered muffalettas at Central Grocery in New Orleans when he was there on a buying trip for his country store. He put his own stamp on the sandwich, as he did on everything, and used pork from the farm instead of the traditional luncheon meats.

This looks lengthy because it has a lot of ingredients, but it only involves making the olive salad (which could be purchased), and roasting the pork before assembling. Serves 6

Olive Salad

1 cup pimento-stuffed green olives, chopped
1 cup pitted black olives, chopped
⅓ cup olive oil
¼ cup coarsely chopped roasted peppers, fresh or jarred
¼ cup chopped fresh parsley
2 cloves garlic, minced
1 tablespoon fresh lemon juice
1 tablespoon drained capers, chopped
1 teaspoon dried thyme
¼ teaspoon salt
¼ teaspoon black pepper
¼ teaspoon cayenne pepper

Roast Pork

1 tablespoon dried thyme
1 teaspoon salt
½ teaspoon black pepper
¼ teaspoon cayenne pepper
1½ pounds pork tenderloin
1 round loaf French bread (24 ounces)
½ cup top-quality mayonnaise
½ pound provolone or mozzarella cheese, thinly sliced

Combine all the ingredients for the olive salad, cover, and refrigerate for several hours or overnight.

Preheat the oven to 350°F. Combine the thyme, salt, and black cayenne peppers and spread them out on a piece of waxed paper or foil. Roll the tenderloin in the spices, pressing the spices onto the surface of the meat.

Place the pork on a rack set in a roasting pan and bake for about 45 minutes, depending on the thickness of the meat. When the meat thermometer registers 155°F, remove the pork from the oven (it will continue to cook while resting). When cool, slice on the bias, about 1/4 inch thick.

To assemble the muffaletta, cut the top third off the French bread and hollow out the bottom by removing as much bread as possible. Leave a solid shell so juices won't leak through. Remove as much bread from the top as possible while leaving a solid shell.

Spread all but 2 tablespoons of the mayonnaise on the bottom and sides of the loaf. Place half the pork in the bottom, cover with half the cheese, then half the olive salad. Repeat layers. Spread the top slice of bread with the remaining 2 tablespoons mayonnaise. Replace the top and press tightly onto the filled loaf.

Wrap well in plastic wrap or foil and place in the refrigerator with a weight on top (such as a brick or heavy can). Refrigerate for at least 1 hour, and up to several hours. Cut into wedges to serve.

LAGNIAPPE **Cajuns love eating outdoors, and the muffaletta makes perfect picnic fare, as it is almost a complete meal, can be made several hours ahead, and is easy to transport. Make sure the sandwich doesn't get warm before eating it: the rule of thumb is that food is safe for 2 hours after it comes to room temperature, but with proteins it's best to be extra careful.**

Sausage Jambalaya with Shrimp

This is Great-Aunt Alice's method of making jambalaya; the sauce is cooked separately and rice is added at the end. She liked all her recipes to stand out as being a bit different. Serves 8

- ¼ cup corn oil
- 4 cloves garlic, minced
- 2 bay leaves
- 1 to 1½ teaspoons cayenne pepper
- Three 14-ounce cans diced tomatoes, drained
- One 6-ounce can tomato paste
- 1 pound andouille or other smoked sausage, sliced
- 2 cups chicken stock
- 2 cups chopped onion
- 1½ cups chopped celery
- 1 cup chopped green bell pepper
- 6 cups cold cooked rice (about 2 cups raw)
- 1 pound raw shrimp, shelled and deveined
- ½ cup sliced green onions

Heat the oil in a large heavy pot or Dutch oven over low heat. Add the garlic, bay leaves, and cayenne and cook for 10 minutes, stirring often. Raise the heat to medium, add the tomatoes and tomato paste, and cook for 15 minutes, stirring often. Add the sausage and cook for 15 minutes, stirring often.

Add the stock, onion, celery, and green pepper, and bring to a boil. Stir, reduce the heat, and gently boil for 1 hour, covered. (Begin cooking the rice about 30 minutes before the jambalaya is done.) Add the shrimp and simmer for 5 minutes. Add the rice, stir gently, and serve sprinkled with sliced green onions. (For a different treatment, spoon the jambalaya on top of rice instead of mixing it in, then sprinkle with green onions.)

LAGNIAPPE **While this recipe uses an entire 6-ounce can of tomato paste, many recipes only call for 1 or 2 tablespoons, leaving an aging can with a residue of tomato paste that soon turns black and unappealing. Before this happens, measure tablespoons of the leftover tomato paste onto a plate covered with waxed paper, and freeze. When the tomato paste is frozen, transfer the spoonfuls of paste to a freezer container or zip freezer bag, for convenient tablespoons of tomato paste measured out for use as needed.**

Seafood

Joseph Pischoff

Grandpa Pischoff Sneaks into the Kitchen

Grandpa Pischoff was a sweet old guy, quite content to putter around the house or in the garden, but happiest when he was cooking. Most Cajun men are known for their outdoor cooking skills, but Grandpa loved being inside the kitchen.

Dad, Grandpa, and Aunt Lorna were always talking about dozens of relatives I had never met, and a farm called Home Place that contained years of their memories and shared experiences. They were bonded together by this place they spoke so fondly of, and I wanted to be involved. I knew the door to being part of Home Place could be entered through the kitchen, so I took the first step toward belonging: I asked Grandpa for cooking lessons.

When Grandpa started teaching me to cook, he considered the first lesson—even before roux—to be familiarity with all the ingredients. So he and I took the streetcar downtown, then caught a cable car to Fisherman's Wharf to buy fresh seafood. It took most of the day, but it was worth it. I'll always remember Grandpa holding me protectively on the cable car, since I begged for us to sit on the outside benches and he was so afraid I would fall off. My stomach mimicked the up-and-down pattern of the cable car as it ascended and descended the steep hills of my native city.

The Wharf itself was an exciting place, so we were not disappointed when our cable car ride ended. Local Dungeness crabs were tumbling in the steaming vats of boiling water, and long displays of fresh clams, oysters, and fin fish rested on crushed ice. Shrimp ranged from small cocktail size to very large—some with their heads still on. Grandpa and I got shrimp cocktails to eat as we walked the length of the Wharf. He would point out the fresh pink color and firmness of the little shrimp underneath the lemony red sauce as we enjoyed one of our favorite snacks, using the color and texture as a tool to show me what to look for in other fish to determine freshness. (In California we call large shrimp "prawns," but there is no such word in Louisiana. "Shrimp" is used for all sizes of the crustacean.)

I felt it impolite not to answer every vendor as they yelled out to us, "Have a shrimp cocktail"; "Fresh crabs here"; "Get the local catch—freshest fish on the wharf." Grandpa would gently grab my hand and pull me along, so I wouldn't get into a conversation with each purveyor.

We bypassed clams: "Not in a gumbo, child."

Oysters: "They're not from the Gulf."

Lobster: "Not a proper food for Cajuns."

"Shrimp!" Grandpa exclaimed suddenly. "Let's have a shrimp and crab gumbo," he said, looking directly at me with dark brown eyes that were sparkling and full of excitement. "You will learn to make gumbo with a roux." We bought raw shrimp with the heads still on so we could use the heads and shells for shrimp stock, and purchased cooked crab, which Grandpa made sure was freshly taken from the boiling water.

Reversing our path and again walking past the vendors with white beards that came to a point, and mustaches that ended in long curlicues, I wondered why we bypassed the row after row of fresh fish displayed in the glass cases. Grandpa gave me an idea when he emphatically stated, "I don't know how y'all can cook without crawfish or decent oysters. I will say, though, that even if Louisiana has the best seafood in the world, your Dungeness crab is something special."

Back home, it was time to learn how to make gumbo. It started, of course, with a roux. Having a jar of pre-made roux, as I had learned to call the ugly brown stuff in a jar, was Grandpa's idea of "fast food." He made up four pints at a time (one light, one medium, and two dark), and kept them in the refrigerator. Having roux on hand negated the process of making the toasty blend of oil and flour every time he wanted to cook. Grandpa heated a large heavy cast iron pot until it was almost smoking and added half the jar of roux.

As Grandpa stirred this mixture in the hot pot, emulsifying the oil and flour back together, that wonderful, familiar aroma began to fill the air. When the roux smoothed out into its golden brown goodness, it was time to begin making the gumbo. First Grandpa added the holy trinity of Cajun cooking (onion, celery, and bell pepper), and began stirring to coat the vegetables evenly with the roux. He cooked this for several minutes, then added the water in which he had boiled the shells and heads from the prawns.

Okra and seasonings were added and cooked for a few minutes, then I was allowed to finish the gumbo by adding the shrimp and the crab. "Now, watch the shrimp carefully, and as soon as they begin to turn from gray to pink, prepare to take the gumbo off the heat before the shrimp get overcooked. You must never, never cook shrimp too long or no self-respecting Cajun will like you."

Grandpa dished up the gumbo and placed a mound of snowy white rice in the center of each serving—a perfect contrast in both color and flavor. Then he instructed me to sprinkle fresh chopped parsley and green onions on top. He brought the steaming bowls of thick, dark gumbo with pieces of shrimp and crab peeking out of the liquid to the table, and we shared a congratulatory smile over our joint project.

After that lesson, I spent hours in the kitchen with Grandpa learning about Cajun cooking, at first just by watching and helping him. However, before I was nine years old, he realized that I had inherited the Cajun passion for food and cooking, and he eagerly brought me into the fold of family cooks, teaching me how to prepare complete meals. Everything I cooked was always "the best he ever tasted." Grandpa was my great fan and supporter. It never occurred to me that any dish or recipe was too difficult for me to prepare, because Grandpa had taught me, and I knew how to cook.

My first lessons were about basics: Grandpa worked with me on making a roux and, echoing the words of his wife, insisted I "get it dark-dark-dark." I learned how to reconstitute dried shrimp and how to clean fresh shrimp. Perhaps most important of all, I was taught how to place shrimp in boiling water until they are just barely done. Teaching me how to make French drip coffee in the two-tiered little pot he kept on the back of the stove was brilliant on his part, as I'd make the coffee for him whenever he asked, thrilled with such a grown-up task. Sometimes I'd try a shortcut to see if I could get away with it, but Grandpa always knew and would gently explain that you don't get the same result from rushing a cooking process. He taught me that nothing needed to be fancy or complicated, but that the ingredients needed to be good quality and fresh, and that spending the time necessary to allow the flavors to develop was the key to good Cajun cooking.

We always had a supply of dried shrimp, salt pork, and four types of pepper (white, black, red, and pepper sauce) for Grandpa's specialties: shrimp gumbo, shrimp jambalaya, shrimp fricassee and, his favorite ingredients next to shrimp, potatoes and vegetables. He had dozens of ways of cooking both and he turned us, as children, into vegetable lovers. He would make maque choux when summer corn and tomatoes were ripe, scraping the cob twice to get all the sweet juice after the kernels were removed, then he added lots of black pepper, though it was never too spicy. He would render some salt pork or bacon and make wonderful potato dishes, and his green beans were requested every time he set foot in the kitchen.

Many of the vegetables came from the garden, where Grandpa would try to sneak a tomato plant, okra, or one year even a raspberry vine within our carefully landscaped yard, hoping my mother wouldn't notice. But eventually, there was the evidence—a red pepper sticking out from under a white camellia bush, or a green cucumber growing from a vine that had climbed to the center of a yellow rose bush. Felix the gardener, who never learned how to pronounce our name correctly, would knock on the door holding a bunch of green onions, or a handful of parsley, and say, "Mrs. Pis-koff, I think your father-in-law has been in the garden again."

Grandpa had a sense of humor that was subtle, but you always knew when he was going to tell a good story because his eyes would twinkle. One of his favorites was about someone at his former place of work, who made a habit of sneaking into Grandpa's locker and stealing some of his chewing tobacco. Grandpa took care of the thief by substituting dried-up cow manure for the tobacco in the tin.

It was always a tearful scene at the end of Grandpa's half year with us, when he would leave to go live with my aunt and her family in Minneapolis for the next six months. As he embraced each of us in turn and held on tight, he said, "I may not see you again; know that I love you." This went on for seven years, until Aunt Lorna and her two children moved to San Francisco in 1962, following the death of her husband. Grandpa would still take turns alternating between the two families, but we were only twenty-five minutes apart, so there were no tears—until two years later.

Grandpa Pischoff passed away in 1964 at the age of ninety. He left us with fond, loving memories of a hard-working man who had quit school after the third grade to help on the farm. He never learned to read or write, but was fluent in three languages and would dictate letters that could have been written by a college graduate. Grandpa advised his family about nutrition long before it was a popular science, and took special care to make sure his children were fed a healthy, balanced diet rich in fruits and vegetables. His sparkling eyes, slow shuffle, and love of life, family, and food will never leave us.

Barbecued Shrimp

One rainy day, shortly after Christmas, Grandpa and Dad decided to cook barbecued shrimp. I wasn't surprised at Dad, because he wouldn't have hesitated to stand out in the rain if the mood to barbecue struck him, but I thought Grandpa was more sensible. I discovered that this dish is truly misnamed, as the sauce is not a barbecue sauce, and they are not cooked on a barbecue. But once you taste them, you won't care what they're called! Serves 4

1 pound raw shrimp, shells on, deveined
5 tablespoons butter
⅓ cup olive oil
2 green onions, sliced
2 cloves garlic, minced
2 tablespoons fresh parsley, finely chopped
1 tablespoon fresh lemon juice
1 teaspoon Worcestershire sauce
1 teaspoon paprika
½ teaspoon salt
½ teaspoon white pepper
¼ teaspoon cayenne pepper
⅛ teaspoon sugar

Spread the shrimp out in a single layer on a 9 × 13-inch baking dish.

Melt the butter in a medium saucepan, and add the remaining ingredients, mixing well. Pour the butter mixture over the shrimp, stir to coat evenly, and marinate for 1 hour (room temperature is okay if it's not a hot day).

Preheat the oven to 325°F.

Bake the shrimp for 5 minutes, stir, and bake 5 minutes longer. (Cooking time depends on the size of the shrimp.) They should be pink and have lost their translucency. Remove from the oven, stir, and dish up into bowls, with plenty of bread to dip in the sauce, and plenty of napkins.

LAGNIAPPE **Shrimp (headless, but with shells) lose about 25 percent of their weight from peeling and deveining, and up to another 25 percent from cooking.**

Catfish and Shrimp Étouffée

Whenever Dad could get freshly caught catfish and fresh shrimp, he liked to make this étouffée. He was so accustomed to the freshest of seafood growing up that there were some dishes he just didn't like unless the fish was absolutely fresh, and he could tell if it wasn't. He wouldn't buy catfish in late summer or fall; he said they just weren't clean tasting that time of year.
Serves 6

- ⅓ cup corn oil
- 2 cups chopped onion
- 2 cups chopped celery
- 1 cup chopped green bell pepper
- 3 cloves garlic, minced
- 1 pound catfish, cut into large pieces
- 1 pound shrimp, peeled and deveined
- 1½ cups fish stock or 1 cup bottled clam juice and ½ cup water
- 2 tablespoons tomato paste
- 1 teaspoon salt
- 1 teaspoon dried thyme
- ½ teaspoon dried oregano
- ½ teaspoon white pepper
- ¼ teaspoon cayenne pepper
- 3 green onions, sliced
- ½ cup chopped fresh parsley

Heat the oil in a large heavy pot or Dutch oven over medium heat. Sauté the onion, celery, bell pepper, and garlic for 10 minutes.

Place the catfish and shrimp on top of the sautéed vegetables.

Whisk the stock with the remaining ingredients, except the green onions and parsley, and pour over the fish. Bring to a boil, reduce the heat to medium-low, and cook, covered, for 30 minutes. Add the green onions and parsley and cook 5 minutes longer. Serve over rice.

LAGNIAPPE The best way to enjoy shrimp is to purchase it fresh, not frozen, and to cook it in the shell. The shells add a lot of flavor, so true shrimp lovers don't mind peeling the shrimp at the table. Whether shelled or not, the shrimp can be cut along the outside curve and the intestinal tract can be removed before cooking.

Crab and Shrimp Sauce Piquante

The "piquante" in this recipe comes from pepper, but we use a rather moderate amount, as Grandpa taught us that it was important to taste all the ingredients, not have them overpowered by spices. Many Cajuns would add more pepper to this, however.
Serves 8

- ½ cup corn oil
- ½ cup all-purpose flour
- 2 cups chopped onion
- 1 cup chopped celery
- 1 cup chopped green bell pepper
- 3 cloves garlic, coarsely chopped
- 2 cups fish or chicken stock (see Lagniappe)
- One 14-ounce can diced tomatoes, drained
- One 6-ounce can tomato paste
- 3 bay leaves
- 1 teaspoon salt
- ½ teaspoon black pepper
- ½ teaspoon cayenne pepper
- 1 pound shrimp, peeled and deveined
- 1 pound crabmeat
- ¼ cup sliced green onions

Heat the oil in a large heavy pot or Dutch oven over medium heat for 2 minutes. Add the flour and cook for 20 to 30 minutes, stirring constantly, to make a medium roux (see page 14).

Add the onion, celery, bell pepper, and garlic and cook for 10 minutes, stirring often. Stir in the stock, tomatoes, tomato paste, bay leaves, salt and black and cayenne pepper. Cover, reduce the heat to medium-low, and cook for 1 hour, stirring occasionally.

Coarsely chop the shrimp if they are large, and add them to the sauce. Stir to combine, and cook for 5 minutes, uncovered.

Add the crab, and gently fold into the sauce. Reduce the heat to low, cover the pot, and cook for 10 minutes. Remove the bay leaves and serve over hot rice, sprinkled with the green onions.

LAGNIAPPE **If you don't make your own fish stock, and can't find it in the store, you can substitute 2 parts bottled clam juice to 1 part water.**

Crab Cakes

These are often called "crab chops" and are shaped like teardrop-shaped chops. I prefer the round cakes, as they are easier to fry and have more surface area to get crisp.

Makes 12 crab cakes; serves 12 as an appetizer, 4 as an entrée

¼ cup corn oil
4 tablespoons (½ stick) butter
1 cup finely chopped onion
½ cup finely chopped celery
½ cup finely chopped green bell pepper
3 tablespoons all-purpose flour
½ cup half-and-half
1 egg, beaten
½ teaspoon salt
½ teaspoon white pepper
¼ cup chopped fresh parsley
1 pound crabmeat (drain off any liquid)
¾ cup dried unseasoned bread crumbs
2 cups corn oil for frying, or more if needed to achieve a depth of ¼ inch in skillet
Garnish: Lemon wedges

Heat the oil and butter in a large skillet over medium-high heat until foam from the butter subsides. Add the onion, celery, and bell pepper and cook, stirring occasionally, for 10 minutes. Add the flour and cook for 5 minutes, stirring constantly. Add the half-and-half, reduce the heat to medium-low, and cook for 3 minutes, stirring constantly. Spread the mixture out in a glass dish to cool.

Add the beaten egg, salt, pepper, and parsley to the cooled vegetables and stir to combine. Add the crabmeat and stir with a fork, gently but thoroughly, breaking up large pieces of crab. Form the mixture into 12 cakes.

Place the bread crumbs on a plate and gently press crumbs onto both sides of each cake; brush off excess crumbs.

Heat the corn oil to a depth of about 1⁄4 inch in a large skillet over medium-high heat. When the oil is hot (350°F), fry the crab cakes for 2 minutes on each side, until golden brown—you will need to do this in two batches. Move to paper towels as they are done (allow the oil to get back up to temperature before frying the second batch). Serve warm with fresh lemon wedges.

LAGNIAPPE **April 2006. I just spoke with Tommy Cobb of Blum and Bergeron, Inc., who have been selling dried shrimp since the early 1900s. Tommy's grandfather sold dried shrimp and other groceries to my Great-Uncle Adolphe, who had a market in Franklin, Louisiana. During the hurricane of 1909, Tommy's grandfather took shelter with Great-Uncle Adolphe in the substantial brick building that housed the market. Tommy, who was spared any devastating effects from the 2005 hurricanes, said that ironically, the seafood is sweeter and better than ever, though there are fewer fishermen going out to gather it. The Cobbs just enjoyed wonderful crab and are seeing the crawfish season open with succulent crawfish.**

Crab Salad

We sometimes have leftover crab following a big crab feed, especially after our annual post-Christmas trip to Half Moon Bay, on the Pacific Coast, for fresh crab. The problem is getting people to shell it the next day, but a promise of this dish usually produces volunteers.
Serves 6

- 2 cups peeled, seeded, and chopped cucumber (see Lagniappe)
- 1 cup chopped red onion
- 1 cup chopped celery
- ¾ cup top-quality mayonnaise
- ¼ cup chopped fresh parsley
- 1 pound crabmeat
- 3 tablespoons fresh lemon juice
- 1 teaspoon salt
- ¾ teaspoon white pepper
- ¼ teaspoon cayenne pepper

Place all the ingredients in a large bowl, and gently toss to combine. May be used as a sandwich filling, stuffed in tomato shells, served over lettuce, or served as a dip to spread on slices of toasted bread (see Crispy Cayenne French Toasts, page 146, for a great complement to the crab salad).

LAGNIAPPE Cajun cooking doesn't fuss a lot with procedures such as peeling tomatoes, trimming the points off artichoke leaves, and fluting mushrooms. When there is a reason, however, an extra step will be taken to prepare an ingredient for its best use in a dish. The cucumbers are peeled and seeded here, as unpeeled cucumbers, while fine in a salad, are a bit tough with the tender flaky crabmeat. The seeds could make the salad watery, diluting the taste and texture. To seed cucumbers, cut them in half lengthwise (after peeling), and simply run a small spoon down the center, scraping out the seeds.

Crawfish Pie

Sometimes we use crab or shrimp in this pie instead of crawfish. It is one of our favorite dishes to serve guests, especially those new to Cajun food, as it is so charming to see this pie coming to the table in a picturesque old black cast iron skillet. Serves 6

- 4 tablespoons (½ stick) butter
- ¼ cup all-purpose flour
- 1 cup chopped onion
- ½ cup chopped celery
- ½ cup chopped green bell pepper
- ¼ cup minced fresh parsley
- 2 cloves garlic, minced
- 1 cup fish stock or ⅔ cup bottled clam juice and ⅓ cup water
- 1 teaspoon paprika
- ½ teaspoon salt
- ½ teaspoon white pepper
- ½ teaspoon black pepper
- ¼ teaspoon cayenne pepper
- 2 pounds cooked crawfish tails (cooked crabmeat or cooked shelled shrimp may be used instead)
- 1 pie crust, purchased or homemade (page 263), rolled out to about 13 inches

Preheat the oven to 400°F.

Heat a cast iron skillet (about 10 inches across) over medium heat and add the butter. When foam begins to subside add the flour. Immediately begin whisking or stirring to combine, and continue to whisk or stir constantly for 10 to 20 minutes, at which time you should have a light roux.

Add the onion, celery, bell pepper, parsley, and garlic and cook for 5 minutes, stirring often. Add the fish stock and spices. Bring to a boil, reduce the heat to medium-low, and simmer for 15 minutes, stirring often.

Remove from the heat and stir in the crawfish tails. Cool a bit and place the pie crust over the filling, crimping the crust over the edges of the skillet. Cut a hole in the center of the crust to allow steam to escape. Bake for 45 minutes.

LAGNIAPPE **You may use a pie plate if your cast iron skillet isn't well seasoned (an unseasoned pan may give an "off" taste to the pie).**

Crawfish Stew

This was my Grandma Olympe's idea of a quick meal, as the roux takes only 10 minutes. It was the one time she disregarded her rule to "get the roux dark, little one, get it dark-dark-dark." I often prepare this recipe in cooking classes to dispel two myths about Cajun cooking: that it is always spicy, and that it is always time consuming. **Serves 6**

- ½ cup corn oil
- ½ cup all-purpose flour
- 4 cups fish or poultry stock
- 4 bay leaves
- 1 teaspoon dried thyme
- 1 teaspoon salt
- 1 teaspoon white pepper
- 2 pounds raw crawfish tail meat
- ½ cup sliced green onions
- ¼ cup chopped fresh parsley

Heat the oil in a large heavy pot or Dutch oven over medium heat for 2 minutes. Add the flour and cook, stirring constantly, for 10 minutes.

Add the stock, bay leaves, thyme, salt, and pepper and bring to a boil. Reduce the heat to medium-low and simmer for 20 minutes, uncovered, stirring occasionally. Add the crawfish, bring to a boil, and reduce the heat and simmer, uncovered, for 5 minutes.

Remove the bay leaves, transfer to a serving dish or plate, and sprinkle with green onions and parsley. Serve over rice.

LAGNIAPPE **There are 100 to 150 crawfish tails in 1 pound of crawfish tail meat; it takes 8 pounds of live crawfish to produce 1 pound (or 3 cups) crawfish tail meat, and 2 pounds of live crawfish to produce ¼ pound (or ¾ cup) crawfish tail meat.**

Creamy Crab Casserole or Dip

We never get tired of crab, and this is one of our most loved crab dishes. Just one pound of crabmeat is needed for this versatile appetizer or light entrée. This atypical roux uses butter, rather than oil, as we prefer a butter roux with delicate crab.

Makes 6 cups (see Lagniappe)

- 2 teaspoons corn oil for greasing
- 4 tablespoons (½ stick) butter
- 5 tablespoons all-purpose flour
- 1 cup chopped celery
- 1 cup chopped red onion
- ½ cup chopped green bell pepper
- 1 teaspoon paprika
- 1 teaspoon salt
- ½ teaspoon white pepper
- 2 cups whole milk
- 1 pound crabmeat
- ½ cup sliced green onions
- ½ cup chopped fresh parsley
- 3 ounces (1¼ cups) grated Cheddar cheese

Preheat the oven to 350°F. Grease an 8-inch baking pan with the corn oil.

Melt the butter in a heavy skillet or Dutch oven over medium heat. Add the flour and cook for 5 minutes, stirring constantly. (Reduce the heat to medium-low after 3 minutes if the roux is sticking to the bottom of the pan.) Add the celery, onion, bell pepper, and spices and cook for 5 minutes, stirring often.

Add the milk, raise the heat to high, and bring to a boil, stirring constantly until the milk is blended into the flour. Reduce the heat to low and cook for 5 minutes, stirring constantly.

Remove from the heat and stir in the crab, green onions, and parsley. Transfer to the prepared pan and sprinkle with cheese.

Bake for 25 minutes.

LAGNIAPPE **This could serve twelve as an appetizer, with toasted French bread slices and raw vegetables to spread the dip onto, or six as a light lunch with buttered noodles and a green salad.**

Dried Shrimp Jambalaya

After finding a note in Aunt Lorna's handwriting that read, "dried shrimp, Houma, LA," I decided to call the phone number, hoping to get more information on dried shrimp. When I explained why I was calling, the warm, Cajun-accented voice on the other end of the line exclaimed to someone in his office, "Get on the extension, I'm talking to Lorna Haggerty's niece!" Aunt Lorna had died nine years before, but people loved her warmth and enthusiasm and never forgot her. A few weeks later I was down in Louisiana and had lunch with Tommy Cobb, the owner of Blum and Bergeron (see Sources, page 267). We discovered that his father had sold my great-uncle the dried shrimp he kept in a wooden barrel in his store—back in the 1920s!

Serves 6

2½ ounces (1 cup) dried shrimp
2 tomatoes
3 tablespoons lard or corn oil
2 cups chopped onion
½ cup chopped celery
2 green onions, sliced
2 cloves garlic, minced
¼ teaspoon cayenne pepper
¼ cup chopped fresh parsley
½ pound andouille or other smoked sausage, sliced
4 cups cooked rice (about 1⅓ cups raw)

Place the shrimp in a measuring cup and add enough water to come up to the 2-cup mark.

Soak the dried shrimp for several hours or overnight. After soaking, drain the shrimp and reserve the water.

Remove the core from the tomatoes. Cut in half across, squeeze out the seeds, and chop.

Heat the lard in a large heavy pot or Dutch oven over medium-high heat. When the lard is hot, add the onion, celery, green onions, garlic, and cayenne and cook for 5 minutes. Add the shrimp and liquid, and bring to a boil; reduce the heat and simmer for 15 minutes.

Add the tomatoes, parsley, and sausage. Bring to a boil, reduce the heat, and simmer 10 minutes longer.

Add the rice, stir gently to heat through, and serve. The jambalaya should be moist, but not juicy.

LAGNIAPPE **Be sure that the dried shrimp you buy have been peeled, otherwise you'll be crunching through dinner. The best dried shrimp (and shellfish, and other Cajun products) come from the source—Louisiana. I suggest making use of the Sources in this book (see page 267).**

Fish Courtbouillon

(Pronounced COO-be-yon.) Though this is not often seen on restaurant menus, courtbouillon is an old-time favorite Cajun dish. It is one of the few served over French bread, rather than rice. It contains a lot of tomatoes, and small pieces of fish. Grandma loved it so much that it is the only dish for which she had two written recipes. **Serves 6**

- 3 tablespoons ("2 pot spoons") shortening or corn oil
- ¼ cup all-purpose flour
- 2 cups chopped onion
- 1 teaspoon salt
- ½ teaspoon white pepper
- 2 cups hot water
- One 28-ounce can diced tomatoes, undrained
- 2 cloves garlic, minced
- 2 tablespoons distilled white vinegar
- ½ cup sliced green onions
- 1½ pounds catfish fillets, cut into 12 pieces
- 6 large slices French bread
- ½ cup chopped fresh parsley

Heat the shortening in a large heavy pot or Dutch oven over medium heat. Add the flour and make a light roux by cooking, stirring constantly, for 10 to 20 minutes (see page 14).

Add the onion, salt, and pepper and cook until the onions "wither," about 10 minutes, stirring often. Add the hot water, stir to incorporate into the roux, and bring to a boil. Add tomatoes, garlic, vinegar, and green onions and bring to a boil. Add the fish fillets, stir, reduce the heat to low, and gently simmer, covered, for 1 hour.

Toast the French bread slices and place one in each serving bowl. Dish up the fish and gravy on top of the bread, and sprinkle with parsley.

LAGNIAPPE Catfish is sometimes looked down upon as it is a "bottom feeder," meaning it swims and feeds at the bottom of a body of water. This is also true, however, of sole, flounder, and halibut and they are not discriminated against, so enjoy the tender, mild flavor of this delicious fish without hesitation. As with most whole fish, catfish has about a 50 percent loss after being skinned, boned, and cleaned, so a 1-pound whole fish will feed two people, yielding two 4-ounce portions, or two 3-ounce portions after cooking.

Fried Catfish

We use this simple treatment with just-caught fish, as it allows the flavor, tenderness, and bright white flesh to come through. When we don't have freshly caught fish, we choose a cornmeal coating or beer batter, as we love those crispy, crunchy coatings.

Serves 6

- 1 tablespoon onion powder
- 1 tablespoon salt
- 2 teaspoons black pepper
- 2 teaspoons garlic powder
- 1 teaspoon cayenne pepper
- 2 cups whole milk
- 2 eggs
- 1½ pounds catfish fillets, cut into 6 or 12 pieces
- 5 cups oil (for a ¾-inch depth in a 10-inch pot or skillet)
- 1 cup all-purpose flour
- Garnishes: lemon wedges, Tartar Sauce (page 215), Sauce Remoulade (page 213)

Combine the spices and divide in half.

Whisk the milk, eggs, and half the spice mixture together in a large bowl. Add the catfish and allow it to sit for at least 10 minutes, while you heat the oil.

Heat the oil to 360°F in a Dutch oven or high-sided pan.

Combine the flour and remaining spice mixture in a pie plate, or similar dish.

Remove the catfish from the liquid and pat dry with paper towels. Place in the flour and coat well, shaking off the excess. Place the fillets in the hot oil, a few at a time (if you crowd them, the oil will cool down). Fry in batches for 2 to 4 minutes on each side (depending on the thickness of the fish). Try to maintain a temperature of about 350°F. Place the fish fillets on paper towels to drain as they are done.

Serve immediately with garnishes of your choice.

LAGNIAPPE **While these could be fried in a skillet, I prefer to use a Dutch oven or other pot with higher sides than a skillet has. This is not only safer, as there is less chance of the oil boiling over or spilling, but cleanup is much easier, since there is not as much spattering of the oil out of the vessel when using one with higher sides.**

Oyster and Pork Jambalaya

This is an oyster lover's dish, and one that was made whenever someone came back from Cypremort Point with a sack of oysters. To make this recipe feasible for those not having access to fresh oysters, I offer the alternative of using fresh oysters in a jar, found in the seafood section of the market. Serves 6

- 1 tablespoon lard or corn oil
- 1 pound fresh lean ground pork
- ¼ cup hot water
- 1 cup chopped onion
- 1 pint shucked oysters with their liquid or two 8-ounce or 10-ounce jars
- 3 cups cooked cold rice (about 1 cup raw rice)
- 3 green onions, sliced
- ⅓ cup chopped fresh parsley
- ½ teaspoon salt
- ½ teaspoon black pepper
- ¼ teaspoon cayenne pepper

Heat the lard or oil in a large heavy pot or Dutch oven over medium-high heat. When the lard is hot, add the pork and cook until most of the pink is gone and it is starting to brown, about 5 minutes, stirring occasionally. Add the hot water and onion and continue cooking until the water cooks out of the pork, about 10 minutes, stirring occasionally.

Cut the oysters into pieces (unless they are very small) so they will break down and merge into the rice. (I find that scissors makes this an easy task.)

Reduce the heat to low, stir the oysters and their liquid into the pork, cover, and cook for 10 minutes. Add the rice, green onions, parsley, and seasonings, and stir to combine all ingredients. Cover and cook for 30 minutes, stirring often, until everything has blended together. (Add a spoonful of water or adjust the heat down a bit if the jambalaya is starting to stick on the bottom of the pot.) The jambalaya should be moist but not wet, and will look like a thick rice dish with the oysters and pork not visible as separate ingredients.

LAGNIAPPE Grandma specified cold rice in several of her recipes, because adding hot rice (in dishes like this one) would result in a gummy texture rather than having the grains of rice separate. There was always cold rice to be found in the refrigerator, as rice was used in some dish at least once a day; scrambled eggs and rice was, and still is, a frequent breakfast for people in our family.

Oyster Po' Boys

These fried oysters have a great texture, with a delicate lacy crust from the egg–baking powder batter, rather than the usual firm, crusty exterior of most fried oysters. Sometimes we just have these fried oysters as an appetizer—easy and delicious. Serves 6

- 3 cups corn oil for frying (for a ½-inch depth in a 10-inch skillet)
- 2 eggs, beaten
- 2 tablespoons baking powder
- 1 teaspoon cayenne pepper
- 18 medium-large fresh oysters or two 10-ounce jars, drained
- 1 cup all-purpose flour
- 1 teaspoon black pepper
- 6 soft sandwich rolls, split and toasted
- Salt and pepper to taste
- Optional garnishes: Tartar Sauce (page 000), shredded lettuce, sliced tomato, sliced dill pickles, lemon wedges, Tabasco sauce

Whisk the eggs with the baking powder and cayenne in a medium bowl, and add the oysters. Soak the oysters in the egg mixture for 5 to 10 minutes.

Heat the oil in a large heavy skillet or Dutch oven to a temperature of 375°F.

Mix the flour and pepper and place in a dish.

When the oil is hot, lift the oysters out of the egg mixture and dip in the flour, gently tossing to coat well. Shake off excess flour. Fry the oysters for about 1 minute on each side, until golden and crusty. Don't crowd oysters when frying, as that will cool the oil. Drain on paper towels.

Place 3 oysters on each toasted roll, and add garnishes of choice. Serve lemon wedges and Tabasco sauce to be added as desired. (The listed garnishes are traditional for po' boys, but I feel that pickles and tomatoes mask the flavor of the oysters, so I just add tartar sauce and lettuce, with a squeeze of fresh lemon and a few drops of Tabasco sauce. If I don't have tartar sauce, I just use mayonnaise with fresh lemon juice and Tabasco, and lettuce.)

LAGNIAPPE **Po' boys are sandwiches that originated in New Orleans, but are now entrenched in Cajun Country as well. Cajun po' boys are usually made of fried seafood or shellfish, sausages, or meatballs and gravy. They were designed to be a hearty and cheap meal for the poor boys who worked on the riverfront during the Depression.**

Pepper-Fried Shrimp

We all looked forward to the huge platter of fried shrimp that often appeared on our dinner table on Friday nights. The array of accompaniments was as welcome as the shrimp themselves: Tartar Sauce (page 215), Mama's Seafood Cocktail Sauce (page 208), Sauce Remoulade (page 213), and fresh lemon wedges. This recipe may successfully be doubled.

Serves 6 as an appetizer, 2 as an entrée

1 cup all-purpose flour plus 2 cups flour for dusting
1 tablespoon salt
½ teaspoon sugar
1 teaspoon black pepper
½ teaspoon white pepper
¼ teaspoon cayenne pepper
1 egg, beaten
1 cup very cold water
2 tablespoons corn oil plus 5 cups for frying (for a 1-inch depth in a 6-quart pot)
1 pound raw shrimp, peeled and deveined (tails may be left on for handles)

Combine the 1 cup flour, salt, sugar, and black, white, and cayenne pepper in a large bowl.

Whisk the egg with the water and the 2 tablespoons oil. Add the egg mixture to the flour mixture in the bowl, stirring just enough to combine the ingredients for the batter.

Dry the shrimp well on paper towels and place it in a bag with the 2 cups flour, shaking to coat the shrimp with the flour. This will help the batter adhere to the shrimp.

Heat the 5 cups oil in a large pot or Dutch oven to 360°F. (This amount is needed for semi-deep-frying). When the oil reaches this temperature, dip the floured shrimp in batter, letting the excess drip off, and carefully drop in the hot oil, cooking a few at a time for about 3 minutes, or until golden brown (don't overcrowd or the oil will cool, and the shrimp will not be crisp). Drain on paper towels.

LAGNIAPPE If you have any leftover fried shrimp, you're obviously not in my house. However, they make wonderful po' boy sandwiches. Remove the tails and layer the shrimp on soft French rolls with sliced tomatoes, shredded lettuce, pickles if desired, and a generous portion of tartar sauce.

Shrimp Boil with Potatoes and Corn

This was always a fun meal when we were kids (and an easy dinner to prepare for company, now that we're adults). With the addition of a salad, it's a complete meal, and lots of fun, as plastic and/or newspapers are spread on the table, and the drained shrimp, potatoes, and corn are either brought in on platters or, if outside on the picnic table, dumped right in the center of the table. After the meal, the newspapers are gathered up, whisking away the shells and corncobs. You don't even have any dishes to do!

Serves 4 as an entrée, 10 as an appetizer

- 1 gallon water
- 1 cup salt
- 1 lemon, thinly sliced
- 1 onion, thinly sliced
- 2 tablespoons cayenne pepper
- 12 small red potatoes (about 2 pounds)
- 6 ears corn, broken in half
- 2 pounds shrimp, 36 to 42 count (see Lagniappe)

Bring the water, salt, lemon, onion, and cayenne to a rolling boil in a large pot, and boil for 5 minutes.

Add the potatoes, bring up to a simmer, and simmer until fork-tender (about 15 minutes).

Add the corn, bring up to a simmer, and simmer for 5 minutes.

Add the shrimp and bring the water to a boil. As soon as the water reaches a rolling boil, shrimp should be opaque and pink, which means they are done.

Immediately drain the boil and transfer to a large platter. The onion and lemon slices may be removed, if desired, but I keep them with the shrimp for flavor.

Serve with a tomato-based sauce, and a mayonnaise-based sauce. My favorites for this dish are Sauce Remoulade (page 213) and Mama's Seafood Cocktail Sauce (page 208) with butter optional for the potatoes and corn.

LAGNIAPPE **Shrimp are sold by the number per pound. The standard counts are: under 10; 10 to 15; 16 to 20; 21 to 25; 26 to 30; 31 to 35; 36 to 42; 42 to 50; 50 to 60. The usual size in restaurants is 16 to 20 per pound. Small shrimp are best for shrimp salad, shrimp cocktails, fricassees, and gumbos; medium are ideal for shrimp boils and deep-frying; large are suited to broiling, grilling, or barbecuing.**

Shrimp Fricassee

Grandpa Pischoff would become upset when anyone overcooked shrimp. He developed a method for teaching children how to cook this crustacean that was almost foolproof: place raw, peeled shrimp in a bowl, pour boiling water over them, cover, and let sit for 2 to 6 minutes, depending on size. Shrimp cooked this way are very tender and never overcooked. Serves 6

- ¾ cup corn oil
- ¾ cup all-purpose flour
- 2 cups chopped onion
- 1 cup chopped celery
- ½ cup chopped green bell pepper
- 2 cloves garlic, minced
- 2 tablespoons tomato paste
- ¾ teaspoon salt
- ½ teaspoon white pepper
- ¼ teaspoon cayenne pepper
- 1 cup fish or chicken stock, or more if needed
- 1½ pounds peeled, deveined shrimp
- ¾ cup chopped fresh parsley
- ¾ cup sliced green onions

Heat the oil in a large heavy pot or Dutch oven over medium heat for 2 minutes. Add the flour, whisk to combine, reduce the heat to medium-low, and cook, stirring constantly, for 30 to 40 minutes to make a dark roux (see page 14).

Add the onion, celery, and bell pepper to the roux, raise the heat to medium, and cook for 10 minutes, stirring often. Add the garlic, tomato paste, salt, and white and cayenne pepper, stirring to combine. Add the stock, bring to a boil, reduce the heat to medium-low, and simmer, uncovered, for 10 minutes, stirring occasionally (if the sauce is too thick, add a bit more stock). Add the shrimp, bring to a boil, reduce the heat to medium-low, and simmer for 10 minutes, uncovered, stirring occasionally. Serve over rice, sprinkled with parsley and green onions.

LAGNIAPPE **The reason that most Cajun dishes call for chopped onion, celery, and so on, rather than minced, diced, finely chopped, or coarsely chopped is that most dishes are cooked so long that the vegetables almost completely break down, helping to form the sauce. It doesn't matter much what size they are when starting out, as they dissolve into the body of the sauce by the end of the cooking time.**

Shrimp Jambalaya with Ham

This was one of Dad's standby recipes when he was cooking for a large crowd. He could make it a day or two ahead, through paragraph 3, then finish cooking it in about 30 minutes.
Serves 8

¼ cup corn oil
¼ cup all-purpose flour
2 cups chopped onion
1½ cups chopped celery
1 cup chopped green bell pepper
3 cloves garlic, minced
1 pound ham, chopped
1 teaspoon dried thyme
½ teaspoon salt
½ teaspoon black pepper
¼ teaspoon cayenne pepper
2 tablespoons tomato paste
4 cups chicken stock
2 bay leaves
One 14-ounce can diced tomatoes, undrained
2 cups raw rice
1 pound cooked shrimp
½ cup chopped fresh parsley
4 green onions, sliced

Heat the oil in a large heavy pot or Dutch oven over medium heat for 2 minutes. Add the flour and cook, stirring constantly, for 5 minutes.

Add the onion, celery, and bell pepper, reduce the heat to low, and cook, stirring often, for 5 minutes. Add the garlic, ham, thyme, and spices and cook, stirring often, for 5 minutes.

Add the tomato paste, and cook for 1 minute, stirring constantly. Add the stock and bay leaves and bring to a boil. Reduce the heat and simmer, stirring often, for 10 minutes.

Add the tomatoes with their juice, and the rice. Bring to a boil, stir well, reduce the heat to a very low simmer, cover, and cook 25 minutes longer. Add the shrimp and cook for 5 more minutes, covered. Remove the bay leaves and stir in the parsley. Sprinkle each serving with green onions.

LAGNIAPPE **Two pounds of whole raw shrimp will yield 1 pound (or 2 cups) of shrimp meat after the shrimp are shelled, deveined, and cooked.**

Shrimp Remoulade

The women in our family seem unable to agree on how remoulade should be made. Great-Aunt Irma always put paprika in hers, but Great-Aunt Alice wouldn't touch remoulade unless it was white, with no paprika. My sister Lorna and I have carried on the dispute; this is her delicious (I admit) version of remoulade (though a better one—mine—is on page 213).

This recipe may successfully be reduced to serve fewer people.

Serves 6 as an entrée, 12 to 16 as an appetizer

Shrimp

- 3 pounds shrimp (medium or large)
- 3 quarts (12 cups) water
- 3 tablespoons salt
- 1 tablespoon white pepper

Remoulade Sauce

- 1 cup olive oil
- ¾ cup distilled white vinegar
- ½ cup stone-ground mustard (Cajun or Creole preferred)
- ¼ cup paprika
- 1 teaspoon white pepper
- 1 teaspoon salt
- ½ teaspoon black pepper
- ½ teaspoon Tabasco sauce
- 1 cup chopped celery
- ½ cup chopped fresh parsley
- ¼ cup chopped onion

Prepare the shrimp by peeling and deveining them. Bring the water, salt, and pepper to a boil in a large pot. Add the shrimp and return the water to a boil; the shrimp will probably be done by the time the water returns to a rolling boil, depending on their size, or they may take another 1 to 3 minutes. As soon as shrimp turn opaque and pink, and are barely firm, drain and place them on a tray. Pour some ice over the shrimp to stop the cooking.

Combine all of the sauce ingredients except the celery, parsley, and onion in a large bowl and whisk to combine. Add the celery, parsley, and onion and stir to mix well.

Lift the shrimp out of the ice in the tray, drain well, and stir into the sauce. Serve slightly chilled or at room temperature.

LAGNIAPPE **We sometimes add mayonnaise to the remoulade for a creamy sauce for shrimp or chicken salad, or to drizzle over a platter of fresh, chilled shellfish, or vegetables.**

Sweet and Savory Bakery

Irma, Victoria, Olympe

Irma Marie Constance Labauve,
Married Albert Pischoff

The Great-Aunts: The Vanilla Lady and the Lonely Trousseau

Dad and Aunt Lorna had two aunts and an uncle who were a big part of their lives: Aunt Alice, Aunt Irma, and Uncle Adolphe. Until they were in high school, Dad and Aunt Lorna lived within minutes of their grandparents' farm and the homes of their aunts and uncle. Most summer days were spent at Home Place, as their own house was rather small and didn't have much of a yard. It certainly didn't have farm animals, a bayou for gathering crawfish, every type of fruit and vegetable that grew in the area, and their cousins Madge, Juanita, and Buster to play with.

Their grandparents were glad to have all of them, and they were a big extended family. Most of their childhood memories revolved around the farm, where there were always a lot of people and much activity. Neither their Aunts Irma and Alice, nor their Uncle Adolphe, had children of their own so they were happy to have their nieces and nephews around.

Irma and her husband, Albert, built a mammoth two-story house near the family farm. There was a gracious, wide porch surrounding the entire house, where they spent their few leisure hours, enjoying each other and family members. The house was filled with gorgeous china, silver, glasses, linens, and furniture. Irma had accumulated these possessions through hard work and years of scrimping and saving to satisfy the taste for fine things that she had acquired while working on Vacherie Plantation as a seamstress.

Irma and Albert's nieces and nephews were fascinated by the fact that they allowed the cattle to find shelter from the hot sun underneath the house. The house was built on piers, and the area under it became everything from a fort to a castle where the children played for hours, using the unsuspecting cattle as cowboys, kings, queens, and spies.

My older sisters, Lorna and Bonnie, would visit Irma's home often during the summers they spent at Home Place as young children. Lorna affectionately remembers some special moments she spent with Irma: "Irma's kitchen was a large room with a farmhouse sink, and wooden sideboards flanked by lots of drawers. There was a long table in the center, and a door at the back on the right side that went out to a tiny cook-house where she did the cooking in the summer. The cookhouse, close to the indoor kitchen, was used so the house wouldn't get hot from cooking during the sweltering months. They almost always cooked hot meals—breakfast, lunch, and dinner—regardless of the weather.

"She was an excellent cook. I vividly remember the fragrance, texture, and taste of her French toast, even some sixty years later. When the house would fill with the aroma of vanilla early in the morning, I would run to the kitchen, because I knew what she was making. She used a lot of vanilla, which I watched her mix with sugar, spices, eggs, milk, and cream. She beat it all until it was smooth and golden, soaked the slices of French bread in the egg-cream mixture for a minute or so, and then fried them. The inside of the French toast was almost like custard, and the outside was crisp and a wonderful caramelized golden brown. She would drizzle melted butter, and cane syrup from a green can, over the top of each slice, put the plate down in front of me, and tell me to 'Eat, eat. You need to put some flesh on those bones.' It was delectable."

Lorna was very fond of her Great-Aunt Irma and her big farm kitchen. She spent a lot of time there, watching Irma cook and learning from her. They found they had a love of cooking in common. This was, and is, a typical way that Cajuns pass on their cooking methods without the younger generation even being aware that they are receiving lessons. This time is also used to pass on family traditions and valuable lessons in life, through stories and pleasant chatter.

Alice's story is the stuff of which dramas are made. She was the baby of the seven children. Petite but strong, she seemed street smart right from the time she was a young child. She was a born businesswoman and started her first successful venture at the age of sixteen by growing and selling watermelons, as evidenced a letter her father wrote in 1906 about Alice and her sisters: "Oréline has great interest in clothes and in helping me with the cattle, while Irma and Olympe are interested in picture-taking with a camera, and Alice's main interest is in watermelon selling."

She was once engaged to a man who deserted her shortly before their wedding. Alice was devastated at first, and then angry. She decided that she wanted no part of romance and would never again let herself fall in love. She kept her intention and never got married. She became an even stronger, more indepen-dent person, and made a life for herself that did not rely on anyone else, especially any man, for success.

Alice began to get more involved in business, enjoying the game of it. She *worked hard managing a local country store, and saving and investing her money. She eventually was able to purchase and open a store of her own, which she ran her entire adult life, amassing what was considered a small fortune at that time.*

Aunt Lorna recalled her childhood visits to the store: "Alice would sit in the store and read magazines and catalogues from all over. She sent for and got joy out of ordering all manner of items, then hoarding them, unused, in the unlived-in house she had built for herself behind the store. She collected a treasure's worth of goods. The house had a beautiful living room–dining room combination. There were two bedrooms in Alice's house and one was stacked with silver dishes, glasses, pots, toasters, set after set of fine china, and set after set of silverware. The room was so chockfull you could hardly walk through. It was like a trousseau that was never used, all of it in original wrappings. Just like a woman who dreamed someday she would get married but then never did.

"Alice," Aunt Lorna continued, "had the Louis XIV bedroom suite that she had purchased from her mother's half brother, her Uncle Solange, who brought it back from France. The set was lovely. That bedroom suite filled her second bedroom. She promised it to me, but I have no idea what happened to it. Alice's house was broken into and cleaned out when she died."

I guess Alice did enjoy her money in her own way, even if that way didn't include personal comforts. According to Aunt Lorna, "Alice was one of the first people in Louisiana to buy one of the large Wurlitzer record players. You could put money into the machine and it would play. She was famous all over the parish because she had such a mammoth record player. She paid over five hundred dollars for it, a crazy amount in those days (almost seven thousand dollars in today's money). People would come from all the surrounding towns to see and hear it.

"One day when I was visiting, Alice put on a record, excitedly telling me to 'listen to this wonderful voice. This woman is someday going to be known the world over.' The woman with the wonderful voice was Ella Fitzgerald."

While she never married, Alice did have a full life, with her large family, her two dogs (Bebe and Doe-Doe), customers, catalogues, property and stock investments, and never-ending additions to her never-to-be-used trousseau.

Bacon-Fried Cornmeal Cakes with Syrup

We like these with Steen's Cane Syrup from Abbeville, but if we're out of that we use pure maple syrup or honey; and we always put a bit of melted butter on top of the cakes before we add the syrup. These taste like fried cornbread with crispy bacon pieces. Serves 6

- 6 slices thick bacon
- 1 cup cornmeal
- 1 cup all-purpose flour
- 1½ teaspoons baking powder
- 1 teaspoon salt
- ½ teaspoon white pepper
- ½ teaspoon baking soda
- 4 eggs, beaten
- 2 cups whole milk
- 1 teaspoon fresh lemon juice
- Corn oil for frying pancakes (about ¼ cup, or more if needed)
- Cane or maple syrup and melted butter for serving

Fry the bacon in a large heavy skillet over medium heat. Remove the bacon from the pan, crumble, and reserve. Transfer the drippings to a dish and reserve; wipe out the skillet.

Sift together the cornmeal, flour, baking powder, salt, pepper, and baking soda in a small bowl.

Whisk the eggs, milk, and lemon juice together in a large bowl; add the dry ingredients to the egg mixture and stir just until combined; don't overmix. Add the crumbled reserved bacon, and 2 tablespoons of bacon drippings; stir to combine.

Heat the skillet over medium-high heat and add 2 teaspoons of the corn oil. When the oil is hot, pour about 3 tablespoons (a bit less than ¼ cup) batter into the pan for each cake; cook for about half a minute, or until bubbles appear all over the surface. Turn, and cook about 1 minute longer, until golden on both sides. Repeat the process, adding more oil as needed, and reducing the heat if the pan gets too hot. Keep cooked cakes warm until all are done. Serve with syrup and melted butter.

LAGNIAPPE **A bit of lemon juice is often added to baked goods when baking soda is the only leavening agent, as the soda needs acid to react with in order to leaven foods. When baking powder is present, as in this recipe, acid is just for flavor.**

Beignets

The first thing we do every time we visit New Orleans is to go to Cafe du Monde for beignets and café au lait, no matter what the time, as they are open twenty-four hours a day. We get our café au lait in cups to go, so after we finish our beignets, we can stroll along the Riverwalk while we sip our coffee.

Makes about 2 dozen

- 3 cups all-purpose flour
- 3 tablespoons baking powder
- 2 tablespoons sugar
- 1 teaspoon salt
- 1½ cups whole milk
- 3 tablespoons corn oil plus oil for frying (about 4 cups)
- 2 tablespoons vanilla extract
- 2 large eggs
- Confectioners' sugar for dusting

Sift the flour, baking powder, sugar, and salt together in a large bowl.

Whisk together the milk, the 3 tablespoons corn oil, vanilla, and eggs. Stir into the dry ingredients until no traces of flour are visible, but don't overmix. The batter will be thick.

Heat the oil for frying in a large heavy Dutch oven (or other large—about 6-quart—pot) to 375°F (use a candy thermometer to gauge the temperature). When the temperature is reached, carefully drop large tablespoons of the dough into the hot oil, and fry a few beignets at a time without crowding, for about 4 minutes, turning once. The temperature will drop when you add the dough; adjust the heat to maintain the temperature between 350°F and 365°F.

Remove the beignets to paper towels, and immediately sprinkle with confectioners' sugar as they come out of the hot oil.

LAGNIAPPE **These are dropped into the hot oil from a spoon, rather than being rolled out and cut before frying. They are not only easier to make this way, as the entire rolling out and cutting steps are deleted, but they have a crispier texture because the surface isn't perfectly smooth, so there are tiny nooks and crannies to get crisp.**

Biscuits Supreme

These were Aunt Lorna's signature biscuits. As they didn't have much sugar in them, they could be used with sweet or savory foods. According to Aunt Lorna, "They are exceptionally tender and may be used for afternoon tea, and used as a base for creamed foods." Make these easy biscuits, even if you don't like baking (see paragraph 4).
Makes 12 medium biscuits

- 2 cups all-purpose flour
- 2 teaspoons baking powder
- 1 teaspoon sugar
- ½ teaspoon salt
- ½ teaspoon baking soda
- ½ cup chilled lard or shortening
- ⅔ cup whole milk
- 2 tablespoons melted butter

Preheat the oven to 425°F.

Sift the dry ingredients into a large bowl. Add the lard, and cut in with a pastry blender or fork until the mixture resembles coarse crumbs.

Add the milk and stir "just until dough follows fork around the bowl," according to Aunt Lorna's phrasing (takes less than 1 minute). The dough should be formed just enough that it can be gathered into a ball and transferred to a lightly floured board. Knead the dough very gently, with floured hands, 6 to 8 times.

Gently roll the dough ½ to ¾-inch thick on a lightly floured surface and cut with a biscuit cutter into 12 biscuits; for light biscuits, don't handle any more than necessary. (If you do not like baking, simply pat the dough out and cut into 12 biscuits of any shape, using a knife or the rim of a glass.) Brush with melted butter.

Bake on an ungreased baking sheet for 12 minutes, or until they are golden brown.

LAGNIAPPE **As long as the biscuits are all the same thickness, the diameter doesn't matter in terms of cooking time. The height of the biscuit determines how long it needs to be cooked until done—the diameter could be miniature or large, and the biscuits will be done at the same time. I often make 6 large biscuits for dinner with half the dough, and 18 small biscuits (one-third of the regular size) with the other half of the dough to use as appetizers. Fill the mini biscuits with ham and pecan butter, or shrimp and remoulade sauce, for an easy, unusual hors d'oeuvre.**

Breakfast Cornbread with Sausage and Apples

Dad loved to make breakfast on Sunday mornings. Once when he was making fried sausages, sautéed apples, and cornbread some friends showed up. Dad looked at the meager pound of sausages and decided to stretch the ingredients to feed everyone. He sliced the sausage links and added them, with chopped apples, to the bottom of a baking dish. He then poured the cornbread batter on top and baked it. We had a new favorite, though were told "FGL," or "family go lightly." Serves 8

- 2 tablespoons plus 4 tablespoons butter, melted and cooled
- 12 pork link sausages (about 1 pound)
- 3 chopped medium apples (about 1¼ pounds)
- 1 tablespoon fresh lemon juice
- 1¾ cups cornmeal
- ½ cup all-purpose flour
- 1 tablespoon baking powder
- 1 teaspoon baking soda
- 1 egg, beaten
- 2 cups buttermilk
- Cane or maple syrup and melted butter for serving

Preheat the oven to 400°F.

Butter a 9 × 13-inch baking dish with 2 tablespoons of the melted, cooled butter.

Cook the sausages in a skillet just until done; slice and place in the dish.

Toss the apples with lemon juice; drain and place in the dish.

Place the dry ingredients in a large bowl, and stir or whisk well to combine.

Whisk the remaining butter with the egg and buttermilk until combined. Fold into the dry ingredients, just until blended. Pour over the sausages and apples, gently spread evenly, and bake for 25 minutes. Serve with syrup and melted butter.

LAGNIAPPE Stretching ingredients by chopping them and adding a starch is typical Cajun cooking. That, essentially, is what jambalaya is—rice with some seafood, poultry, or meat and seasonings. Or, if friends show up, more rice with more of whatever seafood, poultry, or meat is around. This is when smoked meats such as tasso and andouille or dried shrimp are great to have around, as they keep for a long time and can be pulled out in an emergency, and needing enough food to feed unexpected guests is an emergency to hospitable Cajuns.

Coffee-Pecan Bread

Pecans have always been a big part of our lives and our kitchen. The sale of pecans from the family farm helped support our ancestors for generations. Even in California, we felt we were a part of the harvest when Great-Uncle Adolphe would send boxes of fresh pecans to us. Serves 8

- 2 teaspoons corn oil
- 1¾ cups all-purpose flour
- 1 cup chopped pecans
- ½ cup granulated sugar plus 1 tablespoon sugar
- ⅓ cup brown sugar
- 3 tablespoons instant espresso coffee (see Lagniappe)
- 1½ teaspoons baking powder
- 1 teaspoon salt
- 1 teaspoon ground cinnamon
- ½ teaspoon baking soda
- ½ teaspoon ground nutmeg
- 2 eggs, lightly beaten
- ½ cup whole milk
- ½ cup strong coffee, cooled
- 4 tablespoons (½ stick) butter, melted and cooled
- 1 tablespoon vanilla extract

Preheat the oven to 350°F. Lightly oil a loaf pan with the corn oil.

Combine the flour, pecans, the ½ cup granulated sugar and the brown sugar, coffee powder, baking powder, salt, cinnamon, baking soda, and nutmeg in a large bowl.

Whisk the eggs, milk, coffee, butter, and vanilla together in a medium bowl until well mixed. Add the egg mixture to the dry ingredients and stir just until combined; don't overmix.

Transfer the batter to the oiled loaf pan and sprinkle with the 1 tablespoon sugar. Bake for 50 minutes. The bread is done if the top springs back when gently touched in the center, or when a toothpick inserted in the center comes out clean.

LAGNIAPPE Aunt Lorna always had Medaglia D'Oro Instant Espresso Coffee in her pantry. She said that her mother discovered it in the 1940s, and would use it to enhance leftover coffee that she didn't want to throw away, for baked goods and meat sauces.

Coush-Coush

I don't think our family ever tires of cornmeal and its many incarnations. Grandma's favorite was cornmeal with butter and sugar (she called it cornmeal mush); Dad couldn't get enough cornbread; I love cornbread dressings; my sisters adore hush puppies; and my brother loves grits with butter and syrup. Here is yet another way to prepare the yellow grain, and one that we all love, with its crispy, browned pieces of fried cornmeal. We always garnish it the same way: with warmed cane syrup and a drizzle of milk. **Serves 6**

2 cups yellow cornmeal
1½ teaspoons salt
1 teaspoon baking powder
⅓ cup corn oil
Cane or maple syrup, milk, coffee-milk (half coffee, half milk), jam for serving
1½ plus ¼ cups water

Combine the cornmeal, 1½ cups of the water, salt, and baking powder in a large bowl, mixing well.

Heat the oil in a large heavy skillet over medium-high heat. When the oil is hot (but before it is smoking), stir the cornmeal mixture and add it to the hot oil. Spread it evenly with a fork and immediately reduce the heat to medium.

After 5 minutes, carefully lift an outer edge to see if a thick golden crust has formed. If not, allow to cook for 2 more minutes and test again, every 2 minutes (it may take 10 to 12 minutes, depending on the thickness of your pan). As soon as the crust has formed, stir with a fork, scraping the mixture off the bottom of the skillet and distributing the crusty bottom throughout the rest of the mixture.

Add the remaining ¼ cup water and stir again. Cover, reduce the heat to medium-low, and cook for 10 minutes. Stir again to redistribute the newly formed crust throughout the rest of the mixture, then remove the coush-coush from the pan (the mixture should be crumbly and lumpy, but should not be dried out). Serve hot with your choice of accompaniments.

LAGNIAPPE **Some people like jam with coush-coush, but the old-fashioned traditional garnish is café au lait—half coffee and half milk. Café au lait was probably originally poured over the coush-coush so leftover coffee-milk (which was often made up in pitchers before breakfast) could be used.**

Crispy Cayenne French Toasts

We just love these. There's a lot you can do with these versatile, crispy little toasts (see Lagniappe), but they don't usually last long enough to have many to do something with. We make up a double batch before the holidays, as they're great to have around for quick hors d'oeuvres or snacks.

Makes 5 to 6 dozen

- 1 cup olive oil
- 2 teaspoons salt
- 2 teaspoons paprika
- 2 teaspoons onion powder
- 1½ teaspoons garlic powder
- 1½ teaspoons white pepper
- 1½ teaspoons cayenne pepper
- 1 teaspoon sugar
- 1 loaf soft French bread (18 inches long), at least one day old

Preheat the oven to 250°F.

Combine all the ingredients, except the French bread, in a small bowl and blend thoroughly.

Slice the French bread in ¼-inch slices with a serrated knife, and place on baking sheets (you will probably need to do this in two batches, using two baking sheets each time). Note that the French bread is easier to slice if it is a day or two old.

Brush the topping onto the French bread slices (top side only). Divide half the bread slices between the two baking sheets, without overlapping the slices. Place in the oven and bake for 25 minutes. (It's important not to crowd the bread slices so they will get crisp.)

Repeat with the remaining French bread slices.

LAGNIAPPE **These are good just by themselves, but are great crumbled on top of a salad or soup, with cheese, as a base for courtbouillon or other seafood stew or soup, or as a base for small open-faced sandwiches, or crab or chicken salad.**

Fried Okra Corncakes

As very young kids, we maintained that we didn't like okra (we didn't realize that we ate it every time gumbo was served). After tasting these corncakes, however, we realized how good it could be, and started looking for other dishes containing the odd-looking vegetable.

Serves 8

1 cup cornmeal
1 cup all-purpose flour
1½ teaspoons salt
1 teaspoon baking powder
¾ teaspoon white pepper
½ teaspoon black pepper
¼ teaspoon cayenne pepper
2 cups water
1 pound okra (fresh, or frozen and patted dry), sliced ½ inch thick
1 cup finely chopped onion
½ cup chopped fresh parsley
6 tablespoons butter, or more if needed

Sift the cornmeal, flour, salt, baking powder, and black, white, and cayenne pepper into a large bowl. Add the water and stir to blend.

Fold in the okra, onion, and parsley.

Melt 1½ tablespoons of the butter in a heavy skillet over high heat. Add a scant ⅓ cup of the batter for each pancake and cook for 4 minutes. Adjust the heat down to medium-high if the corncakes are browning too fast. Turn over, press down lightly, and cook for 3 minutes on the other side. The cakes should be golden brown and slightly crusty. Repeat until all the cakes are made, replenishing the butter as necessary.

LAGNIAPPE Okra originated in Africa and was brought over by slaves who wanted to bring something from home, and hid the seeds in their hair. The vegetable has been a favorite in the South ever since. The taste has been described as a cross between eggplant and asparagus, and it is a great thickener, as the starch in okra absorbs water and increases in size, thereby thickening the dish containing it. Purchase green, tender but not shriveled pods, and store in the refrigerator. The season is between May and October.

Indian Bannock Bread

Bannock bread is a Native American staple. The oats (bannock means oats) in the bread indicate that it may have originated in Acadia, as many Acadian breads contained oats. This recipe has been in our family for many years, and I don't know where we got it, only that it is absolutely delicious with butter melting over the hot, hearty oat bread.
Serves 6

2 teaspoons corn oil
1½ cups all-purpose flour plus some flour for flouring hands
½ cup rolled oats (not instant oats)
¼ cup sugar
2 teaspoons baking powder
½ teaspoon salt
6 tablespoons butter, melted and cooled
⅓ cup water, or more if needed
Butter and jam for serving

Preheat the oven to 400°F. Use the oil to grease a pie plate.

Combine the flour, oats, sugar, baking powder, and salt in a large bowl.

Add the butter and stir just until combined; add the water and stir just until blended; don't overmix.

Transfer the dough to the pie plate. Flour hands and lightly pat the dough evenly into the plate. Score the dough into six wedges to make cutting easier when the bread is done. Bake in the oven for 25 minutes, or until light golden, and slightly dark golden around the edges.

Cut into six wedges and serve with butter and jam.

LAGNIAPPE **This is a good recipe to use to teach kids the joys of baking. The dough is simple to make, and is just patted into a pie plate—there is no rolling or cutting. The texture is a bit like shortbread, and just sweet enough to be considered a dessert, while not containing much sugar.**

Pain Perdu

This bread holds one of the favorite childhood memories of my sister Lorna. She would sometimes spend weekends with our Great-Aunt Irma in her beautiful farmhouse. Lorna describes waking up in the morning to the aroma of Irma's French toast frying, and she would run to the gigantic kitchen to watch Irma make her favorite breakfast dish. Serves 6

- 9 eggs
- 1 cup sugar
- 3 cups half-and-half
- ½ teaspoon nutmeg
- ½ teaspoon cinnamon
- 3 tablespoons vanilla extract
- 1 whole loaf French bread (16 ounces), at least one day old
- 8 tablespoons (1 stick) butter, or more if needed
- ½ cup corn oil, or more if needed
- Butter, jam, confectioners' sugar, cane or maple syrup for serving

Whisk the eggs and sugar in a large bowl until the sugar is dissolved. Add the half-and-half, spices, and vanilla and whisk to combine.

Cut ends off the bread and save for another use. Slice the remaining loaf into ¾-inch-thick slices; you should have about 22 slices. Dip the slices in the egg mixture, a few at a time, and leave in the mixture for about 1 minute; remove the slices and set them on a baking sheet so they are ready to fry.

Heat about 2 tablespoons of the butter and about 2 tablespoons of the oil in a large heavy skillet over medium-high heat. When they are hot, fry the bread for about 1 minute on each side; turn the heat down to medium and fry the remaining bread for 2 minutes on each side. The bread should be golden brown on both sides; you will need to fry it in several batches so the bread is not crowded and will get crisp.

Remove the bread from the skillet as it is done, transfer to a baking sheet, and cover loosely with foil to keep warm until all the bread is fried. Serve with your choice of accompaniments.

LAGNIAPPE **Pain perdu, in French, means "lost bread," so named by the thrifty Cajuns because it makes use of stale bread, not unlike Bread Pudding (page 248), Crispy Cayenne French Toasts (page 146), or Baked Tomato Casserole (page 168).**

Real Cajun Cornbread

Aunt Lorna gave me this recipe on which she had written, "It's the real thing, from Frances Parkinson Keyes Cookbook, page 100." She copied the recipe from this book, published in 1955. Mrs. Keyes was a wonderful writer of both fiction and nonfiction who lived in New Orleans and in Acadiana for periods of her life while writing about the South. The recipe below is the cornbread I grew up with, and I present it as Mrs. Keyes wrote it, with minor adjustments. It was originally titled simply "Cornbread."

Makes 1 loaf

1½ cups yellow cornmeal
¼ cup sifted all-purpose flour
4 teaspoons baking powder
1 tablespoon sugar
1 teaspoon salt
2 eggs, well beaten
1¼ cups whole milk
¼ cup all-vegetable shortening

Preheat the oven to 450°F.

Sift the dry ingredients into a large bowl.

Whisk the eggs and milk together, and add gradually to the dry ingredients. Stir until the batter is smooth, but don't overmix.

Place the shortening in an 8- or 9-inch square pan, and put into the oven for a few minutes, just until the shortening melts. Cool a bit and swirl the pan to coat the sides and bottom evenly with the melted shortening. Stir the excess shortening into the batter, then turn the batter into the prepared pan and bake for 35 to 40 minutes, until top springs back when touched in the center.

LAGNIAPPE **Yellow cornmeal, white cornmeal, and polenta can be used interchangeably. Yellow cornmeal has a bit more flavor than white cornmeal, and yellow cornmeal and polenta are virtually the same, with polenta being the Italian name for cornmeal. Grits may not be interchanged with cornmeal or polenta, as they are a coarser grind and are made from dried hominy (dried corn from which the hull and germ have been removed) rather than dried corn.**

Cayenne-Roasted Pecans

In June 1918, Great-Uncle Adolphe received a letter from his sister Alice telling him that the pecan trees he planted earlier that year had "all taken root in the pasture. You ought to see your pecan trees, full of leaves." After years and years of traveling, it was the pecan trees full of leaves that finally brought Adolphe home to settle down. He harvested the pecans and sold the crop, using the money to open the store on the corner of the Home Place property. This store would be the local country store, post office, and gathering place for the local residents for the next fifty years. ***Makes 4 cups***

2 tablespoons butter
2 tablespoons corn oil
4 cups fresh pecan halves
1 teaspoon salt
1 teaspoon cayenne pepper
¾ teaspoon white pepper
½ teaspoon black pepper
½ teaspoon Tabasco sauce

Heat the butter and oil over medium-high heat in a large heavy skillet. When the foam from the butter subsides, add the pecans and remaining ingredients and cook, stirring constantly, for 2 minutes. Reduce the heat to medium and cook, stirring frequently, for 8 minutes longer.

Remove from the heat and drain on paper towels. Cool and store in an airtight container.

LAGNIAPPE **These go well with ice-cold beer on a hot day. Also, with a sharp Cheddar cheese, a glass of sherry, and a roaring fire on a cold winter day. But they are suitable for more than just snacks; I keep some frozen in a zip freezer bag and grab a few to toss on salads for texture and added flavor. Or I'll coarsely chop them and sprinkle on soups, casseroles, or vegetables to give some flair and spice to an otherwise unembellished dish.**

Savory Roasted Pecans

In 1918, Great-Uncle Adolphe planted pecan trees in the orchard. He was so proud of his pecans, and knew the variety of each tree. One type was a 4- to 5-inch-long, slim-shaped pecan, a "paper shell" variety that he was especially proud of. He sent pecans to us in California every year after the harvest. We must have had a dozen nut crackers of every conceivable type, and they were well used when the harvest came in each year as the family shelled pecans for a dessert, or just to enjoy fresh and unadorned. **Makes 4 cups**

2 tablespoons butter
2 tablespoons corn oil
4 cups pecan halves
1 teaspoon dried oregano
1 teaspoon dried thyme
1 teaspoon salt
1 teaspoon garlic powder
½ teaspoon white pepper
¼ teaspoon black pepper
⅛ teaspoon cayenne pepper

Heat the butter and oil over medium-high heat in a large heavy skillet. When the foam from the butter subsides, add the pecans and remaining ingredients and cook, stirring constantly, for 2 minutes. Reduce the heat to medium and cook, stirring frequently, for 8 minutes.

Remove from the heat and drain on paper towels. Cool and store in an airtight container.

LAGNIAPPE **If pecans (or any nuts) should become stale, simply heat on a baking sheet in a 200°F oven until crisp.**

Savory Onion Hush Puppies

These are way up there on our list of family favorites—so wonderfully crispy, and full of savory onion flavor. When we're deep-frying chicken or fish, we usually make these as an accompaniment, since the batter is so easy to make and we have a pot full of hot oil anyway. ***Makes about 24***

- 1 cup yellow cornmeal
- 1 cup all-purpose flour
- 2 teaspoons baking powder
- 1 teaspoon salt
- ½ teaspoon white pepper
- ½ teaspoon baking soda
- ½ cup finely chopped onion
- ½ cup finely sliced green onions
- 1 egg, beaten
- ¾ cup buttermilk
- 4 cups corn oil for frying (for a ¾- to 1-inch depth in a 6-quart pot)

Mix the cornmeal, flour, baking powder, salt, pepper, and baking soda in a large bowl. Add the onion and green onions and toss to coat evenly with the flour mixture.

Whisk the egg and buttermilk together and stir into the dry ingredients. Don't overmix; stir just until combined.

Heat the oil in a deep pot to 375°F. As soon as the oil reaches that temperature, drop the batter into it by tablespoons. Don't crowd the hush puppies; you will need to cook them in batches. Cook for about 3 minutes, until golden brown, turning halfway through. Remove the hush puppies to paper towels to drain as they are done. (Adjust the heat up or down as necessary to maintain a frying temperature of 350° to 365°F.)

LAGNIAPPE The story about how these little cornmeal fritters got their name supposedly comes from the time when outdoor cooks wanted to keep the dogs from barking and would toss them scraps of this fried batter, with the command to "Hush, puppy."

Sweet Hush Puppies

These crispy, crunchy, golden hush puppies are one of our favorite Sunday breakfasts. I've heard that leftover hush puppies aren't as good after a few hours, but I wouldn't know (leftover hush puppies?). They are often served with pork sausages, but we serve them with chicken or turkey sausages to make the meal a bit lighter. Some people like syrup drizzled on them, but we find sugar and cinnamon to be the ideal garnish. ***Makes about 30***

1 cup yellow cornmeal
1 cup all-purpose flour
½ cup sugar
2 teaspoons baking powder
½ teaspoon salt
1 egg, beaten
¾ cup buttermilk
2 teaspoons vanilla extract
4 cups corn oil for frying (for a ¾- to 1-inch depth in a 6-quart pot)
Sugar for sprinkling
Cinnamon for sprinkling

Mix the cornmeal, flour, sugar, baking powder, and salt in a large bowl.

Whisk the egg, buttermilk, and vanilla together and stir into the dry ingredients. Don't overmix; stir just until combined.

Heat the oil in a deep pot to 375°F. As soon as the oil reaches that temperature, drop the batter into it by tablespoons. Don't crowd the hush puppies; you will need to cook them in batches. Cook for about 3 minutes, until golden brown, turning halfway through. Remove the hush puppies to paper towels to drain as they are done, and immediately sprinkle liberally with sugar and cinnamon. (Adjust the heat up or down as necessary to maintain a frying temperature of 350° to 365°F.)

LAGNIAPPE If you want to serve sweet hush puppies with fried chicken or fish, or want to cook both savory and sweet hush puppies, cook the sweet ones before the savory ones, or before frying chicken or fish. That way, you can use the oil for both recipes, but the sweet hush puppies won't taste like onion.

Green Onion Biscuits

This recipe has always been one of the first baking projects taught to the kids in our family, as the dough can be simply patted out and cut with a table knife. It's an easy way to introduce children to the satisfaction of baking, and to the slight bite that the three different types of pepper—essential elements in Cajun cooking—offer to food. Makes 18

- 1 teaspoon corn oil for greasing
- 1¼ cups all-purpose flour
- ½ teaspoon baking powder
- ½ teaspoon salt
- ½ teaspoon black pepper
- ½ teaspoon white pepper
- ¼ teaspoon cayenne pepper
- ⅛ teaspoon baking soda
- 4 tablespoons (½ stick) cold butter, cut into pieces
- ½ cup finely chopped green onions
- 1 egg, beaten
- ⅓ cup sour cream

Grease a baking sheet with the oil. Preheat the oven to 400°F.

Combine the flour, baking powder, salt, black, white, and cayenne pepper, and baking soda in a large bowl. Add the butter and cut into the dry ingredients using a fork or pastry blender, until the pieces are the size of coarse crumbs.

Add the green onions and stir into the flour mixture.

Combine the egg and sour cream and add it to the flour mixture, stirring just until the ingredients are combined. The dough will be stiff, so use your hands to mix if necessary, but try not to overmix.

Turn the dough out onto a lightly floured board and gently press into an 8-inch square; using a sharp kitchen knife, cut into 12 biscuits, of any desired shape. Place on the prepared baking sheet and bake for about 18 minutes, until light golden brown.

LAGNIAPPE **What the Cajuns call *green onions* (or sometimes shallots or onion tops) are called scallions by much of the country. While green onions are used in many dishes, they are probably used more often to sprinkle on top of finished dishes—usually along with chopped fresh parsley. Some Cajuns sprinkle just the green tops on finished dishes, but we've always used the whole green onion.**

Shrimp Fritters

Most people love the crisp exterior and tender interior of properly fried food. When I was working at the Culinary Institute of America in the Napa Valley, it was known that a solution to what to serve could be answered with "fry something, they'll love it."

Makes about 2 dozen

- ¼ cup corn oil plus 1 cup oil for frying, or more if needed
- ½ cup finely chopped onion
- ¼ cup finely chopped fresh parsley
- ¼ cup finely sliced green onions
- ½ teaspoon salt
- ½ teaspoon white pepper
- ¼ teaspoon cayenne pepper
- 1 cup finely chopped cooked shrimp
- 2 eggs, beaten
- 4 slices soft white "sandwich" bread
- ½ cup all-purpose flour

Heat the ¼ cup oil in a large heavy skillet over medium heat. Add the onion, parsley, green onions, salt, and white and cayenne pepper and cook for 5 minutes, stirring often, until the vegetables are softened. Add the shrimp and cook 5 minutes longer, stirring often. Transfer to a dish and cool a bit. Wipe out the skillet.

Beat the eggs in a large bowl. Tear the bread in small pieces and add to the beaten eggs, mashing together with a fork until blended into a thick paste. Add the cooked, cooled shrimp mixture to the bread and eggs and mix thoroughly to combine.

Place the flour on a plate. Begin heating the frying oil to about 350°F (medium-high to high) in the same large skillet.

Form the shrimp mixture into firm balls, then flatten slightly. Roll them in the flour, shaking off the excess.

When the oil is hot, add the fritters, a few at a time, and cook for about 1 minute on each side. Don't overcrowd—you will have to do this in batches—transferring the fritters to paper towels to drain as they are done. Regulate the heat as necessary to maintain 350° to 365°F. Serve the fritters hot, with fresh lemon wedges.

LAGNIAPPE **Using bread as an ingredient was very common in the past. Casseroles were topped with toasted bread, beaten eggs were poured over toasted bread and cheese and baked, and meatloaf was extended with the use of bread soaked in milk.**

Skillet Cornbread

I love the old-fashioned look of a cast iron skillet being brought to the table with hot, steaming cornbread. The edges are crispier than those of a cornbread baked in a baking dish. This cornbread is a bit lighter in texture than most Cajun cornbreads, as it has a higher proportion of flour to cornmeal than most. Serves 8

- 1 tablespoon corn oil for greasing plus ½ cup oil
- 2½ cups yellow cornmeal
- 1 cup all-purpose flour
- ¼ cup sugar
- 3 tablespoons baking powder
- 2 teaspoons salt
- 4 eggs, well beaten
- 2½ cups whole milk

Preheat the oven to 400°F. Oil a 10-inch cast iron skillet with the 1 tablespoon of corn oil.

Sift the dry ingredients together in a large bowl.

Whisk the eggs, milk, and the ½ cup of corn oil together until blended. Stir into the dry ingredients, mixing just until combined and smooth; don't overmix.

Transfer the batter to the skillet. Bake for 30 minutes, or until the cornbread springs back lightly when touched in the center, and a toothpick inserted in the center comes out clean.

LAGNIAPPE The kitchen in the farmhouse at Home Place had cast iron pots, pans, and skillets hanging on the wall. Cast iron has been around for hundreds of years, and was originally used over open fires, suspended over the fireplace by a hook. It is particularly ideal for baking, as the even, high heat helps to form golden crusts on baked goods.

Bay Leaf Tea

My father's cousin Madge swears that this tea is "good for cold weather and indigestion." Since Madge is ninety-six as of this writing and still plays the piano and enjoys her weekly game of bingo, I tend to believe anything she says. **Makes 1 mug**

5 dried bay leaves
2 cups water
½ teaspoon sugar

Bring the bay leaves and water to a boil in a small saucepan. Boil for 10 minutes.

Strain into a mug, add the sugar, and stir to dissolve. Serve hot.

LAGNIAPPE **This tea is so quick and easy to make that I boil a cup as I want it, rather than making it up ahead of time. It has a gentle, earthy taste and more flavor than many of the flavored teas that cost several dollars for a package of twenty tea bags.**

Vanilla Mint Iced Tea

This is the way Aunt Lorna liked her iced tea on special occasions, but I suspect she learned it from Great-Aunt Alice, as it has vanilla, which Alice put in everything that didn't move! Aunt Lorna said they drank gallons of iced tea on afternoons when it was too hot to do anything but sip a cold beverage and talk. This tea is intentionally strong so its flavor won't be diluted by the ice.
Makes about 1 gallon

1 gallon water
12 tea bags
1 cup sugar
1 bunch fresh mint
1 tablespoon vanilla
Optional garnishes: lemon slices and/or fresh mint leaves

Bring the water to a boil in a large pot. Add the remaining ingredients and remove the pot from the heat. Let sit for 20 minutes to allow the flavors to blend.

Lift the tea bags and mint out of the pot, squeezing both over the pot to extract the flavors.

Cool and refrigerate. Serve over lots of ice, with lemon slices or additional mint leaves as garnish, if desired.

LAGNIAPPE While we make this when we want something special, our usual daily beverage is plain iced tea, with sugar—the amount depending on individual taste. Lemonade is a popular beverage during the summer, although we drink iced tea year-round. Cocktails, particularly mixed drinks borrowed from our New Orleans neighbors, such as Bloody Marys, mimosas, mint juleps, and old-fashioneds, are enjoyed by many. Beer is the usual beverage of choice to accompany meals, as it is ideal with the hearty, flavorful Cajun dishes. If you choose to drink wine with Cajun food, drink a full-bodied wine (whether red or white) that will stand up to the strong character and seasonings of Cajun cookery.

Vegetables and Beans

Theodore Adolphe Labauve, 1906

Great-Uncle Adolphe: The Country Store on the Farm

When my two sisters and I drove into Baldwin, Louisiana, near the birthplace of our father, and stopped in the drugstore to ask directions to the house of family friends we had not yet met, an elderly man sitting on a chair in the corner spotted us and asked, "Are y'all the Labauve sisters, going to see Pete and Mary Boudreau?"

"Our grandmother was a Labauve and, yes, we are going to the Boudreaus' house. They are going to take us to Home Place, the farm at—"

"I **know** *the farm.* **Everybody** *knows the farm. It's pretty run-down now, but full of history. Welcome to your daddy's hometown, we're glad to have you. Turn left at the first light and go down to the green house across from the graveyard."*

We got back in the car and followed directions. We weren't even out of the car when two strangers came down the steps of their home and enveloped us in hugs. Pete and Mary had offered to take us to see Bill Douglas, the man who purchased our family farm after Uncle Adolphe died twenty years before, and Bill had agreed to let us visit the property and take a look around. My sisters hadn't been there in almost fifty years, and I had never seen it, so we got in the backseat of Pete and Mary's car and headed down the highway to Home Place.

When Pete slowed the car down, and my sister Bonnie pointed to a corner piece of land and said, "There it is—the farm our great-grandfather built," the relatives I had been hearing about all my life weren't just names—they were people who grew up right there, on that piece of land where my family had lived for 120 years.

I had been hearing about Home Place since I was a small child, and here it was. And here I was, standing in the middle of it. It was beautiful. Beautiful for its history, knowledge, and sheltering of decades of my Labauve ancestors. My eyes were blinded to the condition of the farm. I was standing in what was once the garden where my great-grandparents would come to get cucumbers and tomatoes for their salad, and flowers for the table, looking at the porch on which my great-great grandparents sat when they visited my great-grandparents. The very same land, the very same porch, the very same farmhouse.

We walked through the kitchens, indoor and outdoor, where the family recipes I now make had once been prepared and served. We saw the bedroom that had held my great-grandparents' massive and beautiful bedroom set from France, walked through the side entryway where the squawking chickens had frightened my older sister Lorna when she was a little girl, and peeked up the staircase that led to the attic where she found Great-Grandma Clara's ball gowns in a trunk.

Pete assessed our fascination with the house, and asked, "Would you like to see the old store? It's in a pretty dilapidated condition, too."

I couldn't wait to see the country store Great-Uncle Adolphe ran for almost fifty years. We entered through the back, as the front steps had crumbled away long ago. We stepped carefully, avoiding the rotting floorboards. Dust-encrusted windows, an L-shaped glass counter with a flaking wooden base, and shelves holding broken pieces of pottery were remnants of this once lively center of activity. A large, straight, and sturdy chimney stood, undamaged, next to the cash register.

Looking up, one saw a metal roof dripping with cobwebs, and dusty rafters that were host to bare yellowed light bulbs dangling askew over the counter. To the left of the counter was a beam-balanced scale with two pans. In one, Adolphe would put the merchandise to be weighed, and in the other he would place the weights. The sale was then rung up on the old-fashioned cash register that stood five feet tall, and contained dozens of tiny compartments and drawers to keep track of inventory. If ten cents' worth of beans and twenty-five cents' worth of calico were sold, he would place the dime in the bean drawer and the quarter in the calico drawer. Adolphe's brown paper was then used to wrap each and every purchase, regardless of whether or not the customer wanted the item wrapped. The holder for the roll of brown paper was still bolted to the counter. The building had housed the Ashton Post Office, which was just beyond the counter, evidenced by the small barred window area with a collection of pigeonhole post boxes.

There was a large alcove across from the cash register, which, according to my sister Lorna, in the early 1940s was lined with shelves devoted solely to dry goods. A long, wide table used to measure and cut the bolts of cloth stood in the center. In the main room, shelves on the wall opposite the counter held all kinds of hardware and garden supplies. Seeds for every type of fruit and vegetable that grew in that climate were available, as were the necessary tools for gardening, planting, and harvesting.

My cousin Bill Schmaltz describes a visit to the store in the early 1960s when he was still a child. The layout of the store and the contents of the alcove had changed over twenty years: "When we visited, we would sit in the alcove opposite the counter and chat with Uncle Adolphe. We would sit there if he was busy, or when we were waiting for him to close the store for lunchtime at Aunt Irma's. To this day, I can recall a beautiful emerald green banner advertising a Remington shotgun. The stock in the picture had the richest, warmest brown wood grain I have ever seen. Beneath the banner were two wooden rockers, and stacks of buckets and baskets.

"There were a number of things jammed in this cramped alcove. There was an old fan on a heavy stand, with a chrome bullet-shaped motor on the back. There was an ancient, rattling refrigerator with a handle that would shock you when it was touched, where Uncle Adolphe kept his refrigerated items, mainly cold drinks and luncheon meat. There was a fifty-five-gallon wooden barrel with a wooden top, which sat half in the wing and half in the aisle and contained dried shrimp. Not the dried shrimp you see today. In those days, they must have dried the jumbo shrimp. These were very large, very salty, and very flavorful. When the top of the barrel was removed, an incredible aroma filled the store. The barrel was lined with a waxed brown paper and a special small scoop was kept inside to dole the shrimp out. They were so expensive that if Uncle Adolphe offered you a taste, it was just one shrimp.

"The store was known for miles around and was a landmark . . . it was indeed the local General Store. People lingered to talk and visit with their neighbors and get caught up with the latest news, gossip, or joke. There was much laughter to be heard in that old store. We had to wear our coats inside sometimes (as there was no heater), but the atmosphere was warm and friendly.

"Everything had seen its better day, but that was part of its appeal to me. The dusty, musty smell and rustic atmosphere lent a sense of adventure to my visits there. Each visit was special."

Our friend Pete Boudreau loved to reenact a typical conversation of the type that took place between Adolphe and a customer, as Adolphe was honest to a fault and would only sell an item if it met the customer's specific need. With great respect, Pete would imitate T.A.'s formal, French-accented, clipped way of speaking and begin:

Customer: "I'd like a box of double-0 buckshot."

Adolphe (T.A.): "My good friend, what are you going to shoot with this double-0 buckshot?"

Customer: "I'm going to hunt squirrel."

Adolphe: "I'm sorry, but I will not sell you this double-0 buckshot. That is for a large animal, a deer or a bear."

And another:

Customer: "I would like to buy some cabbage seeds."

Adolphe: "My friend, what are you going to do with this cabbage seed?"

Customer: "Well, I just got through working my garden up; I'm going to plant."

Adolphe: "I'm sorry, but I'm not going to sell them to you. The moon is not right for planting cabbage seeds." And he wouldn't sell the customer the seeds.

During our visit in the early 1990s, the hustle and bustle of the well-stocked store was alive only in our willing imaginations. We moved on to the back of the business counter, where there was a doorway leading to Adolphe's sleeping quarters, through a tattered curtain that had once offered privacy. The simple room was sparsely furnished with a bed and a lamp for reading. I spotted an envelope with familiar handwriting on the only shelf in the room, and picked it up to discover a letter sent from my Aunt Lorna to Adolphe in 1968. Wondering if there were more family mementos, I began to sift through the jumble of old papers strewn on the floor. I discovered Adolphe's ledger from 1938/1940 and asked Pete why the edges were frayed. "From a rat nibbling on it." "Yeah," said my sister Bonnie, with a huge smirk on her face, "probably the same rat making that noise in the pile of papers by your foot."

I quickly turned to leave, but stopped short in front of a round white enamel bowl with a red rim. "Oh, look," I said to Pete and my sisters, "wouldn't that look cute on a table with a plant set in it? Bill Douglas said we were welcome to anything we found of sentimental value, I think I'll bring this home." I knew by the look on Pete's face that there was something wrong with this idea.

"Do y'all know what that is?" asked Pete. "Mr. T.A. was the most dignified man I've ever known, and he would be horrified if he knew his great-niece came all the way from California to see the remains of his store, and took home his chamber pot."

"Well, it looks like a clean but dusty white bowl, and Great-Uncle has been dead for twenty years, so home it goes." I later found a lid in a nearby antique store that fit it perfectly. The chamber pot currently adorns a metal stand on my outdoor deck, filled with seashells I collected in Alaska. Definitely, I believe, a more creative use for it.

I was fascinated with the uncle of my father and aunt. I met him only once, when I was eight years old and he traveled to California to visit us. I still remember sitting on the porch and talking with him for the longest time. Just Great-Uncle Adolphe and me. He *later told my Aunt Lorna that "Darrell's daughter Terri kept company with me as nice as a grown person." I treasured that affirmation of my value to this intriguing old French gentleman. The trip to California was his last one, as he was almost eighty years old. He returned to Louisiana and continued running the store until he was no longer well enough to do so. Adolphe died in 1972 at the age of ninety-five.*

Baked Tomato Casserole

My freshman year, I went to college in San Francisco, just a bus ride away from Aunt Lorna's house. My best friend, Dianne, and I would often go to Lorna's for the weekend. Even though Dianne's father owned one of the best restaurants in San Francisco at that time, she and I loved to have a weekend of Aunt Lorna's home-cooked meals. This simple tomato dish was always hot and waiting for us when we walked up the hill from the bus stop. We spent half the weekend in our bathrobes studying, and the other half cooking wonderful dishes to bring back to the dorm. Between Dianne's father and my aunt, we were always coming back to campus with food to share with our cafeteria-weary classmates. Serves 6

1 large onion
¼ cup corn oil
6 slices day-old French bread
4 tablespoons (½ stick) butter, softened
Three 28-ounce cans whole tomatoes, drained
1 teaspoon sugar
1 teaspoon salt
½ teaspoon white pepper
¼ teaspoon garlic powder

Preheat the oven to 350°F.

Cut the onion in half vertically, and then cut across in slices. Heat the oil in a skillet over medium-high heat and sauté the onion for 10 minutes, stirring often.

Toast the French bread and spread with the softened butter.

Place the tomatoes, onion, sugar, salt, white pepper, and garlic powder in a 9 × 13-inch baking dish and stir to combine (cut large tomatoes in half so they cover the bottom of the dish). Top with the buttered toast and bake in the oven for 30 minutes.

LAGNIAPPE **This recipe is typical both of country cooking and of an old-fashioned dish; it puts together common ingredients that are usually in the pantry. Combining textures is another element of old-fashioned country cookery. The crisp, buttery toast topping the tomatoes makes what is really just baked tomatoes seem hearty and satisfying. Reading old magazines from the 1940s makes it clear that the use of bread or toast in vegetable dishes was prevalent during the Second World War, when housewives were encouraged to stretch food, and to use as little meat as possible.**

Black-Eyed Pea and Andouille Bake

Beans of all types have always been loved by our family, but black-eyed peas (or black-eyed Susans) are by far the favorite. Serves 8

- 1 pound dried black-eyed peas
- ¼ pound sliced bacon
- 1 cup chopped onion
- ½ cup chopped celery
- ¼ cup chopped green bell pepper
- 2 cloves garlic, finely chopped
- ½ pound andouille, chopped
- 2 cups chicken stock
- 1 teaspoon salt
- ½ teaspoon black pepper
- ¼ teaspoon cayenne pepper
- ½ cup chopped fresh parsley

Bring 6 cups water to a boil in a medium saucepan and add the black-eyed peas. Bring to a boil again, reduce the heat, cover, and simmer for 2 hours, stirring occasionally. Drain.

Heat a large heavy pot or Dutch oven over medium heat and put in the bacon. Cook until the bacon is crisp, then remove, crumble, and set aside. Add the onion, celery, bell pepper, and garlic to the bacon drippings and cook, stirring often, for 10 minutes.

Add the drained cooked beans, andouille, stock, salt, and black and cayenne pepper, bring to a boil, then reduce the heat to low. Cook over low heat for 1 hour, covered, stirring occasionally. As you stir, mash some of the beans to add texture and thickness to the liquid. When tender, dish up and serve sprinkled with the reserved bacon and chopped parsley.

LAGNIAPPE **In order to diminish the effects of gas from eating beans, place the beans in a large pot, cover with water, and bring to a boil. Cover the pot, boil for 2 minutes, and then turn off the heat. Soak for 1 hour (or longer, but the longer you soak the more nutrients you will lose when you drain off the water). Drain and rinse the beans, and proceed with the recipe, using fresh water. Eating rice with beans is said to reduce the gaseous effects of the legume.**

Buttered Potatoes and Turnips

Turnips were one of Great-Uncle Adolphe's favorite vegetables: he liked them raw, boiled, and fried, alone, or in combination with other vegetables. They have a slight sweetness when cooked that makes them an interesting complement to sharp-tasting vegetables such as mustard greens, and a pleasant companion to rather mild-flavored potatoes. Serves 6

- 6 medium russet potatoes (about 2 pounds), peeled and coarsely chopped
- 2 medium turnips (about 1¼ pounds), trimmed and coarsely chopped
- 4 tablespoons (½ stick) butter
- 1 teaspoon salt
- ½ teaspoon white pepper
- ¼ teaspoon sugar
- ¼ cup sliced green onions
- ¼ cup chopped fresh parsley

Bring a large pot of water to a boil. Add the potatoes and turnips and bring back to a boil.

Boil for 10 minutes, or until the vegetables are tender but not overcooked. Drain.

While vegetables are cooking, melt the butter with the salt, pepper, and sugar.

Transfer the vegetables to a serving dish and add the hot melted butter, green onions, and parsley and gently toss to coat. Serve hot.

LAGNIAPPE **Turnips have a bit of a bad reputation with some people, probably because they have either had old turnips, which can be very strong, or overcooked turnips, which are very strong. A fresh turnip, cooked only until done, and served with a bit of butter and salt is a wonderful vegetable. Turnip greens, again if they are fresh, are delicious cooked in the same way as any other green, such as collard greens, mustard greens, spinach, or chard.**

Collard Greens and Tasso with Pot Likker

Grandpa Pischoff often served greens this way, but I had to try many times to get mine to taste the way his did. I finally realized that I was using stock as the cooking liquid, and the stock masked the flavor of the greens. Grandpa, I'm now certain, used water to allow the taste of the collard greens to predominate. *Serves 8*

1 pound collard greens or mustard, chard, or turnip greens
2 tablespoons corn oil
1½ cups chopped onion
½ pound tasso or ham, chopped
½ teaspoon salt
½ teaspoon sugar
¼ teaspoon black pepper
¼ teaspoon cayenne pepper

Wash the collard greens and strip the leaves from the stems. Coarsely chop the stems. Stack the leaves, roll up, and slice across into thin strips.

In a large heavy pot or Dutch oven, heat the oil and sauté the onion and tasso for 10 minutes, or until the onion is golden brown, stirring often. Add the salt, sugar, and black and cayenne pepper and stir for 1 minute. Add the collard greens and chopped stems, and just enough water to cover (about 6 cups). Bring to a boil, stir, and reduce the heat. Simmer for 45 minutes, uncovered.

LAGNIAPPE **Boiled greens are traditionally served in a bowl, with cornbread to dip in the liquid (pot likker). A bit of sugar is always added to greens, and usually to other vegetables, as sugar enhances the flavor.**

Corn and Okra Stew

Aunt Lorna loved to cook this stew slowly, over low heat, to give the vegetables and spices a chance to meld together. This is the dish I serve when I introduce okra to people who think they don't like it. With leftover shrimp or chicken added, this is a full meal if served over rice.

Serves 6 as an entrée, 12 as a side dish

- 2 tablespoons butter
- 2 tablespoons oil
- 2 cups chopped onion
- 2 cups chopped celery
- 2 cups chopped green bell pepper
- 1 clove garlic, minced
- 1 teaspoon sugar
- 1 teaspoon paprika
- 1 teaspoon dried thyme
- ½ teaspoon salt
- 4 medium ears fresh corn, kernels removed (about 4 cups)
- 3 cups chopped fresh tomatoes or one 28-ounce can chopped tomatoes, drained
- 1 pound fresh okra or 20 ounces frozen, defrosted okra, sliced

Heat the butter and oil in a large heavy pot or Dutch oven over medium heat. When the butter melts, add the onion, celery, and bell pepper and cook for 15 minutes, stirring occasionally.

Add the garlic, sugar, paprika, thyme, and salt and cook for 5 minutes, stirring occasionally. Add the corn kernels and tomatoes and cook for 5 minutes, stirring occasionally. Add the okra; reduce the heat to low, and barely simmer, covered, for 1 hour, stirring occasionally.

LAGNIAPPE **Okra, from the same family as hollyhock and hibiscus, is a versatile vegetable that is wonderful fried as an appetizer, served alone or mixed with other vegetables, or put in a gumbo or soup where it is an essential thickener.**

Corn Custard

Cajuns love corn. They make it into pudding, salad, and soup; grind it and make meal for bread, or fried cornbread such as hush puppies, corncakes, or coush-coush; cook it as a vegetable, alone or in combination with other vegetables; use it as a batter to coat seafood; and eat it as a cereal.
Serves 6

- 2 tablespoons butter, softened
- 2 cups milk
- 4 eggs
- 3 tablespoons all-purpose flour
- 1 tablespoon sugar
- ½ teaspoon salt
- ¼ teaspoon black pepper
- ⅛ teaspoon cayenne pepper
- 1 cup fresh corn kernels
- ½ cup sliced green onions

Preheat the oven to 325°F. Spread a 2-quart baking dish with the butter.

Place the milk in a blender with the eggs, flour, sugar, salt, and black and cayenne pepper. Add the corn and green onions to the blender and process for 2 to 3 seconds. Transfer to the prepared baking dish.

Place the baking dish on a low rack, or a folded towel, set in a 9 × 13-inch pan, and pour boiling water into the pan to a depth of 1 inch. Set the custard on the rack or towel and bake for 50 to 60 minutes. Remove the custard from the oven when a knife inserted near the edge of the dish comes out clean; the center will not be completely set, but will finish cooking while the custard cools a bit. Allow to cool for 10 minutes, and serve warm.

LAGNIAPPE Custard recipes often call for scalded milk. Scalding was employed to kill bacteria in the days before milk was pasteurized. Milk is scalded now as it makes the cooking process a bit quicker, but in most dishes it is an unnecessary step (and leaves another pan to wash). When milk is scalded it should be gently heated to about 180°F, or the point where bubbles start to appear around the edges of the pan.

Fried Okra

We like this with just a squeeze of lemon or tangerine juice (see Lagniappe), but Sauce Remoulade (page 213), Tartar Sauce (page 215), or Nice Pink Sauce for Shrimp (page 207) are all good accompaniments.

This makes a wonderful hors d'oeuvre. Serves 6

- ¼ cup cornmeal
- 1 cup all-purpose flour
- 1 teaspoon salt
- ½ teaspoon black pepper
- ½ teaspoon garlic powder
- ¼ teaspoon cayenne pepper
- ¼ teaspoon sugar
- ⅓ cup buttermilk
- 1 pound okra, cut into ½-inch-thick slices
- 4 cups corn oil (for a ½-inch depth in a 10-inch skillet)
- ½ cup chopped fresh parsley
- Salt as desired
- Optional garnish: lemon or tangerine wedges

Combine the cornmeal, flour, and seasonings in a large bowl.

Pour the buttermilk in a medium bowl and add the okra slices. Soak for 10 minutes and drain.

Heat the oil in a 10-inch cast iron skillet, or other large heavy skillet, to 350°F.

When the oil is hot, toss the okra slices in the flour mixture, a few at a time, shaking off excess flour. Place the okra in the oil and fry in batches so the oil won't cool down, until golden brown. As you remove the okra from the oil, place it on paper towels to drain. Sprinkle with parsley and salt while still hot.

LAGNIAPPE Citrus fruits grow well in Southwest Louisiana, and the satsuma, which are thin-skinned mandarin oranges, are wonderful squeezed on fried okra. In fact, they are an interesting substitute for either oranges or lemons: for oranges in fruit salads, and for lemons with fried food where you would normally use fresh lemon to squeeze over the food.

Green Beans with Salt Pork

Grandpa loved cooking with salt pork, but complained that what was in the markets wasn't the same meaty salt pork he had been used to. He taught me to "cook the onions until they are tired," which puzzled me as a child, since they never looked tired, just soft.

Serves 6

- ¼ pound salt pork, chopped
- 2 cups chopped onion
- 1 pound fresh green beans, trimmed, cut into about 1-inch pieces
- ½ teaspoon sugar
- ¼ teaspoon salt
- ¼ teaspoon black pepper
- ⅛ teaspoon Tabasco sauce
- 1½ cups chicken stock

Heat a large heavy pot or Dutch oven over medium heat and add the salt pork. Cook for 10 to 15 minutes, stirring occasionally, until the fat is rendered and the pork pieces are golden and crisp.

Add the onion and cook for 5 minutes, stirring occasionally, until it is wilted or "tired," as Grandpa always said. Add the beans and seasonings and cook for 5 minutes, stirring occasionally. Add the stock, bring to a boil, reduce the heat, cover, and simmer over medium-low heat for 20 minutes.

Serve over rice, or in a bowl with cornbread for dunking.

LAGNIAPPE **Many people feel that Cajuns cook their vegetables too long and in too much water. It is, however, the long cooking that gives the distinct flavor to the vegetables, and since the cooking liquid is consumed along with the vegetables, any nutrients leached into the liquid are not lost.**

Tomato Maque Choux

Another everlasting debate within Cajun cooking is whether maque choux (pronounced mock-shoe) should contain tomatoes. There are tomato maque choux people, and those who would never add the red stuff to this favorite of corn dishes (see Maque Choux, page 183). The flavor of sweet summer corn comes through better without the tomatoes, but it seems a shame not to add fresh summer tomatoes at the prime of their season, as they complement corn so well. We regularly eat both versions throughout the summer. Serves 6

3 large ears fresh corn
¼ pound bacon
1 cup chopped onion
½ cup chopped green bell pepper
½ teaspoon salt
½ teaspoon black pepper
1 large tomato, cut in half horizontally and seeds squeezed out

Cut the corn off the cob by placing the stem end on a board and slicing down to remove the kernels; slice down again, scraping against the cob, to remove the sweet, milky liquid.

Cook the bacon over medium heat in a heavy skillet until the bacon is crisp. Remove, crumble, and set aside.

Cook the onion and bell pepper in the bacon fat for 10 minutes. Add the corn and its liquid, salt, and pepper and cook 10 minutes longer. Add the chopped tomato and cook for an additional 10 minutes. Sprinkle with the crumbled bacon, if desired, or save for another use.

LAGNIAPPE **For a fun treatment of corn on the barbecue, pull back the husk from the tip of the corn, leaving it attached at the stem end; remove silk; take off one strip of husk and use it to tie the pulled-back husk, so the husk can be used as a handle; butter, season, and place corn on the grill (not over direct heat) until warm and browned. (To keep husks from burning, either extend them over the edge of the barbecue, or place a sheet of foil under them.)**

Marinated Mirliton

We sometimes like vegetables in an oil and vinegar marinade instead of butter. We use the method below for 2 pounds of any cooked vegetable. If the marinade is ready when the vegetable is done it makes a great hot dish, and can be served cold as a vegetable salad the next day. Serves 8

- 4 medium mirlitons (chayote squash) (about 2½ pounds)
- ½ cup olive oil
- ½ cup chopped fresh parsley
- ½ cup sliced green onions
- 2 tablespoons fresh lemon juice
- 1 tablespoon red wine vinegar
- 1 teaspoon dried thyme
- 1 teaspoon onion powder
- 1 teaspoon salt
- ½ teaspoon garlic powder
- ½ teaspoon white pepper
- ¼ teaspoon cayenne pepper
- ¼ teaspoon sugar

Bring a large pot of water (about 8 cups) to a boil.

Halve the mirlitons lengthwise and add to the boiling water. Boil, uncovered, until fork-tender, about 40 minutes. Chop into cubes about ½ inch in size.

While the mirlitons are boiling, add the remaining ingredients to a large bowl and whisk to combine well. Add the mirliton cubes to the dressing while still warm, and gently toss; serve hot or chilled.

LAGNIAPPE Mirlitons are known in much of the country, and in Central America, as chayote, and in France as christophene. They are actually a fruit, although used as a vegetable, pale green in color, and about the size of a large pear (indeed, they are also known as "vegetable pear"). The mild flavor might be described as a cross between cucumber and summer squash. It isn't necessary to peel them, or to remove the soft seed in the center. As they are quite mild in flavor, they take on the taste of whatever seasonings they are paired with. They are a favorite vegetable in Acadiana, and much loved for stuffing. The height of the season is during the winter, although they can be found most of the year in supermarkets.

Mixed Greens with Bacon

The most commonly used greens in Cajun Country are collard, mustard, turnip, and spinach. I like to mix two or more, as this gives more variety in terms of both flavor and texture. I think Grandpa would have made greens every night, if he hadn't met with protests from kids! Serves 6

- 12 slices bacon
- 2 cups chopped onion
- 1½ pounds greens (any combination), coarsely chopped
- 6 cups water
- ½ teaspoon salt
- ¼ teaspoon black pepper
- ⅛ teaspoon cayenne pepper
- ⅛ teaspoon sugar

Fry the bacon in a large pot or Dutch oven over medium heat until crisp. Remove from pot, drain, crumble, and set aside.

Add the onion to the pot and sauté in bacon drippings over medium heat for 5 minutes, or until onions are softened. Add the greens, tossing to coat with bacon drippings. Add the water, salt, black and cayenne pepper, and sugar and bring to a boil. Reduce the heat to medium-low and simmer, uncovered, for 45 minutes.

Serve in soup bowls with plenty of liquid in each bowl; sprinkle each serving with crumbled bacon. Serve with cornbread, biscuits, or French bread to dip in the liquid (pot likker).

LAGNIAPPE **We frequently had greens and cornbread as a meal. With either shrimp, chicken, or sausage added, it was "fast food," and turned whatever seafood, poultry, or meat we had into a quick and delicious meal.**

Mustard Greens with Turnips

When there were a lot of turnips in the garden, Grandpa would pick some of them when they were very small—only about an inch across. They were so sweet and tender. He would remove the tops, then parboil the turnips for about a minute, drain them, and toss them in melted butter in a skillet for a couple of minutes. Then he added the tops, and cooked the baby turnips and tops together until the tops were just wilted. I think it's the only dish he ever made without adding any seasonings. The boiled greens are an ideal accompaniment to the buttery turnip cubes. Serves 6

- 4 tablespoons (½ stick) butter
- 1 large firm turnip (about 1 pound), cut into ¼-inch cubes
- 1 cup sliced green onions
- 1 teaspoon sugar
- ½ teaspoon salt plus 1 tablespoon salt
- ¼ teaspoon black pepper
- ¼ teaspoon cayenne pepper
- 8 cups water
- 1 pound mustard greens, coarsely chopped (other greens may be used)

Melt the butter in a large heavy skillet over medium heat. When the foam subsides, add the turnip cubes, green onions, sugar, the ½ teaspoon of salt, and black and cayenne pepper, stir, and cook for 5 minutes, uncovered. Reduce the heat to medium-low, cover, and cook until the turnips are fork-tender, about 30 minutes, stirring often to prevent sticking.

While the turnips are cooking, bring the water to a boil in a large pot and add the additional 1 tablespoon of salt and the greens. Bring the water back to a boil, and immediately drain the greens (if using greens other than mustard, cook a bit longer if needed until the greens are tender). Transfer to a serving dish and cover to keep warm until the turnips are ready.

Top the greens with the turnips and any juices in the pan.

LAGNIAPPE **Turnips are a round white root vegetable with a purple top. Part of the cabbage family, they are a cousin to the rutabaga and may be used in the same way. As a young vegetable, turnips are wonderful raw, similar to radishes in that they have a slight bite. Avoid turnips that are large and soft, as they will be woody and pithy, and strong in taste.**

Shrimp-Stuffed Mirliton

We always have at least one stuffed vegetable for holidays and important occasions, and this is the one we serve most often, partly because we love the shrimp filling and crusty, buttery top, but also because it is quick and easy to prepare. *Serves 8*

- 2 teaspoons butter plus 4 tablespoons (½ stick) melted butter
- 4 mirlitons (about 2½ pounds)
- ¼ cup corn oil
- 1½ cups chopped onion
- 1½ cups chopped green bell pepper
- 1 cup chopped celery
- 1 cup sliced green onions
- ½ cup chopped fresh parsley
- 1 teaspoon salt
- ½ teaspoon white pepper
- ½ teaspoon Tabasco sauce
- ¼ teaspoon sugar
- 2 cups cooked rice (about ⅔ cup raw)
- 1 pound cooked shrimp meat
- ¼ cup dried unseasoned bread crumbs

Preheat the oven to 350°F. Butter a 9 × 13-inch pan with the 2 teaspoons butter.

Bring a large pot of water to a boil and add the mirlitons. Boil for 45 minutes and drain. When cool enough to handle, cut in half lengthwise and scoop out the pulp, leaving a ½-inch-thick shell. Place the shells in the buttered pan.

Heat the oil in a large heavy skillet over medium-high heat. When the oil is hot, add the onion, bell pepper, celery, green onions, parsley, salt, pepper, Tabasco sauce, and sugar and cook for 15 minutes, stirring often. Remove from the heat. Add the rice and shrimp to the mixture in the skillet, and gently toss to combine.

Divide the filling among the mirliton halves, mounding it and allowing it to spill over if necessary. Sprinkle with bread crumbs and drizzle with the melted butter. Bake for 40 minutes.

LAGNIAPPE **The mirliton (pronounced mirl-uh-tan) is a favorite food of Cajuns; they love to pickle, fry, and boil the vegetable (technically a fruit), but stuffing it—with shrimp, chicken, meat, or vegetables—is the favored treatment.**

Smothered Cabbage with Andouille

We serve this with cornbread or biscuits for dipping in the broth, much the way greens with pot likker are served. Sometimes we add four whole sausages, in addition to the cup of chopped sausage, and serve it over rice as a complete meal for four people.

Serves 8

2 tablespoons corn oil

1 cup (about 6 ounces) chopped andouille sausage

1 cup chopped onion

1 large head of cabbage (about 3 pounds), cored and coarsely chopped

2 cups chicken stock

1½ teaspoons salt

1 teaspoon black pepper

1 teaspoon sugar

½ teaspoon cayenne pepper

Heat the oil in a large heavy pot or Dutch oven over medium heat. When the oil is hot, add the sausage and onion and cook for 10 minutes.

Add the cabbage, stock, salt, black pepper, sugar, and cayenne, and stir to combine.

Bring the stock to a boil, cover, reduce the heat to medium-low, and cook for 40 minutes, stirring occasionally (the cabbage should be soft and tender when done).

Turn the heat to medium-high, uncover, and gently boil for 10 minutes to reduce liquid.

LAGNIAPPE Cabbage has a delicious buttery taste when cooked. It is also inexpensive, and a wonderfully healthy vegetable. It is mild (unless overcooked, but that's not the cabbage's fault) and takes on the flavor of whatever seasonings are put with it. Inexpensive, tasty, and accommodating—a winning combination.

Smothered Okra

Okra was such a part of growing up in Louisiana that Dad couldn't imagine our dislike for its texture. "You can't be Cajun and not like okra; you can't eat gumbo and not eat okra," he would tell us. Determined to get us to like the vegetable, he introduced us to fried okra, with which he would serve one of our favorite sauces for dipping. When we agreed that we liked okra cooked that way, he made this smothered okra, full of tomatoes, seasonings, and spices, and we were, once again, converts to one of Dad's food passions.

Serves 8

- 1/4 cup corn oil
- 2 tablespoons butter
- 2 pounds fresh okra, sliced 1/2 inch thick (see Lagniappe)
- 2 cups chopped onion
- 1 cup chopped celery
- 1/2 cup chopped green bell pepper
- 1 teaspoon salt (1 1/2 teaspoons if using fresh tomatoes)
- 1 teaspoon garlic powder
- 1 teaspoon black pepper
- 1/4 teaspoon cayenne pepper
- 1/4 teaspoon sugar
- 3 cups chopped fresh tomatoes or two 14-ounce cans diced tomatoes, drained

Heat the oil and butter in a large heavy pot or Dutch oven over medium-high heat (do not use a cast iron pan, as it may discolor the okra).

When the butter has melted, add the remaining ingredients, except the tomatoes, and cook for 5 minutes, stirring often. Cover the pan and cook 5 minutes longer (adjust heat down a bit, if vegetables are sticking to bottom of the pan). Add the tomatoes and cook for 5 minutes, uncovered, stirring often (return heat to medium-high if it was adjusted down).

Reduce the heat to the lowest setting, cover, and cook for 30 minutes, stirring occasionally.

LAGNIAPPE **Frozen okra may be used. Defrost on a baking sheet that is covered with paper towels to absorb the water as the okra defrosts. It is best to purchase whole okra and slice it, as the sliced frozen okra will be more adversely affected by the freezing process, since there is more exposed surface area.**

Maque Choux

We have several ways to prepare our favorite vegetables. Corn is one vegetable we never tired of, and this recipe for maque choux is for the "tomatoes-don't-belong-in-maque-choux" contingent. Aunt Lorna didn't have a written recipe for maque choux, so I stood next to her, with a notepad and pen, and watched her make it—writing down ingredients, amounts, and instructions every step of the way. This is how her mother taught her to make the dish, and the way we have all been making it for years. Serves 6

- 6 medium ears fresh corn
- 3 tablespoons lard or corn oil
- 1½ cups chopped onion
- 1½ cups chopped green bell pepper
- 1 teaspoon salt
- ½ teaspoon sugar
- ¼ teaspoon white pepper
- ⅛ teaspoon cayenne pepper
- 2 tablespoons milk

Cut the corn off the cob by placing the stem end on a board and slicing down to remove the kernels; slice down again, scraping against the cob, to remove the sweet, milky liquid.

Heat the lard in a large heavy skillet over medium heat. Add the onion and bell pepper and cook for about 15 minutes, or until the onion is "withered" (Grandma Olympe's terminology). Add the corn and its liquid, salt, sugar, and white and cayenne pepper and continue cooking over medium heat until most of the liquid is absorbed and the corn is tender, about 20 minutes, stirring occasionally. Add the milk, stir, and cook 10 minutes longer, stirring often. If the liquid is absorbed before the corn is tender, add a bit of milk or butter to keep the corn moist until it is done.

LAGNIAPPE Corn is actually a fruit, with each individual kernel being its own fruit-producing seed. Every element of this fruit can be used: the kernels for food, the silk for tea, the husks for making tamales, and the cobs as food for animals.

White Beans and Ham Hocks

Both Dad and Grandpa loved white beans. With the exception of the occasional meal of red beans and rice (we usually had white beans and rice) I never saw them cook red beans, or any beans other than white, and black-eyed Susans (which are white with a black "eye" on their inner curve). During fall and winter, there was almost always a pot of beans, or bean soup, either cooking on the stove, or cooked and waiting in the refrigerator to be dished up as desired. Serves 6

- ½ pound dried white beans
- 3 cups water
- 2 cups chopped onion
- 1 cup chopped celery
- 1 large ham hock or shank (about 1½ pounds)
- 2 large cloves garlic, sliced
- 2 teaspoons brown sugar
- 1½ teaspoons distilled white vinegar
- 1 teaspoon black pepper
- 1 teaspoon baking soda
- ¼ teaspoon salt

Place the beans and all remaining ingredients in a large heavy pot. Bring to a boil, stir, reduce the heat to medium-low, cover, and simmer for 1 hour to 1 hour and 15 minutes, until the beans are very tender.

Remove the ham hock and take off the meat; return the meat to the beans, stir, and serve.

LAGNIAPPE **Soda is supposed to speed the cooking time and soften the beans, and vinegar (or other acid) is said to slow down the cooking time and toughen the beans. Dad added soda because he liked a somewhat mushy pot of beans rather than having individual beans intact, and soda breaks down the skin of the beans to give this result. He added vinegar because he liked the acid flavor, but vinegar is said to keep the skin of the beans intact. So, in theory, the soda and vinegar in Dad's beans canceled each other out. Whatever the chemical reaction, or lack of it, these are very good!**

Salt is said to prevent beans from softening, but I've never found that to be true.

A serving of beans is ¼ cup (2 ounces) dried beans.

White Beans and Rice

White beans are more common in Cajun Country than red beans, although "red beans and rice" is the traditional Monday dish. Monday was wash day, and a pot of red beans was put on to cook, unattended, while the laundry was being done—an all-day task in the olden days. At the end of the day, rice was cooked and the red beans were spooned over the rice. With an occasional exception, we made red beans and rice as white beans and rice.
Serves 8

½ pound bacon, coarsely chopped
6 cups water
2 cups chopped onion
2 cups chopped green bell pepper
1 pound dried white beans
2 bay leaves
1½ teaspoons salt
1½ teaspoons white pepper
1 teaspoon Tabasco sauce
1 teaspoon garlic powder
6 cups cooked rice (2 cups raw)
1½ cups sliced green onions
¾ cup chopped fresh parsley

Heat a large heavy pot or Dutch oven over medium heat and put in the bacon. Cook until crisp; remove and set aside.

Add the remaining ingredients, except the rice, green onions, and parsley. Bring to a boil, stir, and reduce the heat to medium-low. Cover and simmer, stirring occasionally, for about 1 hour and 30 minutes until the beans are tender but not mushy. Remove the bay leaves.

Remove about 3 cups of beans from the pot and mash with a fork or in a blender. Return to the pot, stir, and heat through (the mashed beans thicken the pot of beans).

Serve over rice, sprinkled with green onions, parsley, and the reserved bacon.

LAGNIAPPE **The age of dried beans, differences in altitude, hardness of water, and the moisture in the beans can all change the suggested cooking time. Soaking beans saves only about 15 minutes of cooking time. I never bother soaking them, so I am free to decide to cook a pot of beans a couple of hours before dinner.**

Salads, Salad Dressings, and Sauces

Darrel Joseph Pischoff, Tulane graduation, twenty-one years old

Dad and the House Under the Redwoods: Cajun in California

My father's zest for life was infectious. Our family left San Francisco in 1955 and moved to a lovely house, thirty minutes south of the city, which Dad immediately turned into a playground. No one enjoyed it more than he did. We had a badminton court, a perfect level rectangle of a front lawn for croquet, holes made from tuna cans in the sloping back lawn for an unsophisticated miniature golf course, a Ping-Pong table, a sandpit with poles for high jumping, a basketball court, and a horseshoe pit. Three hammocks hung in a triangle of redwood trees, to plop into when we were worn out from all the fun.

There was no place Dad would rather be than at home, surrounded by his family. He was a typical Cajun male in his love of outdoor cooking, and never did anything in a small way. Dinner for four somehow ended up being dinner for a lot more than expected; people were always dropping by, and they couldn't escape Dad without agreeing to join us for dinner. As soon as the weather got warm enough, and often before it was warm enough, we started eating outside. Dad wheeled the three large barbecues out from the shed, and unearthed the huge pots used for fish fries and for crawfish, shrimp, or crab boils. He stocked the freezer with food that he could defrost when he wanted to spend time cooking instead of going to the store: pork roasts, ribs, the biggest shrimp he could find, catfish, crawfish when he could get them, and frozen corn. The pantry was bursting with boxes of cornmeal, grits, tomatoes, dried beans, and cans of beans that would be the base of one of his "homemade" hot bean dishes or bean salads in an emergency. We didn't can our own food but rather used the freezer to keep a stash of ingredients. Of course, we purchased fresh food most of the time, but the freezer and pantry enabled us to have instant gatherings.

I loved to go grocery shopping on Saturday mornings with Dad, especially in the spring when he was stocking up for the coming months. Nothing was off limits, it seemed, and we could toss anything we wanted into the cart. Unless it was something foolish, like a cellophane-wrapped package of ham when there was already a ham in the cart, or canned shrimp, which was, to Dad, a mortal sin. He was always generous and wanted us to be enthusiastic about Cajun food and cooking, which, he knew, started with ingredients.

He used these shopping trips to teach us about the cuisine of his childhood, as we walked up and down the aisles, sampling the foods that the store promoted on Saturday mornings. We spent a lot of time in the spice section, as each spring Dad bought fresh bottles of Tabasco sauce, cayenne pepper, black pepper, white pepper, garlic powder and onion powder, and extra filé in case we ran out of what Uncle Adolphe made and sent us each year. We'd pass by the hot dogs and Dad would tell us about andouille sausage and boudin that put hot dogs to shame; in the bakery aisle he would talk about beignets and hush puppies that make packaged doughnuts unappealing; and in the canned goods section he told us the only canned foods we would buy were beans, corn, tuna, and canned tomatoes. We sometimes had two carts full of groceries, and it took all morning to unload and put them away, wrapping and preparing some of the food for the freezer.

The first barbecue of the year was an announcement of summer (even if it was in the early spring), and as eagerly anticipated as any major holiday. It was usually a shrimp boil with corn and potatoes, and a large pork roast cooked for a long time in the covered barbecue (after it had been seared to achieve a crispy dark outside). The entrée was always accompanied by Dad's famous cucumber and red onion salad. And ever present was a loaf of the French bread Dad loved as a child: sliced, the slices brushed with cayenne-infused garlic butter, and wrapped in foil to set on the back of the grill until it was warm, fragrant, crusty, and buttery. Sometimes, however, we would sneak in a loaf of our local San Francisco sourdough French bread; after all, we would buy it from Boudin Bakery, and Boudin is a wonderful Cajun sausage as well as a Cajun name.

With every barbecue there was always a tense moment when Dad would bring in the entrée, having forgotten, once again, to give Mom "fifteen minutes' notice, Darrell. You were supposed to give me fifteen minutes' notice before the barbecued food was done, so I could have the rest of the meal ready." I don't think he ever did; it became a ritual without which a party would have been missing something. My gregarious Dad was usually interspersing a badminton game with watching the barbecue, drinking his Chivas Regal or icy cold beer, and visiting with guests. He was always proud as a peacock over whatever he produced, and had such a sad, sheepish expression when my mother was displeased with him over the fifteen-minute rule, that the tension quickly passed.

A bread pudding was usually put together from the stale bread we saved in *the freezer for that purpose, and ice cream with pecans would substitute when we didn't have time to make dessert. Except during blackberry season. Then we would have berry pie, berry cobbler, berry ice cream, or just freshly picked berries with a drizzle of cream. Dad would pull out saucepans with handles and lead his kids down into the creek at the side of the house. Each excursion was an adventure with him, and every berry-picking trip evoked a new Louisiana story. I realize now that because Dad and his siblings, as children in Louisiana, were given the job of picking berries during the summer, these outings with us brought him back to his years as a boy on the family farm.*

Dad's imagination was wonderful. We were never just in the creek next to our house, but rather in some exotic southern locale, often looking for an elusive treasure. One time the creek would be a bayou and we would have to watch for alligators; another visit would have us tromping through the bushes looking for a riverboat; sometimes we tried to spot old rifles from the Civil War; and more than once we were lost in the swamp with our native California redwood trees serving as moss-covered weeping willows. These visits transported us to the old family farm halfway across the country, and forty to one hundred years into the past, the creation of the time and place depending on Dad's mood of the moment.

The large yard encircling our house was meant for entertaining, and offered a favorite spot for everyone. Those not interested in sports usually ended up in the covered patio area. This was my choice. I loved to be near the outdoor fireplace that lengthened summer evenings, and gave us an excuse to sit under the fragrant jasmine-covered arbor until long past dark. I didn't realize, until I went to Louisiana as an adult, how much of the feeling of Home Place Dad had brought to our home. Besides abundant plantings of jasmine, growing wherever there was a trellis or pole to climb, a wisteria vine graced the overhang of the porch, and an apple tree was espaliered on the side wall in the front of the house. There was a huge magnolia tree, lots of camellia bushes, gardenias, azaleas, and several types of citrus trees.

The wonderful house that was home to our family for almost fifty years was also perfect for parties. And it's a good thing. Cajuns love to have a houseful of people, and Dad was no exception. Sometimes I would be awakened at one or two A.M. on a Sunday morning by the sounds of Benny Goodman on the stereo downstairs, which turned into Cajun music as the frolicking rolled on and Dad took control of the records. Laughter, voices, frying pans clattering, and ice clinking told me that my parents had returned with a group of friends from a dance or party, just not ready to let the evening end.

Bacon was frying, grits were bubbling away, eggs were being scrambled, and a few diehards were still tripping the light fantastic. As I got older I would come downstairs and join them for eggs and conversation, feeling disloyal to my Irish grandmother in the bedroom next to mine, who thought this was nonsense that my parents should have outgrown long ago.

In addition to the many impromptu dance and breakfast parties, there were spur-of-the-moment game parties. My father would have taken some clients out to lunch and, in his southern hospitality mode, invited them to come to the house for an afternoon of croquet and dinner, notifying my mother that two, three, four or more people would be coming over, with their wives later joining us for a barbecue. Mom thought of this as supporting my father in the family business, and just got used to it, as she got used to all his Cajun ways.

Thanksgiving and Christmas dinners were out of another era: the house decorated with candles and holly; fireplaces in the living and family rooms glowing and offering a wonderful spicy aroma; unexpected visitors, sometimes unseen for years, dropping in to wish us a Merry Christmas; and all those Cajun specialties. Oyster bread stuffing was a must, along with at least one shrimp-stuffed vegetable, cornbread-stuffed turkey, sweet potatoes, fruit salads, pecan pie, and bread pudding. And these were just the fixed dishes each year; there were always new additions.

As teenagers and young adults, we would sometimes get so involved with conversation and visiting with siblings or cousins who had married and moved away, that we forgot whoever was in the kitchen slaving away while we laughed and enjoyed embellishing the same old stories. We became forever aware that no one belonged in the kitchen alone when my sister Lorna appeared at the entrance to the family room one Christmas Eve and said, "Would **somebody** peel the goddamn shrimp!" That's still our cue, some twenty years later, that help is needed in the kitchen.

A day or two after Christmas, we would go to Half Moon Bay on the Pacific Coast and pick up fresh crab. Lots of fresh crab. We'd call cousins, aunts, and uncles, and Dad would fix a crab boil. Nothing but crab, fresh lemons, and corn and potatoes cooked in the highly seasoned water. We'd lay plastic and newspapers on the dining room table and set the platters of crab, corn, and potatoes in the center. It was a mess, and the highlight of the holidays. Someone always brought in dishes of melted butter for those non-purists who liked a dip for their crab. The cooking water was seasoned enough that the food supposedly didn't need further embellishment, but the butter always disappeared quickly, very quickly.

Friday night was story night when we were kids, and Dad would make either pecan or coconut pralines, which he learned how to make from his mother and had been making since childhood. Occasionally, he would choose a new *candy to make for us. The trouble was, Dad didn't know how to make any candy other than pralines. He sometimes chose something called* **penuche** *from his mother's old green cookbook. Lacking the patience (he was a very impatient man) to use a candy thermometer and wait until the bubbling sugar mixture reached the correct temperature, Dad would suddenly exclaim "It's ready," and pour the candy onto a buttered baking sheet. If it was underdone, it would still be soft when it set—somewhat like very firm taffy—and we would have to pull and twist it apart to each get a portion. When it was cooked too long it was brittle, and we wouldn't have to wait more than a few minutes before we could crack it—with a hammer. Either way, it was okay with us unless Dad wasn't pleased with it, and decided that adding something else before it set would make it better. The something else was usually raisins, and totally ruined any chance of our enjoying the confection.*

Sometimes we just had popcorn, and if Dad was very tired he would simply cut up apples or watermelon, sprinkling salt on it to our dismay, insisting that salt made the fruit sweeter. Whatever the snack, we relished the Friday night stories, because these were the funny tales about our relatives. Always staying one step short of disrespect, Dad would tell us about young Irma spending most of her money on clothes, or Alice sleeping with a shotgun by her bed. We loved hearing about the miserly side of our ancestors and how they hid their money so well that it was sometimes never found, even after their deaths. Dad revealed that our kind and gentle great-grandfather believed that there was nothing more important than family, and on the occasions when he announced that there would be a family picnic at Charenton Lake he expected to see the entire family there. Everyone knew that it wasn't an invitation, it was a proclamation and they had better attend.

Most of our ancestors were only names to us, yet we felt that we knew them all: from the kind-hearted great-great-uncle who played the fiddle, but also shot and killed a man, to the great-aunt who fell into a deep depression following the death of her newborn twins and spent much of her life in what was then called an insane asylum. Dad was a born storyteller and didn't hesitate to relay to us the quirky side of these relatives, as well as the stories of their daily lives on the farm in "the old days." I think he kept their memories alive for himself in the telling of these tales; he wanted us to know his family even though they lived so far away. By the time my sisters and I went down to Louisiana as adults, it was with great familiarity that we walked into the Cajun farmhouse kitchen, by the old barns, across the bayou, and through Uncle Adolphe's store.

As we grew older and moved away from home, the four of us came back to Mom and Dad's house as often as we could, bringing new generations with us in our own children and grandchildren—making five generations of Cajuns who swung on the hammocks under the redwoods, ate Dad's wonderful seafood boils, fricassees, and gumbos, and vied to be the winner at horseshoes or croquet. We'll always remember the times Dad spent joyfully cooking, and dragging whatever kids were around and willing to the stove or barbecue to share the process with him.

No one could leave in the morning after a visit at Mom and Dad's without breakfast, and I mean **breakfast.** There would be eggs, andouille sausage, Grandpa Pischoff's smothered potatoes, cornbread or hush puppies, lots of whatever fruit was in season cut up and arranged on a platter, and pitchers of juice, coffee, and hot milk to put in the coffee. Dad would get up before everyone else and make breakfast as quietly as he could, which was about as quietly as a locomotive roaring through the house. He wanted to surprise everybody and have this wonderful feast on the dining room table when people got up.

In later years, children and grandchildren would be gathered at Mom and Dad's house because they were in the area to go to a game, wedding, class reunion, or shopping in downtown San Francisco. There was a long drive home facing most of the group, who lives in Southern California, and they wanted to break up the trip with stops for breakfast and lunch. Not only would Dad have made the huge breakfast that everyone told him they wouldn't have time to eat before they left, but the dining room table would be loaded with enough food for a dozen or more people, even if there were only two guests (who didn't want breakfast). He would also have packed a huge lunch for the travelers to eat on the way home. Words meant nothing to Dad, if they weren't the words he wanted to hear, and "please don't fix breakfast for us" didn't register with his generous heart, or conform to his method of doing everything with a southern hospitality flare.

Dad didn't know how to live life or any part of it in a diminutive way. Eventually he was just too tired to make such a feast in the morning, especially when he finally realized that people weren't eating most of it. He simply would not believe that people did not need something to eat before they left, and he would still get up at dawn and put out cereal, fruit, cornbread, juice, and coffee, then go back to bed for a nap. We would put everything away before he got up from his early morning nap, and then leave a note thanking him for the breakfast, thereby perpetuating the behavior. Yet, it was so important to him to nurture his family physically as well as emotionally that we all played along with it and let him be the dad who loves his family by feeding them. And feeding them. And feeding them.

His health was failing as Dad approached the age of eighty-eight. He was tired and his heart was weak. My *husband, Dick, and I went down to Louisiana the spring before Dad's eighty-eighth birthday, and were bringing our pictures of Home Place and our relatives to show him on Father's Day. We decided that instead of buying a gift, we would prepare a special Cajun dinner for him as a present.*

I had my heart set on making a crawfish boil for him—his favorite meal, unless he could get oysters just brought from the Gulf and savor them fresh on the half shell. There wasn't a seafood market listed in the phone book that I didn't call, but no one had any crawfish—live, refrigerated, or frozen. Saddened that I wouldn't be able to boil up a mess of crawfish, potatoes, and corn for my dad, I stopped by my usual market to get some large shrimp for a shrimp boil instead.

In the frozen seafood section were two boxes of crawfish tails. I was astonished. This store had never had crawfish before (nor have they had them since). I grabbed both boxes—just the right amount for Mom, Dad, Dick and me—and tossed them into the shopping cart. Dad had tears—happy tears—in his eyes throughout the meal. Three different people called me that week to tell me how overjoyed Dad was with the crawfish boil; he couldn't stop talking about it.

Five days later, I got a call that Dad had suffered a heart attack and wouldn't recover. But he went the way he wanted to go—quickly and suddenly, with no suffering. And, I like to think, still dreaming of that crawfish dinner.

Cajun Mustard Sauce

Sauces have always been important to us, possibly because we have a lot of unadorned dishes such as shrimp boils, cracked crab, barbecued steak, grilled fish, and roasted turkey. A variety of sauces (we usually have two or three with meals such as those just mentioned) makes a simple meal seem festive. Our family likes this recipe, as it is so versatile. We use it with seafood, poultry, or meat, on sandwiches, or even on hot vegetables as a topping, or with fresh raw vegetables as a dip. It can also be diluted with milk to a pouring consistency and used as a salad dressing.

Makes about 2 cups

- 1 cup top-quality mayonnaise
- ⅔ cup stone-ground mustard (preferably Cajun or Creole)
- 2 tablespoons prepared horseradish (see Lagniappe, page 213)
- 2 tablespoons chopped fresh chives
- 2 teaspoons fresh lemon juice
- ½ teaspoon salt
- ¼ teaspoon white pepper

Combine all the ingredients. Cover and store in the refrigerator.

LAGNIAPPE This sauce could be combined with cooked potatoes or macaroni for an instant potato or macaroni salad, with all the seasonings already included. Since mayonnaise is the main ingredient, use a top-quality one. A whole grain or stone-ground mustard is the favored mustard of Cajuns. Creole mustard, very popular in Cajun country, has whole seeds that are marinated in wine before the mustard is made.

Coleslaw

We have made coleslaw the same way for years and are very definite about how we like it: a blend of shredded cabbage, mayonnaise, and seasonings; nothing more, nothing less—just simple perfection. Vinaigrette dressings make coleslaw translucent, watery, and very unhappy. Olives, pineapple, and other inappropriate additions mask the crisp, clean taste of the cabbage, which needs only the creaminess provided by mayonnaise and the zest from the seasonings. It should be made with the next day in mind, when it is even better, and can be piled on lots of thinly sliced barbecued pork or chicken, for the ultimate sandwich.

Serves 6 (with leftovers for sandwiches)

2 medium heads of cabbage (about 2½ pounds total)
1 cup top-quality mayonnaise
¾ cup sliced green onions
3 tablespoons fresh lemon juice
1 teaspoon salt
½ teaspoon white pepper
¼ teaspoon sugar

Quarter the cabbage and remove the core from each quarter. Discard the core and any blemished outer leaves. Slice downward—lengthwise, not across—thinly shredding the cabbage.

Place in a large bowl and toss well with the remaining ingredients. It's best at least 2 hours, and up to one day, after making.

LAGNIAPPE **If you have trouble digesting cabbage, know that you are not the first. In the book *Food History* by Reay Tannahill, the author states, in writing about the effects of gas-producing foods such as cabbage, "Medieval man was oblivious to cause and effect. He knew only that, despite the odds, he should 'always beware of [his] hinder part from guns blasting.' "**

Corn and Bell Pepper Salad

It's always embarrassing when people ask for this recipe, as it is so easy that I feel as if I didn't go to any trouble for my guests. A fixture on the buffet table when I have a big party, it literally takes minutes to prepare. And people love it! Of course, it is best when made with fresh corn, but frozen corn allows us to enjoy it year-round. Serves 6

5 cups fresh corn kernels or 20 ounces frozen corn, defrosted and drained
3/4 cup chopped celery
1/2 cup chopped red or green bell pepper
1/2 cup chopped red onion
6 tablespoons olive oil
2 tablespoons red wine vinegar
1 teaspoon salt
1/2 teaspoon black pepper
1/4 teaspoon Tabasco sauce
1/4 teaspoon sugar

Combine all the ingredients and toss. The salad may be made up to 2 days ahead.

LAGNIAPPE Corn is one of the few vegetables that I will purchase frozen (besides okra, out of necessity for making gumbo year-round). Since the sugar in corn begins to convert to starch almost as soon as it is picked, corn that is picked, removed from the cob, and frozen soon after picking will actually be sweeter than fresh corn that is a few days old. Corn is the only vegetable (other than tomatoes and, sometimes, beets) that I will consider purchasing canned.

Crab Salad with Summer Vegetables

This is a favorite toward the end of the summer, when cucumbers, corn, and bell peppers are making their last appearances, and crab is just coming in. It's ideal when the weather is hot, and a chilled entrée salad is perfect for a lazy supper. Serves 6

1 large cucumber
2 medium ears corn
1 cup chopped green bell pepper
1 cup chopped red onion
1 pound crabmeat
¾ cup Mama's Nice Pink Sauce for Cold Shrimp (page 207)
1 tablespoon fresh lemon juice
¾ teaspoon salt
½ teaspoon white pepper
¼ cup chopped fresh parsley

Peel and chop the cucumber.

Cut corn kernels off the cob.

Combine all the ingredients and gently toss.

Serve with French bread and a tossed green salad for a complete but light meal.

LAGNIAPPE Many recipes would have you scoring the skin of cucumbers, peeling and seeding tomatoes, and preparing foods for better presentation. But this isn't the Cajun Country way of cooking. When the cuisine was being developed, seeding tomatoes or decorating cucumber skins was the last thing on the mind of the cook who had to get outside to tend to the farm animals, or harvest the crops or the food from the garden. Cajun cooks put their cooking energy into the taste of the finished dish rather than its presentation.

Dad's Cucumber Salad

This was always a requested dish during the dozens of years that we gathered for dinners at our childhood home. It was one of Dad's specialties, and we pleaded with him not to get creative and stray from the recipe as he was sometimes likely to do. I once caught him putting some rather old pineapple yogurt in it, so the yogurt wouldn't go to waste! (In the process, of course, he ruined the salad.) He was a fabulous cook most of the time, but his creativity was sometimes misguided, usually when he was trying to use up leftovers—something he did indiscriminately, and not well. Serves 6

- 2 large cucumbers (about 2 pounds), peeled and sliced
- 1 large red onion (about 8 ounces), halved vertically and thinly sliced
- ½ cup top-quality mayonnaise
- 1½ teaspoons salt
- 1 teaspoon sugar

Mix all the ingredients in a large bowl and allow to sit in the refrigerator for several hours. Any remaining dressing can be saved to use as a dressing on green salads another day.

LAGNIAPPE **While nothing gets wasted in a Cajun kitchen, there are times when you just can't make something good from leftovers—such as the case of Dad adding pineapple yogurt to the cucumber salad and ruining it. A bit of leftover this or that, especially if it's getting old, is better tossed away. Old food will not metamorphose into new food by mixing the two together; undesirable leftovers that no one wants to eat are going to remain what they are, diminishing the quality of whatever they are combined with.**

Dark Sweet Cherry Salad

This recipe of my grandmother's required some investigation. She called for a #303 can of dark sweet cherries which, I came to realize, is how a 15-ounce can is now designated. The package of cherry gelatin left me wondering if she was referring to a 3-ounce or a 6-ounce package, and if it was the same "Jell-O" that is commercially available today. After testing the recipe, I realized that she meant a 3-ounce package. And after speaking with the Jell-O division of Kraft Foods, I discovered that Jell-O was popular by the turn of the century, and the cherry flavor was introduced and readily available by 1916. Canned cherries were also widely distributed by that time and, I suspect with these two "store-bought" items, this salad was a treat for holiday meals. Serves 8

One 15-ounce can dark sweet cherries
One 3-ounce package cherry gelatin
½ cup plus ½ cup sour cream
2 tablespoons sugar
2 teaspoons vanilla extract
16 pecan halves

Drain the cherries, reserving the juice. Add enough water to the cherry juice to measure 2 cups liquid.

Bring the liquid to a boil, add the gelatin, remove from the heat, and stir until the gelatin is dissolved.

Transfer to a 6-cup serving dish, cool, and refrigerate until thick, but not set.

Add ½ cup of the sour cream to the thickened gelatin and stir to combine. Add the drained cherries and stir again. Chill until firm.

Mix the additional ½ cup sour cream, the sugar, and the vanilla.

Serve the salad topped with a tablespoon of the sweetened sour cream and 2 pecan halves on each serving.

LAGNIAPPE **Before powdered, packaged gelatin (either flavored or plain) was available, home cooks used sheets of prepared gelatin. These had to be clarified by boiling them with egg whites and eggshells, then dripping the mixture through a jelly bag. You can make flavored gelatin using your favorite juice simply by dissolving a 3-ounce package of cherry gelatin in 2 cups boiling juice, according to the directions on the envelope. I often make cranberry, orange, or pineapple gelatin (from juice) for a refreshing dessert.**

Garlic Shrimp Mayonnaise

Garlic Shrimp Mayonnaise came about when Aunt Lorna wanted to make use of a bit of shrimp she had left after making Shrimp Fritters (page 156). This is so good that it quickly became a traditional accompaniment to the fritters. Whenever we have just a bit of extra shrimp, we make this mayonnaise and serve it instead of tartar sauce or remoulade with Crab Cakes (page 118), Fried Catfish (page 126), Pepper-Fried Shrimp (page 129), or Oyster Po' Boys (page 128). ***Makes about 3 cups***

2 cups top-quality mayonnaise
½ cup cooked shrimp, finely chopped
¼ cup finely chopped celery
3 tablespoons finely chopped onion
1 tablespoon white wine vinegar
1 teaspoon stone-ground mustard (preferably Cajun or Creole)
¼ to ½ teaspoon salt (depending on saltiness of shrimp)
½ teaspoon dried thyme
½ teaspoon dried oregano
¼ teaspoon Tabasco sauce
¼ teaspoon white pepper
4 cloves garlic, minced

Combine all ingredients and refrigerate immediately after making. Serve within one day. Do not allow to stand at room temperature for more than a brief time, especially if using homemade mayonnaise.

LAGNIAPPE **Since homemade mayonnaise must be carefully handled and refrigerated, I sometimes wonder if my ancestors ever got food poisoning from dishes like this one, in which mayonnaise was combined with seafood. As there was no refrigeration, I suppose they must have made just enough for one meal and served it immediately after preparation. In reading old letters and diaries of other families, in addition to those of my family, I found indications that people were subject to brief illnesses on a relatively frequent basis, perhaps due to food bacteria, or what we now term "food poisoning." Commercial mayonnaise does not carry the same risk as homemade mayonnaise, because of the preservative in it. It is actually the protein that the mayonnaise is combined with that causes the problems (with chicken salad, deviled eggs, potato-egg salad, and so on), not the mayonnaise itself.**

Gravy

While gravy is usually formed as a dish cooks, there are times when gravy is needed, such as when there is a leftover roast, or some chicken, or some naked rice. Cajuns love rice and gravy, and could have it at every meal—indeed, perhaps as *a meal on occasion. Most Cajun cooks save drippings from chicken, beef, pork, and duck in the refrigerator and use them for gravy, or for frying. The drippings from each kitchen give the cook's food a distinctive taste and, in turn, define her or his reputation as a cook.*

Makes about 7 cups

¾ cup reserved drippings, lard, or corn oil*
1¼ cups all-purpose flour
6 cups chicken stock
1½ cups sliced green onions
1 teaspoon salt
1 teaspoon black pepper
1 teaspoon onion powder
¼ teaspoon cayenne pepper

*When I don't have drippings from a roast, from frying chicken, or from another source, I use a combination of lard and/or corn oil, with strained bacon drippings added for flavor.

Heat the drippings in a large heavy skillet or Dutch oven over medium-high heat for 2 minutes. Add the flour and whisk constantly to combine. As soon as the drippings and flour are combined, reduce the heat to medium and cook for 10 minutes, whisking constantly.

Add the remaining ingredients and, whisking constantly, bring to a boil. Reduce the heat to medium-low and simmer for 20 minutes, whisking often.

LAGNIAPPE Here are some tips for making gravy:

When you are roasting meat or chicken, place the amount of flour you are likely to use when making the gravy in a small dish in the oven when the roast is almost done. The toasted flour will give a deeper flavor to your gravy.

Darken your gravy with a couple of spoonfuls of leftover coffee, to give it a dark color without affecting the taste.

If gravy is too thin, stir 2 tablespoons flour and 2 tablespoons soft butter into a paste and stir it into the boiling gravy. Repeat if the gravy is still too thin. Thin out too-thick gravy by adding a bit of stock.

Lemon-Parsley Rice Salad

If leftover rice didn't go into rice pudding, it was made into rice salad, or jambalaya, unless we were having gumbo that night, in which case the rice had a note on it with an emphatic "SAVE FOR GUMBO." This makes a light entrée when shrimp or chicken is added and is one of our hot-weather favorites, served with a tomato or cucumber salad. Serves 6

4 cups cooked rice (about 1⅓ cups raw), cooled
¾ cup top-quality mayonnaise
2 tablespoons fresh lemon juice
1 teaspoon stone-ground mustard (Cajun or Creole)
½ teaspoon salt
¼ teaspoon white pepper
½ cup chopped celery
½ cup sliced green onions
½ cup chopped fresh parsley

Combine the cooled rice with the mayonnaise, lemon juice, mustard, salt, and pepper. Toss gently to combine. Add the remaining ingredients and gently toss again.

LAGNIAPPE **Innocent-seeming rice can be a source of bacterial spores, some of which can occasionally survive cooking. If handled correctly, this isn't a problem—serve rice shortly after cooking, and refrigerate leftover cooked rice. Rice salads, such as this one, should have some form of acid—lemon juice, vinegar, or pickles.**

Lorna's Sauce Piquante

Piquant means so hot that it hurts . . . not my idea of enjoying food. This version is hot but allows the flavors of the other ingredients to come through. Sauce Piquante is so popular in Louisiana that there is a yearly Sauce Piquante Festival with endless variations of this dish. Sauce Piquante usually refers not to just a sauce, as in this recipe, but to a stew-type dish made with tomatoes, poultry, seafood, meat, game, or even vegetables.

Serves 6

4 tablespoons (½ stick) butter
2 cups chopped onion
1½ cups chopped green bell pepper
½ cup chopped celery
3 cloves garlic, minced
2 cups chicken stock
One 14-ounce can diced tomatoes, drained, or 1½ cups diced fresh tomatoes in season
2 bay leaves
1½ teaspoons salt
1½ teaspoons white pepper
1 teaspoon black pepper
½ teaspoons cayenne pepper
1 tablespoon cornstarch
1 tablespoon cold water

Melt the butter in a large heavy skillet or Dutch oven over medium-high heat. When the foam subsides, add the onion, bell pepper, celery, and garlic and cook for 10 minutes, uncovered, stirring occasionally.

Add the remaining ingredients except the cornstarch and water, bring to a boil, and reduce the heat to medium-low and simmer for 20 minutes, partly covered, stirring occasionally.

Bring the mixture to a boil again, mix the cornstarch and water together, and stir into the boiling liquid. Simmer for 5 minutes to thicken.

Serve with poultry, seafood, meat, game, vegetables, or leftovers.

LAGNIAPPE **Fresh tomatoes, as with all varieties of produce, are much preferred over canned. However, as tomato season is only June through September in most areas of the country, good-quality tomatoes that are processed and canned shortly after harvesting are better than the off-season, flavorless tomatoes found in markets from fall through spring. Store tomatoes stem up, at room temperature, and out of direct sunlight. Refrigeration makes them pulpy and flavorless. Place unripe tomatoes in an open paper bag with an apple.**

Macaroni Salad

I remember making this as a young bride, because the ingredients were so inexpensive, and it could be made into a main course with the addition of leftover chicken or other protein. Cajuns think nothing of serving several starches with a meal, and it wouldn't be unusual to find this on the table with beans, rice, and perhaps even potato salad. ***Serves about 16***

16 ounces "salad" macaroni (see Lagniappe), cooked
3 cups chopped celery
3 cups top-quality mayonnaise
1½ cups chopped onion
¾ cup chopped dill pickles
1 tablespoon fresh lemon juice
1 tablespoon stone-ground mustard (Cajun or Creole)
1 teaspoon salt
½ teaspoon sugar
½ teaspoon white pepper

Put the macaroni in a large bowl, add the remaining ingredients, and toss to combine. Store in the refrigerator.

LAGNIAPPE Noodles and pasta are not used regularly in Cajun Country, except for two dishes that are much loved by Cajun people: macaroni salad and macaroni and cheese. For both dishes our family uses the "salad" macaroni, which is tube shape with a straight cut, but some folks prefer "elbow" macaroni, which is a tube shaped that is curved, like an elbow. I think the salad macaroni tends to hold the dressing better than the elbow, but both are perfectly acceptable in either dish.

Mama's Nice Pink Sauce for Cold Shrimp

I love the title of this simple recipe of Great-Grandma Clara's. So gentle and unassuming, yet I'm sure she knew that hers was the best, and the only, sauce for cold shrimp! (Cajuns are not generally shy about their preferences, or about their cooking.)

Makes about 1½ cups

1 cup top-quality mayonnaise
½ cup ketchup
1½ tablespoons fresh lemon juice
½ teaspoon salt
½ teaspoon paprika
¼ teaspoon white pepper
¼ teaspoon Tabasco sauce
⅛ teaspoon cayenne pepper

Combine all the ingredients and store in the refrigerator for no more than a few days.

LAGNIAPPE **We use this with crab and crawfish, as well as with shrimp. It also makes a good dip for raw vegetables. Grandma would thin this out with milk if there was any left over, and use it as a salad dressing; it's very similar to the dressing for a Shrimp or Crab Louis.**

Mama's Seafood Cocktail Sauce

In researching the recipes in this book, and the food and eating habits I was able to study from generations of family letters, I was surprised at the amount of manufactured foods available at the turn of the last century. I was also startled at the number that my family seemed familiar with, even out in the country. Ketchup and chili sauce were in company with ingredients that they purchased on occasion for holiday meals: canned cherries, cherry-flavored gelatin, dried coconut, Worcestershire sauce, canned tomatoes, prepared horseradish, and capers. ***Makes about 1¼ cups***

½ cup catsup
2 tablespoons chili sauce
1 tablespoon fresh lemon juice
1 teaspoon prepared horseradish (see Lagniappe, page 213)
1 teaspoon Worcestershire sauce
½ teaspoon celery salt

Combine all the ingredients. Store in the refrigerator, but bring to room temperature before serving.

LAGNIAPPE Chili sauce (sold near ketchup in the market, in a similar bottle), introduced by Heinz in 1895, was one of the few store-bought condiments used by both my grandmother and great-grandmother. It is a combination of tomato puree, vinegar, corn syrup, dehydrated onions, spices, and seasonings. My grandmother thought it very convenient to use this condiment along with ketchup as the base for her cocktail sauce, instead of having to cook down the tomatoes to a thick puree and add her own minced onion and seasonings. To Great-Grandma Clara, this was probably like flavored oils and vinegars are to us today.

Rice Salad

This has just a little bite to it from the pepper and Tabasco, but it is mild enough to pass as "not spicy." However, the amount of heat varies according to the person making it. Dad was known to add more pepper when the chef-of-the-day wasn't looking! We often heard someone say, "I don't understand why this is spicy—I made it according to the family recipe." At which point everyone looked at Dad, who was invariably looking down at his plate with his sheepish grin. It was difficult to be upset with him when his mistake was simply a passion for a bit more pepper. Serves 6

3 cups cooked rice (about 1 cup raw), cooled
¾ cup top-quality mayonnaise
½ cup sliced green onions
½ cup chopped green bell pepper
3 hard-cooked eggs, chopped
2 tablespoons chopped bread and butter pickles or 2 tablespoons capers (see Lagniappe)
1 teaspoon Dijon mustard
1 teaspoon salt
½ teaspoon black pepper
½ teaspoon paprika
¼ teaspoon cayenne pepper
⅛ teaspoon Tabasco sauce

Place the rice and mayonnaise in a large bowl and gently toss to combine. Add the remaining ingredients and gently toss to combine.

LAGNIAPPE For a different flavor, 2 tablespoons capers may be used instead of pickles. While capers are not a traditional Cajun ingredient, there are a few dishes to which we like to add them. This salad is one (I always use capers instead of pickles in this, as did Aunt Lorna), and tartar sauce is another. Rice Salad could be a light entrée with a bit of leftover shrimp, crab, or chicken folded in—add a green salad and you've got a complete meal.

Potato Salad

For my siblings, spring meant the annual parish picnic with sack races and swimming. For me, however, it meant potato salad that my mother would only make once a year. Her recipe was the ideal combination of potatoes and mayonnaise, studded with bits of onion and celery, flecked with parsley and enhanced with salt and pepper. If he could get away with it, my Cajun father would sneak cayenne and paprika into the salad just before packing it, so we never knew if it would be red or white, but we knew we would adore either version. Since this is a Cajun cookbook, I snuck Dad's cayenne and paprika into the recipe. Serves 6

- 2 pounds russet (Idaho) potatoes (about 3 large)
- ¾ cup top-quality mayonnaise
- ¾ cup chopped celery
- ½ cup chopped onion
- ¼ cup chopped fresh parsley
- 2 hard-cooked eggs, chopped
- 1 teaspoon stone-ground mustard (preferably Cajun or Creole)
- 1 teaspoon salt
- 1 teaspoon paprika
- ½ teaspoon cayenne pepper
- ¼ teaspoon Tabasco sauce
- ¼ teaspoon white pepper

Boil the potatoes for 45 minutes, or until tender, and drain. When cool enough to handle, peel, and cut into ½-inch-thick slices.

Place the potato slices in a large bowl. Add the mayonnaise and gently toss with the potatoes. Add the remaining ingredients and toss gently, but thoroughly, to combine well. Some of the potato slices should remain intact, while some will become a bit mashed, providing a creamy texture to the salad.

For traditional potato salad without the Cajun kick, omit the paprika, cayenne, and Tabasco sauce and increase the white pepper to ½ teaspoon. (This I suggest in honor of my Irish mother, who boiled and peeled and cut all those potatoes each spring for endless years.)

LAGNIAPPE We always use russet potatoes (also called Idaho or baking potatoes) for our potato salad. They have a low moisture and high starch content that soaks up and meshes with the dressing. We also prefer these potatoes for baking and use them in stews. Small red or white round potatoes are great for roasting (with olive oil, salt, and pepper).

Salad Dressing from Mama

This simple recipe is very special to me. It is my great-grandmother's recipe, handwritten on a yellow, lined scrap of paper by my Grandmother Olympe for her daughter, my Aunt Lorna, who passed it down to me. Before finding this recipe and reading Grandma's note, I didn't know that green salads were part of Cajun cooking in days past, as there never seemed to be a reference to them. This is the only indication I have that fresh salad greens were used, and tossed with a dressing, just the same as the salads we make today.

Grandma's instructions: "This salad dressing is enough for two salad servings." Serves 2

2 tablespoons tomato juice
1 teaspoon top-quality mayonnaise
1 teaspoon fresh lemon juice

Combine all the ingredients for a quick and refreshing salad dressing.

LAGNIAPPE I know that my great-grandmother made her own mayonnaise, at least until 1912. Richard Hellmann owned a delicatessen in New York City, and his wife, Nina, made a dressing for sandwiches and salads that was so popular he began to sell the spread in 1912. Hellmann's mayonnaise is known as Best Food's mayonnaise west of the Rocky Mountains, and is the only one our family will use, choosing to make our own if Best Food's/Hellmann's isn't available.

Sauce Remoulade from Great-Grandma

My sister Lorna and I have had endless discussions about how remoulade sauce should be made. There is no definitive answer, and we will never agree, but every time we go to a restaurant that serves the sauce we order some. If it is pink (usually from paprika) my sister Lorna wins; if it is white with no evidence of pink, I'm the winner. However, this is our great-grandmother's recipe, so it rules! And, it is not pink. I win. The recipe below is exactly as great-grandma made it.

Makes about ¾ cup

½ cup top-quality mayonnaise
2 tablespoons finely sliced green onions
1 tablespoon finely chopped fresh parsley
1 teaspoon stone-ground mustard (Cajun or Creole)
1 teaspoon prepared horseradish (see Lagniappe)
¼ teaspoon salt
¼ teaspoon white pepper
1 small "bud" (clove) garlic, minced
1 hard-cooked egg, chopped

Combine all the ingredients and mix well.

LAGNIAPPE Horseradish is a plant with a very hard root, shaped something like a carrot. It is scraped or grated for culinary use; its pungent, sharp fragrance is paired most often with beef and fish. Prepared horseradish is sold in a jar and is much milder than fresh, as it is combined with vinegar, water, oil, salt, and starch.

Seasonal Fruit Salads from the Farm

Dad liked fruit salad with Sunday dinner, and he always chose the same seasonal fruits he had on the farm when growing up: pears, apples, and grapes in fall and winter; peaches, plums, and strawberries in summer. He remembered his grandmother setting a pitcher of milk on the counter, at room temperature, to let it sour. A crust would form over the milk that would protect it, and she would stir the sour milk into the fruit. However, I've taken enough classes in food science that I'm not comfortable experimenting with milk this way, so I use commercial sour cream. Serves 6

¾ cup pecan halves

Dressing

¼ cup sour cream
¼ cup fresh orange juice
2 tablespoons mayonnaise (homemade or top-quality purchased)

Winter fruits

2 large apples, cored and chopped
2 large pears, cored and chopped
3 cups seedless grapes, stemmed

Summer fruits

3 medium peaches, pits removed, chopped
3 plums, pits removed, chopped
12 ounces strawberries (about 3 cups), stemmed and halved lengthwise

Garnish

¼ cup chopped fresh mint leaves or 2 tablespoons dried

Toast the pecan halves in a dry skillet over medium heat for 10 minutes.

Whisk the sour cream, juice, and mayonnaise together in a large bowl to make the dressing.

Combine either the winter fruits or summer fruits with the dressing, and transfer to a serving dish. Sprinkle with the pecan halves and the mint.

LAGNIAPPE To get a nice even cut with the mint leaves, stack the leaves and roll them lengthwise in a tight cylinder. Slice across the rolled leaves and you will have uniform pieces, referred to in culinary terms as a chiffonade. This works well for basil leaves and any medium to large leaves of herbs or greens.

Tartar Sauce

This is another very old recipe, judging from the tattered note card on which it was written. It fell out of my Great-Uncle Adolphe's one cookbook: ***European and American Cuisine****, by Gesine Lemcke; New York and London; D. Appleton and Company, 1919. This book was passed back and forth between Adolphe and my Grandma Olympe until the binding was broken, and the pages yellowed and stained. That is currently its condition as it sits safely tucked away on the top shelf of my bookcase.*
Makes about 1½ cups

1 cup top-quality mayonnaise
¼ cup finely chopped onion
2 tablespoons capers
2 tablespoons chopped fresh parsley
2 tablespoons chopped dill pickles
2 teaspoons fresh lemon juice
¼ teaspoon white pepper

Combine all the ingredients. Serve with fish.

LAGNIAPPE It continues to surprise me that my ancestors out on the farm had access to ingredients like capers, but I think my Great-Uncle Adolphe brought these foods back from New Orleans. He would go there for products with which to restock his country store, and apparently he usually returned with one or two items that were new culinary curiosities to him—he was fascinated with food his entire life.

Tomato and Cucumber Salad

Dad loved cucumbers so much that I've seen him eat them for breakfast. They were as much a staple in our kitchen as salt and pepper. This simple salad was served almost every night during the summer, when we could walk out to the garden and pick fresh tomatoes and cucumbers. We always picked at least one extra cucumber, as Dad would quarter one lengthwise, sprinkle it with salt, and munch on it while he was preparing the salad. Serves 8

- 6 medium tomatoes (about 1½ pounds)
- 2 medium cucumbers, peeled
- 3 green onions, sliced
- ½ cup chopped fresh parsley
- ½ cup olive oil
- ½ cup red wine vinegar
- 1½ teaspoons salt
- ½ teaspoon black pepper
- ½ teaspoon garlic powder

Chop the tomatoes (discarding the cores) and cucumbers and place in a large salad bowl.

Add the remaining ingredients to the tomatoes and cucumbers and toss gently to combine. This salad may be made ahead and refrigerated, but is best served at room temperature. For a light meal, Dad would slice some smoked sausage and toss it with the salad, spooning some of the salad dressing over slices of French bread.

LAGNIAPPE **The ends of the cucumber should be discarded, as they can be bitter. However, Dad taught me a trick to removing the bitterness: cut a piece (about 1 inch) off one end of the cucumber, then rub the exposed end of the cucumber and the exposed end of the cut piece together in a circular motion for about 1 minute. Repeat with the other end of the cucumber. This motion causes the cucumber to release the bitter substance, in the form of a liquid-like gel—simply wipe it away, discard the end pieces, and proceed as usual to peel and chop the cucumber.**

Dressings, Potatoes, and Grits

Aunt Lorna in her twenties

At Aunt Lorna's Table

Aunt Lorna had the same love of cooking as the rest of our Cajun family, and it was part of what bonded us together. From the time I was a little girl and she visited us in California, to right before she died at the age of eighty-six, Aunt Lorna and I would spend hours talking about and preparing food. These were such enchanting sessions, learning about the Cajun recipes and history of our family. As I got older, we sometimes chatted and cooked well into the night.

Aunt Lorna and I liked to cook bits and pieces of food. I think this was because the stuffed vegetables and the cookies and fried pastries we so loved to prepare took lots of time to make, but little concentration. This allowed us to talk, gossip, and repair the ills of the family and the world while we stood together and shelled crawfish, battered and fried shrimp, or cut out dough. These were some of my happiest moments as my beloved aunt and I joyfully prepared food, often finding old, untried recipes in her files as we talked about, and cooked for, people we both loved.

Her kitchen was always my favorite part of Aunt Lorna's house. The little café table with two chairs was just the right size for our cozy visits. When she made a pot of her French roast coffee, poured milk in the antique cream pitcher, and took the old-fashioned peppermint chews down from the top shelf, I knew the meal we were preparing would be late . . . we were in for a memory-making visit.

Our conversation didn't even begin until after the rituals were performed. Aunt Lorna set two Limoges cups carefully on the table. With great dignity, she ceremoniously poured steaming, fragrant coffee into each cup. As she picked up the pitcher of milk, I knew I was going to be treated to a story about its original owner, Great-Aunt Alice. With her hand a full foot above the cup, she slowly poured a steady stream of milk into the center of the coffee, merging its pure whiteness with the outer circle of black—dark as night and thick as syrup. When the coffee became just the right shade of peanut butter, she set the pitcher down and began her tale.

Lorna was the storyteller of the family, and she didn't take requests. I learned early on that a tale she was telling was like a picture an artist was painting. It was destined to be told at the particular moment in time that she chose to relate it to the listener. The air was like a blank canvas, which she painted with her words. And when she began, it was because she had something to say.

Like Dad, Aunt Lorna kept her Cajun family, traditions, cooking, and memories alive by passing them on to her children, grandchildren, and nieces and nephews. Aunt Lorna was Dad's older sister, and enjoyed telling tales about his funny antics as a little boy. She took her role of the oldest child seriously, and had been the one to walk Dad to school on his first day. Dad was six years old and had never left home before. Aunt Lorna loved to relate that Dad "was crying like a baby because he had to leave Mama. He got so bad I had to take him back home. The next day Mama gave me a nickel and I bought Darrell a Johnny Crook Bar; a chewy, coconut, caramel candy bar that took forever to eat. A great big thing to a child of that age. He chewed and chewed on it. He was so happy with the candy he didn't mind going to school. The bribe worked." To his dying day, Dad loved any type of caramel candy bar, and more than a few times had to go to the dentist after losing a filling to one of the chewy sweets.

My Grandmother Olympe was adamant about educating her children in every way possible. They were strongly encouraged to apply themselves and obtain good grades. Additionally, she brought Dad, Aunt Lorna, and Rhea to every lecture, concert, and performance possible, as well as regularly taking them to the library and passing on to them her love of reading and books.

They were all still in the early years of grade school when Grandma Olympe took the children to a lecture given by Dr. Bernard McFadden, who was becoming well known for his work in the then-new field of nutrition. Grandma was especially interested in anything relating to medicine and health, and read medical textbooks out of sheer passion for the subject. She began to apply the suggestions of Dr. McFadden to her own cooking, much to the dismay of my grandfather, who regularly lamented that "my wife was a fabulous cook until she went to hear that doctor." Her children were equally distraught when they were told that they could no longer eat the candy kisses that were wrapped in metal foil, because of some element in the foil (long since corrected) that Dr. McFadden felt was harmful.

Aunt Lorna credits her lifelong passion for theater and opera to her mother's interest in the arts. "There used to be a playhouse theater on a boat that traveled up and down the Bayou Teche from New Orleans. Mama was very interested in the arts. She and I went to the riverboat to see a production of **Stella Dallas**. Either Darrell and Rhea were too young to go, or Mama could only afford two tickets, but I'll never forget that play."

Grandma Olympe and Grandpa Pischoff moved their family to Lake Charles, Louisiana, in 1918, as there were more opportunities for Grandpa to find work there than in their small hometown areas of Ashton, Baldwin, and Franklin. The children missed their grandparents terribly, and began spending entire summers on the farm in Ashton. By this time, their Uncle Adolphe was running a store on the highway frontage of the Home Place property. After dinner, Adolphe would bring the children back to the store, which he kept open until late in the evening. Dad and Lorna would have to sit on a high stool in his office area and read the **New Century Dictionary and Cyclopedia**. Lorna remembers, "I couldn't get off the stool, even to go to the potty, until I had finished whatever it was he instructed me to read. I would be furious. I would start at nine and read until midnight. The windows were kept open because it was so hot. I would have on a little short dress and the mosquitoes would bite my bare legs."

Uncle Adolphe was insistent that his nieces and nephew educate themselves, and in their adult lives they thanked him for pushing them so hard. This pursuit of and love for education lasted their entire lifetimes. Being the oldest of the three children, Aunt Lorna was the first to enter college, enrolling at Southwestern Louisiana Institute, now known as the University of Louisiana at Lafayette, in September 1927. She attended for one year and enthusiastically exclaimed that "I loved every minute." Her college education was interrupted the following year when Dad graduated from high school and received a $2,500 four-year tuition scholarship to Tulane University in New Orleans. There wasn't enough money for Lorna to continue her studies, as she needed to go to work and help pay for her brother to attend Tulane.

After leaving college following her freshman year, in 1928, Aunt Lorna went to work for JCPenney's doing accounting and business reports. One day, a young auditor by the name of Joseph Francis Haggerty came to Lafayette to audit Aunt Lorna's books. They soon married. A few months after the wedding, Lorna wrote home to her parents: "I love him so much I still think I am dreaming." Lorna and Joe had two children, my first cousins Joe Haggerty and Eleanor Haggerty Code. Their marriage was cut short after only twenty-three years, when Joe passed away after a long illness. Lorna and her two children moved to San Francisco to be near our family, the only bright spot resulting from the death of their husband and father.

Lorna and I became very close. She nurtured in me not only a love of cooking and all things Cajun, but a love of music, opera, reading, museums, and the theater. We spent many happy hours together from 1962 when they moved to California, until she passed away in 1994. I think of her daily and am reminded of her not only in my kitchen, but in all the rooms of my house that contain treasures she gave me, like Great-Aunt Alice's coffeepot, her favorite Limoges cup, and *photos of Lorna smiling and full of joy, always finding something to celebrate, even on the dreariest day. She lived by the Cajun saying* **laissez les bon temps rouler** *(let the good times roll).*

Above all she is part of my daily life through the recipes she handed down to me. From Great-Grandma Clara, to Grandma Olympe, to Aunt Lorna, to me, and now to my children and my grandchildren, we link past and future together. It is the Cajun way.

Baked Spicy Cheesy Grits

These grits are convenient, as they bake in the oven and you don't have to stand at the stove at the last minute, stirring them while you're trying to get the rest of the dinner on the table. This is one of our standby dishes for a large group, so the recipe is for twelve although it may be halved and baked in a 6- to 8-cup baking dish. Serves 12

- 1 tablespoon corn oil
- 4 cups water
- 4 cups whole milk
- 2 cups quick grits (not instant)
- 3 cups grated Cheddar cheese (8 ounces)
- 8 tablespoons (1 stick) butter, cut into several pieces
- 1½ teaspoons dried thyme
- 1 teaspoon salt
- 1 teaspoon white pepper
- 1 teaspoon paprika
- 1 teaspoon onion powder
- ½ teaspoon cayenne pepper
- 4 eggs, beaten

Preheat the oven to 350°F. Use the oil to grease a 9 × 13-inch baking dish.

Bring the water and milk to a boil in a large heavy pot. Slowly add the grits, stirring constantly, and return to a boil. Reduce the heat to low, cover, and simmer for 15 minutes, or until thickened, stirring every 3 to 4 minutes. Remove from the heat.

Add the remaining ingredients, except the eggs, to the grits and stir vigorously until well combined. Add about a cup of the grits to the eggs, and stir to combine; stir the egg-grits mixture back into the pot of grits. Transfer to the greased dish and bake for 1 hour. Allow to set for 10 minutes before cutting.

LAGNIAPPE **Tempering refers to the technique of heating something gradually—in this case heating the eggs gradually by adding a bit of hot grits to them, and then putting the egg-grits mixture into the potful of hot grits. If the eggs were put directly into the potful of grits, without tempering them, they would be likely to curdle.**

Black-Eyed Pea and Ham Dressing

What some people call "stuffing," we call dressing. Dressing can be made with rice, cornbread, or French bread, and can be served alone as a side dish, or stuffed into poultry (stuffed chicken or turkey), fish (stuffed crab), or vegetables (stuffed mirliton or bell peppers). Dressings are sometimes hearty enough to be a complete meal, and no holiday table would be complete without at least one dressing.

Plan to serve 8 people with 8 cups dressing. Serves 8

- 3 cups water
- 1 cup chopped onion
- 1 pound ham, chopped
- ½ pound dried black-eyed peas
- 2 cloves garlic, sliced
- 3 cups cooked rice, cooled (1 cup raw)
- ½ cup chopped fresh parsley
- ½ cup sliced green onions
- ½ teaspoon black pepper
- ¼ teaspoon salt
- ¼ teaspoon cayenne pepper

Combine the water, onion, ham, black-eyed peas, and garlic in a large heavy pot. Bring to a boil, stir, reduce the heat to medium-low, cover, and simmer for 1 hour, or until the beans are tender. Drain, reserving the liquid, and transfer to a large bowl.

Add the remaining ingredients to the black-eyed peas and gently stir to combine. Add the reserved liquid, as desired, to moisten the peas (I add about ½ cup). The dressing should be moist, but thick enough to stuff into a vegetable, if desired, and not watery.

LAGNIAPPE **We use black-eyed peas interchangeably with white beans, but the black-eyed peas seem to have a bit more flavor. Black-eyed Susans is the name my family uses for these white "beans," which are actually members of the pea family. Although they are popular in southern cooking, they are native to China and were originally planted in this country as food for animals.**

Breakfast Grits

We serve these grits with little dishes of butter, cinnamon, pecans, raisins, milk, brown sugar and, Great-Uncle Adolphe's favorite, peanut butter. Each person has the fun of garnishing their own bowl of grits just the way they like them. If we're serving eggs with the grits, we leave out the sugar and butter and fold some grated cheese in at the end. Serves 6

- 2 cups whole milk
- 2 cups water
- 4 tablespoons (½ stick) butter
- 2 tablespoons sugar
- 1 teaspoon salt
- 1 cup quick grits (not instant)
- Optional garnishes: butter, cinnamon, pecans, raisins, milk, brown sugar, peanut butter

Bring the milk, water, butter, sugar, and salt to a boil over medium-high heat in a medium saucepan. Slowly add the grits, stirring constantly until smooth (adding them slowly helps prevent lumps). Reduce the heat to medium-low, cover the pan, and cook for 5 to 6 minutes, or until smooth, stirring several times. Serve with your choice of garnishes.

LAGNIAPPE **We generally use quick grits, which cook in just a few minutes, rather than stone-ground or old-fashioned grits, which take up to an hour to cook. The stone-ground and old-fashioned grits are delicious, but very difficult to find outside of the South. For this reason (not because of the time element), all the recipes in this cookbook use the quick grits. We never, never use instant grits as they are very finely ground and don't produce a good texture.**

Cornbread Dressing

We make cornbread so often that there are usually the 4 cups needed for this recipe in the refrigerator. But to make sure cornbread for dressing is always on hand, I freeze it in 4-cup increments in zip freezer bags when we have leftovers. Serves 6

- 1 tablespoon plus 6 tablespoons butter
- 1½ cups chopped onion
- 1½ cups chopped celery
- 2 teaspoons dried thyme
- 1 teaspoon salt
- 1 teaspoon white pepper
- 1 teaspoon poultry seasoning
- ¾ cup chicken stock
- 4 cups leftover crumbled cornbread

Preheat the oven to 350°F. Use 1 tablespoon of the butter to grease a pie plate.

Heat the remaining 6 tablespoons butter in a large heavy skillet over medium heat. Add the onion, celery, thyme, salt, pepper, and poultry seasoning. Cook for 15 minutes, stirring often. Add the stock and stir to incorporate. Remove from the heat.

Add the cornbread and gently toss to combine all ingredients. Transfer to the prepared pie plate and bake uncovered for 1 hour.

LAGNIAPPE **This dressing makes a good stuffing for peppers, eggplant, mirlitons, or other vegetables. If shrimp, andouille sausage, or other protein ingredients are added to give it more substance, it makes a complete meal. If you use this to stuff vegetables, do so before baking the dressing, as it will be cooked when you bake the stuffed vegetable.**

Cornbread Dressing with Andouille

My father remembered his grandfather smoking meats to preserve them. Spicy, smoky andouille sausage goes into this flavor-packed dressing, which we always prefer to a plain starch, such as potatoes, noodles, or bread. As you may have guessed by now, Cajuns never tire of cornbread, and have endless ways to prepare it—often using leftovers, as in this dish, to create something wonderful. My handwritten note on top of this recipe in my file reads, "I love this." Serves 8

1 tablespoon plus 3 tablespoons corn oil
1 cup chopped onion
½ cup sliced green onion
½ cup chopped celery
⅓ cup chopped green bell pepper
3 cloves garlic, minced
1 teaspoon salt
1 teaspoon thyme
½ teaspoon black pepper
¼ teaspoon cayenne pepper
1 pound andouille sausage, chopped
4 cups leftover crumbled cornbread
1 cup chicken stock

Preheat the oven to 350°F. Use 1 tablespoon of the oil to grease a 9 × 13-inch baking dish.

Heat the remaining oil in a large heavy skillet over medium heat. Add the onion, green onion, celery, bell pepper, garlic, salt, thyme, and black and cayenne pepper and sauté for 5 minutes, stirring often.

Add the andouille and cook for 5 minutes, stirring often. Remove from the heat and add the cornbread and stock, tossing gently to combine. The dressing should be moist, but not wet.

Transfer to the prepared pan and bake, uncovered, for 1 hour.

LAGNIAPPE This dressing can be stuffed into bell peppers, eggplant, or other vegetables, or used to stuff fish or poultry. By definition, a dish like this is stuffing if stuffed in something, and dressing if it is baked in a dish, but most Cajuns use the term "dressing" in either case. I like this baked and served as a side dish rather than stuffed in something, as the top gets so beautifully browned and crusty.

Crawfish Dressing

A crawfish dressing (or other shellfish dressing) is an important part of a party, holiday, or large meal. While Cajuns are cost conscious in terms of not wasting food, they are by no means miserly in terms of what they spend to make a favorite dish. I once asked a Cajun cousin who lives in Acadiana if she feels dishes such as this one are expensive to serve as mere side dishes, since they usually have 2 pounds of fish, poultry, or meat (our family sometimes has dressings like this as an entrée). Her response was that she simply feels these are good side dishes; the expense isn't relevant when preparing food for a gathering. The old "live to eat" theory may not have originated with the Cajuns, but it certainly describes them! Serves 8

8 tablespoons (1 stick) butter
2 cups chopped onion
1 cup chopped celery
2 cloves garlic, minced
1 teaspoon salt
½ teaspoon white pepper
¼ teaspoon cayenne pepper
2 pounds crawfish tail meat, coarsely chopped
4 cups cooked white rice (1⅓ cups raw)
1 cup sliced green onions
½ cup chopped fresh parsley

Melt the butter in a large heavy skillet over medium-high heat. When the foam subsides add the onion, celery, garlic, salt, and white and cayenne pepper and cook for 15 minutes, stirring occasionally. Reduce the heat to medium-low, add the crawfish tail meat, and simmer for 15 minutes longer, stirring often.

Add the rice, green onions, and parsley, and cook for 10 minutes, stirring often.

LAGNIAPPE Here are some crawfish equivalencies:

8 pounds live crawfish equals 1 pound, or 3 cups, crawfish tail meat.

It takes 100 to 150 crawfish tails to yield 1 pound crawfish tail meat.

For a crawfish boil, allow 5 pounds live crawfish per person.

Eggplant Dressing

We didn't like eggplant as young kids, for the same reason we didn't like okra until we became familiar with its wonderful taste: the texture is an acquired affection. Grandpa made this dressing and stuffed it into vegetables that we liked—peppers or tomatoes—to introduce us to the flavor and encourage us to be open-minded about trying other eggplant dishes. The taste will win you over, eggplant lover or not.

Makes 8 cups dressing, serves 8 as an entrée, 16 as a side dish

- 1 pound ground beef
- 1 pound ground pork
- 2 cups chopped onion
- 1½ cups chopped celery
- 1 cup chopped green bell pepper
- 2 medium eggplants (about 1½ pounds), peeled and chopped
- 1 cup beef stock
- 1 teaspoon salt
- ½ teaspoon black pepper
- ¼ teaspoon cayenne pepper
- 4 cups cooked rice (about 1⅓ cups raw)
- 1 cup chopped fresh parsley

Brown the meat in a large heavy pot or Dutch oven over medium heat until the pink color is gone and the meat is crumbled.

Add onion, celery, and bell pepper and cook for 10 minutes, stirring often.

Add chopped eggplant, stock, salt, and black and cayenne pepper, and reduce the heat to medium-low. Simmer for 1 hour, uncovered, stirring periodically. The eggplant will break down and combine with the beef into a velvety texture.

Add the rice, stir to combine, reduce the heat to low, and cook for 10 minutes, stirring often. Dish up and sprinkle with parsley. (Cooked eggplant and cooked ground beef do not present the most attractive color combination, so sprinkle with the parsley after transferring the dressing to a serving dish.)

LAGNIAPPE This is a delicious side dish that might be served as part of a big holiday meal, potluck, or family gathering to go along with main courses, vegetables, breads, and other side dishes. It is versatile, as it could also be an entrée; the filling for stuffed peppers, tomatoes, mirlitons, or other vegetables; or a casserole if combined with macaroni, topped with cheese, and baked.

French Bread–Pecan Dressing

Most people don't put nuts in their French bread dressings, but our family loves pecans so much that we are always looking for ways to add their flavor and crunch to dishes. I don't bother making a single portion of this dressing; I always double it and leave one dish out on the sink for people to snack on, so they'll leave alone the dressing for the party or holiday meal the next day. This is most definitely a family favorite. Serves 8

- 8 tablespoons (1 stick) butter plus 2 tablespoons (¼ stick) melted butter, and some for greasing
- 2 cups chopped onion
- 2 cups chopped celery
- 1 tablespoon poultry seasoning
- 1 teaspoon dried thyme
- 1 teaspoon salt
- ½ teaspoon black pepper
- 1 pound loaf French bread, cut into small cubes
- 1 cup chopped fresh parsley
- ½ cup chopped pecans
- 1½ cups chicken stock

Preheat the oven to 350°F.

Heat the 8 tablespoons butter in a large pot over medium-high heat. When the foam subsides, add the onion, celery, and seasonings and sauté for 10 minutes, stirring often.

Remove the pan from the heat and add the French bread, tossing to combine well. Add the parsley and pecans and toss. Add 1 cup of the stock and toss.

Grease a 9 × 13-inch dish with some butter and transfer the dressing to the prepared dish. Bake for 30 minutes. Add the remaining ½ cup stock, stir to redistribute the crispy and soft bread cubes, drizzle with the 2 tablespoons melted butter, and bake 15 minutes longer.

LAGNIAPPE **Pecans are the only major nut native to North America. They are revered for their accessibility near waterways, the fact that they are not as difficult to shell as other nuts because the shell is softer and, of course, because of their wonderful flavor.**

Grandpa's Smothered Potatoes

Grandpa Pischoff made these potatoes every weekend, sometimes on both Saturday and Sunday. When he passed away, Dad started making them using a "French fry cutter," which was a simple stainless steel contraption that held a potato on a small spike, with a grid top that was lowered onto the potato and cut it into large French fries. (This was innovative twenty years before food processors appeared on the scene.) Dad probably made these at least once a week until he passed away. Whenever siblings, children, and grandchildren are gathered together and, as always, Daddy's name comes up, someone invariably says, "Remember his potatoes?" He never wrote the recipe down, but I've tried and tried, and think these are just about the way he would make them if we were lucky enough to still have him here. Serves 6

- 1/4 pound sliced bacon
- 2 cups chopped onion
- 6 medium baking potatoes (2 to 2 1/2 pounds), unpeeled
- 1 teaspoon salt
- 1/2 teaspoon black pepper
- 1/8 teaspoon sugar
- 1/2 cup sliced green onions

Cook the bacon until crisp in a large heavy skillet over medium heat. Remove the bacon from the skillet, crumble, and set aside.

Add the onion to the hot bacon drippings and cook for 5 minutes, stirring often.

Cut the potatoes into cubes (about 1/2 inch) and add them to the skillet with the salt, pepper, and sugar and cook for 15 minutes, stirring often; scrape up any bits on the bottom of the skillet and incorporate them into the potatoes.

Add 1/2 cup water and stir well. Reduce the heat to medium-low and cover the pot. Cook 45 minutes longer, stirring occasionally.

The potatoes should be very tender and just a bit mashed. Serve sprinkled with the green onions and reserved bacon.

LAGNIAPPE **These can be cooked over a higher heat for less time, but the long cooking gives the texture that Dad's potatoes had. Not that Dad aimed for that texture for any particular reason—it's just the way his potatoes always turned out. He was a totally instinctive cook and was right on target about 90 percent of the time. But, oh, his mistakes could be awful!**

Green Onion Mashed Potatoes

Everyone in our family had their own way of preparing mashed potatoes, and deciding on whose method to use made holiday dinners very hectic at serving time. The recipe below has become our standard, as it is easy at the last minute. All the ingredients—milk, butter, salt, and pepper are heating while the potatoes are boiling, so when the potatoes are drained, they can be mixed with everything at once. Also, as the milk, butter, and seasonings are hot, the potatoes don't get cooled down from adding cold milk and butter.

Serves 6

6 medium baking potatoes (about 2½ pounds)
1⅓ cups (about ½ bunch) sliced green onions
¾ cup milk
3 tablespoons butter
1 teaspoon salt
½ teaspoon white pepper

Peel the potatoes and cut into quarters.

Bring a large pot of water to a boil over high heat; add the potatoes and bring back to a boil. Boil for about 10 minutes, or until the potatoes are tender but not falling apart. Drain in a colander and transfer to a serving bowl.

While the potatoes are boiling, heat the remaining ingredients together and keep warm over low heat until the potatoes are done (reheat gently if the mixture has cooled down).

Mash the potatoes with a potato masher, or put through a ricer or food mill, just until all the lumps are gone. Add the milk mixture and gently fold into the potatoes. Keep warm by covering with foil.

LAGNIAPPE There's a reason for using potato mashers, ricers, or food mills for mashing potatoes: they gently get the lumps out without beating the potatoes. Both electric mixers and food processors overwork the potatoes, which releases the starch and makes the potatoes gluey. We discovered this one Thanksgiving when Dad had just purchased his first food processor. Being Dad, he didn't take the time to read the instruction manual, and in his enthusiasm he ran the potatoes through the food processor; and ran them through and ran them through. The huge pile of boiled potatoes was reduced to a heavy, gluey mess. But they did match the rest of the meal, as Dad had also put all the ingredients for the shrimp dressing through the food processor; chopped the vegetables in the food processor; sliced the fruit in the food processor; and made the oyster dressing for stuffing the turkey in the food processor. It was a well-pureed meal; an ideal one for anyone without teeth. Pecan pie was the only food on the table that holiday with any texture.

Grits and Sausage Bake

For major holidays, or when we have a houseful of guests, we prepare this a day ahead and bake it in the morning. That way, we can have a nice hearty breakfast without any effort, and without messing up the kitchen—especially appreciated on Thanksgiving and Christmas, when we'll be spending most of the day cooking.

Serves 8 as an entrée, 12 as a side dish

1 tablespoon butter
1½ pounds bulk pork sausage
3 cups water
3 cups whole milk
1½ cups quick grits (not instant)
½ pound Cheddar cheese, grated
½ teaspoon salt
¼ teaspoon garlic powder
¼ teaspoon white pepper
⅛ teaspoon cayenne pepper
5 eggs, beaten
½ cup sliced green onions

Preheat the oven to 350°F. Grease a 9 × 13-inch baking dish with the butter.

Cook the sausage in a skillet until it is browned and crumbly. Drain and reserve.

Bring the water and milk to a boil in a large heavy saucepan. Slowly add the grits, stirring constantly, and bring to a boil. As soon as they boil, immediately reduce the heat to the lowest setting and cover the pan. Cook for 8 minutes, stirring occasionally.

Remove the grits from heat and add the cheese (reserving 1 cup), salt, garlic powder, and white and cayenne pepper. Stir to combine. Add the sausage and stir well, then add the eggs, stirring rapidly so the eggs don't cook. Transfer to the prepared dish.

Bake for 1 hour. Remove from the oven and sprinkle with the reserved cheese and the green onions; allow to sit for 10 minutes before serving.

LAGNIAPPE **Making your own bulk sausage is very simple: mix 1½ pounds ground pork with 1 teaspoon salt, 1 teaspoon dried sage, ½ teaspoon black pepper, ¼ teaspoon dried thyme, and 1/16 teaspoon ground nutmeg.**

Mirliton and Rice Dressing

Buttery is the way to describe this dressing. It has lots of flavor, yet it is mild. This is what I make to introduce someone to mirlitons if they haven't had them before, as everyone seems to like this dish. Something wonderful happens when you combine butter, mirlitons, and rice. Serves 6

- 2 mirlitons (about 1½ pounds)
- 6 tablespoons butter
- 1 cup chopped onion
- 1 cup chopped celery
- ½ cup chopped green bell pepper
- ¼ cup chopped fresh parsley
- 1 teaspoon salt
- ½ teaspoon black pepper
- ½ teaspoon Tabasco sauce
- 2 cups cooked rice

Bring a medium-size pot of water to a boil. Halve the mirlitons lengthwise, and add to the boiling water. Boil, uncovered, until fork-tender, about 30 minutes. Chop the pulp into ½-inch cubes; set aside.

Melt the butter in a large heavy skillet over medium-high heat and sauté the onion, celery, and bell pepper for 15 minutes, until softened.

Add the remaining ingredients, reduce the heat to medium-low, and cook for 5 minutes, stirring often. Return the chopped mirliton to the skillet and cook, covered, for 30 minutes, stirring a few times.

LAGNIAPPE **As with most dressings, this is versatile. It may be served as it is for a side dish, or used to stuff other vegetables, poultry, or fish. It may also be topped with bread crumbs and dots of butter, or cheese, and baked as a casserole and, perhaps best of all, it can be made a day ahead and gently reheated.**

Oyster–French Bread Dressing

Dressings have always been one of the most important dishes on our holiday table. We usually have two dressings: one made with French bread and one with cornbread. If there is a third, it is a rice dressing. Whichever type doesn't make it to Thanksgiving dinner appears at Christmas. Serves 6

- 8 tablespoons (1 stick) butter plus 4 tablespoons (½ stick) melted butter
- 1 pound loaf day-old soft French bread, cut into 1-inch cubes
- 2 cups chopped onion
- 1 cup chopped celery
- ½ cup sliced green onions
- ½ cup chopped fresh parsley
- 1 teaspoon salt
- 1 teaspoon black pepper
- 18 fresh small oysters (or two 8-ounce jars small or extra small oysters), liquid reserved
- ½ cup fish or chicken stock or more if needed

Preheat the oven to 350°F. Use 1 tablespoon of the stick of butter to grease a 9 × 13-inch baking dish.

Place the bread cubes in a large bowl.

Melt the rest of the stick of butter in a large heavy skillet over medium-high heat. When the foam subsides, add the vegetables, salt, and pepper and cook for 10 minutes, stirring often.

Add the oysters and their juice, and cook for 2 minutes, stirring often.

Pour the oyster mixture over the bread cubes, and toss well to combine. Add enough stock to moisten the bread cubes without making them soggy (I use about ½ cup) and transfer to baking dish. Drizzle with the ½ stick melted butter.

Bake for 20 minutes, uncovered.

LAGNIAPPE Here are some approximate equivalents of jarred and fresh oysters:

> **A jar of extra small oysters is 8 ounces, which equals 1 cup (with liquid), which equals about 10 fresh extra small oysters.**
>
> **A jar of medium oysters is 10 ounces, which equals 1¼ cups oysters (with liquid), which equals 8 or 9 fresh medium oysters.**
>
> **One dozen fresh large oysters equals 1 pint, or 16 ounces—about one and a half 10-ounce jars.**

Pecan-Stuffed Sweet Potatoes

This is a sweet potato variation of "twice baked potatoes," and one that we serve often. It has so much flavor, is easy and quick to prepare, can be made a day or two ahead and baked just before dinner, and it is festive. Sometimes we use half bourbon and half orange juice for "Bourbon Pecan-Stuffed Sweet Potatoes." Serves 6

- 3 large sweet potatoes (about 2½ pounds)
- 1 tablespoon corn oil
- 2 large ripe oranges
- 4 tablespoons (½ stick) softened butter
- 1 teaspoon salt
- ½ cup chopped pecans

Preheat the oven to 350°F. Oil the potato skins with the corn oil, and lightly score in half horizontally, so the potatoes will cut evenly when done.

Bake the potatoes for 1 hour, until they are fork-tender; allow them to sit until they are cool enough to handle. Cut in half horizontally, and scoop the insides into a large bowl, leaving a shell thick enough to support the filling, about ¼ inch thick.

Zest the outside of one orange, then squeeze the juice from it. If you don't have 1 tablespoon zest and ¼ cup juice, use the second orange.

Mash the potato centers with a fork, and then add the butter, orange juice, and salt, mixing until light and fluffy.

Spoon the potato mixture back into the shells and sprinkle with the orange zest, then the pecans. Bake for 20 minutes.

LAGNIAPPE **There is a lot of confusion about sweet potatoes and yams. While they are similar in appearance, yams are a tuber and not related to the potato or sweet potato. The skin and flesh of a yam are lighter than those of a sweet potato, which is a variety of potato, and has a dark red-orange skin and bright orange flesh. Sometimes sweet potatoes are mistakenly called yams, but to be sure, look for the dark orange, almost purplish skin and a bright orange flesh. Sweet potatoes were once given to children as dessert in Cajun Country, as they are naturally sweet and satisfying.**

Rice Dressing with Shrimp and Oysters

I usually serve rice dressings like these shortly after they are made, as opposed to bread dressings, which I make ahead and bake. The bread dressings get crusty on the top, which adds to their goodness, while the rice dressings tend to dry out in the oven. Serves 6

- ¼ cup corn oil
- ¼ cup all-purpose flour
- 1 cup chopped onion
- 1 cup chopped celery
- ¼ cup sliced green onions
- ¼ cup chopped fresh parsley
- ½ teaspoon salt
- ½ teaspoon white pepper
- ½ pound fresh raw shrimp, peeled, deveined, and chopped (tails removed)
- 3 cups cooked rice (1 cup raw)
- 9 fresh small oysters (or one 8-ounce jar small or extra small oysters), liquid reserved
- 1 cup fish or chicken stock

Heat the oil in a large heavy skillet over medium heat for 2 minutes; add the flour and stir constantly for 10 to 20 minutes for a light roux (see page 14).

Add the onion, celery, green onions, parsley, salt, and pepper and cook for 5 minutes, stirring constantly. Add the shrimp and cook for 5 minutes, stirring often. Reduce the heat to medium-low and add the rice and oysters and their liquid, gently stirring to combine. Add the stock, heat for 5 minutes, and serve.

LAGNIAPPE **My family in Cajun Country has easy access to those wonderful Gulf oysters, but not everyone across the country can get fresh oysters, and certainly not year-round. So to accommodate all readers, the recipes using oysters call for fresh oysters sold in 8- or 10-ounce jars in the seafood section of the market. While they aren't "just shucked," they are bottled fresh and have a short shelf life (meaning they're not kept around for long). So they're the next best thing to living in Louisiana with all its wonderful shellfish. Of course, if you have access to fresh oysters, by all means use those instead (see Lagniappe, page 236, for more information on equivalents of fresh and jarred oysters).**

Sweet Potato Fries

The kitchen in the house where I grew up had a "cooler," a low cupboard that was vented to the outside of the house. That is where potatoes, both sweet and white, onions, and garlic were kept. There were always sweet potatoes in the cooler; it was just one of those foods that we kept in stock. We probably had sweet potatoes two or three times a week, usually just baked and split in half, with a pat of butter melting in the center. But when the mood struck, someone would gild the lily by getting fancy with the sweet potatoes and making these fries, or combining the potatoes with roasted onions, or with slices of apple. Serves 6

- 1½ pounds sweet potatoes, unpeeled (about 3 medium)
- ¼ cup corn oil
- 1 teaspoon salt
- ½ teaspoon white pepper
- ¼ teaspoon cayenne pepper

Preheat the oven to 375°F.

Cut the potatoes into large "steak" fries, about 4 inches long and ½ to 1 inch across. Place the fries in a large bowl and add the corn oil, and toss to coat evenly. Add the salt and white and cayenne pepper and toss to coat the potatoes evenly.

Transfer the fries to a baking sheet, using a rubber spatula to get all the oil-spice mixture in the bowl onto the potatoes. Spread out in a single layer on the baking sheet. Bake for 20 minutes; take out and turn over with a metal spatula so the bottoms don't adhere to the pan, and return to the oven to bake for an additional 20 minutes. These are best if served right away, while golden and hot.

LAGNIAPPE Sometimes the simplest things are the best. I love this easy recipe for sweet potatoes, which treats them as savory rather than sweet. I've never been one to load sweet potatoes with marshmallows, pineapple, coconut, or other sugary garnishes, although most Cajuns like their sweet potatoes with sweet accompaniments. The taste of these fries is wonderful, as the salt-dusted potatoes caramelize while they are baking, bringing out an entirely different flavor than sugar does.

Sweet Potatoes with Apples

This is a standard dish for holiday dinners at our house. I remember Grandma Olympe zesting and squeezing fresh oranges for this the day before Christmas, and grating nutmeg on a tiny, flat tin grater. This was always one of the first dishes to disappear.
Serves 8

- 2½ pounds sweet potatoes (about 4 large), unpeeled, quartered
- 3 medium Granny Smith or pippin apples (about 1½ pounds), unpeeled
- 2 large ripe oranges
- ½ cup brown sugar, packed
- ½ teaspoon ground cinnamon
- ¼ teaspoon freshly grated nutmeg
- 2 tablespoons butter, melted, plus 4 tablespoons (½ stick) chilled butter, cut into pieces

Preheat oven to 350°F.

Bring a large pot of water to a boil, add the potatoes, and boil for about 20 minutes, until the potatoes are just fork-tender. Drain and allow to cool slightly, then peel and slice ½ inch thick.

Cut the apples in half, remove the cores, and slice. Zest the outside of one orange and squeeze the juice from the orange. If you don't have 2 teaspoons zest and ¼ cup juice, use the second orange.

Combine the orange juice, zest, brown sugar, cinnamon, and nutmeg.

Grease a casserole dish with the 2 tablespoons butter and layer with one-third of the potato slices, one-third of the apple slices, and one-third of the brown sugar mixture. Repeat to make three layers. Sprinkle the butter pieces on top of the casserole.

Bake for 45 minutes, uncovered. Baste the potatoes and apples with the juices from the bottom of the dish, thoroughly moistening them. Bake for 15 minutes longer.

LAGNIAPPE **Sweet potatoes and fruit are a terrific complement to one another, especially tart fruit, such as oranges, cranberries, or tart apples. Cranberries, with their jewel-red color, are stunning in a sweet potato dish next to the vibrant orange.**

Desserts

Bayou that runs through the old Labauve farm between the general store, house, and under Vacherie Road

Our Cajun Kitchen Today

My birthday request every year is for our three young adult daughters to come over and spend the day cooking Cajun food with me. To make certain I pass down the cooking techniques as well as the family recipes, the day always starts with a basic lesson that I want to instill as permanent in their repertoire. They have mastered roux, are good friends with the holy trinity of Cajun cooking, and have firsthand knowledge of the differences among stew, fricassee, and étouffée, and among gumbo, bisque, courtbouillon, and bouillabaisse. They know at least two dozen uses for corn, save leftover bread for bread pudding, and never run out of filé or okra in case the mood for gumbo suddenly strikes.

Yet, the little nuances are best learned with a hands-on approach. For example, a hands-on approach can teach someone that a very large skillet cooks roux to a dark brown sooner than a smaller skillet cooks the same amount of flour and oil; shrimp must be scooped out of boiling water the instant they are past the translucent stage; and if the bourbon sauce for the bread pudding is too clear, it needs some cream. One learns by stirring, smelling, seeing, tasting, and even touching—by cooking with someone to whom these culinary practices are second nature.

Also, cooking together is just plain fun. One year we tested the old Cajun saying that the time it takes to make a roux is "the same amount of time it takes to brew and drink a pot of coffee." It's not true: the roux takes longer, but then there were four cooks in the kitchen drinking coffee that day. The second adage is that roux is made "in the amount of time it takes to drink a six-pack of beer." That was true, but I don't know how accurate, as we each had 1½ beers and we made a 40-minute roux. If the cook is supposed to drink the entire six-pack, I wonder if he or she would care what color the roux was by the end of beer number six.

As we talk and laugh and dirty every pot in the kitchen, I often think of my great-grandmother and her five daughters, and wonder if their kitchen was this lively, noisy, messy, and fun. I do know they also loved to disagree, and did often, about such things as whether to use black or white pepper; or whether the gumbo should be thickened with filé or okra; or if the roux should be peanut butter colored or dark chocolate colored; and, always, whether remoulade should be pink or white. Then, as today, the arguments raged, and then, as today, they were really all in fun.

I discovered early on that our daughters had learned an immense amount through watching, helping, and "by osmosis," just from being around Cajun food and cooking. So when they were in their early teens, we decided to have the five members of our family alternate cooking Sunday dinners. My husband, Dick, also took a turn using our Cajun recipes. We chose the dishes from the file of recipes handed down by the Labauve ancestors. The girls eventually became so familiar with Cajun cooking that they wanted to make the entire meal without help. I stayed available in case the roux wasn't looking right, or the jambalaya was too thin, but I let them go at their own pace, as I wanted them to develop their own feeling for Cajun food and cooking.

They particularly delighted in inviting my parents and Aunt Lorna over to the dinners they prepared, and my Cajun father sat through the whole meal misty-eyed, telling them how wonderful the food was and how it tasted just like the dishes his grandmother used to make. I never asked him if that was true, because it didn't matter. What mattered was that family history was being made as we all gathered around the old oak table where each of the three girls had sat in a high chair not all that long before, and dined on food that one of them had prepared for our Sunday dinner.

Our daughters grew up and left home, but not without copies of our family recipes. My husband and I are fortunate and grateful that all of our girls live in Northern California, within two hours of our home. When one of them calls and asks, "What are you and Dad doing this weekend?" I know that we're about to have three daughters, three spouses, and three fabulous grandchildren descend on us for three days, because when one of them is spending the weekend, the others are attracted home like magnets. For that, we thank our lucky Cajun stars, take a look at what's in the freezer, and head to the market to supplement what we have with enough food for eleven people for two or three days (actually, ten people; baby Lily is only three weeks old as of this writing). At the top of the agenda is the eager question, "What are we having to eat?"

When our first grandchild, Jordan, was about two years old, she began to take an interest in what was going on in the kitchen. She would lick the bowl when a cake was made, help sprinkle parsley on étouffée, and add pecans to the bread pudding. Her favorite kitchen task was to make what she called "soapsuds soup," by standing at the sink filled with soapy water, and filling and emptying plastic storage containers, while stirring the brew with wooden spoons and her hands. This kept her occupied for an hour or more, and gave us the freedom to get some cooking done while enjoying her company at the same time. As she got older we gave her bigger and better jobs, like cutting out cookies, and dipping buttermilk-soaked okra in the seasoned flour/cornmeal mixture before we fried it (after which she needed soapsuds soup to wash her hands). Jordan's younger brother, Kyle, has shown at least as much interest in the goings-on in the kitchen as his older sister. They sometimes are more interested in what is happening in the kitchen than what is happening in the playroom (especially if they are hungry and scrounging for before-meal snacks).

So I take this wonderful opportunity of being a grandmother to cook with my incredible grandchildren, Jordan and Kyle, and to look forward to cooking with beautiful newborn baby Lily when she gets a bit older. When I did the final test for the seasoning salts and spice mixtures for this book, I had all the ingredients measured out and let Jordan and Kyle "make" the recipes. They also made both the Spicy Pecans and the Savory Pecans, again with everything measured out for the final test. The competition for which was better, Kyle's Spicy Pecans or Jordan's Savory Pecans, went on for days. Their pride in what they made will always be with them. It has encouraged more interest in cooking Cajun food, in cooking with other family members, and in cooking with me. It has also laid a foundation of confidence; they know they can successfully cook food they are proud to call their own.

As our children and grandchildren watched me compile this book, they began to feel a real part of family history, especially as we began to gather 100-year-old photos and letters along with the recipes. They started to tie these people in the letters to the recipes on the yellowed pieces of paper, and to the photos taken on the family farm. I have laid the foundation, and will enjoy the building of the new generations' association with its Cajun history for decades to come.

Apple-Pecan Cobbler

Apple Cobbler is the first dessert we make when we feel fall in the air. As autumn seems to be the favorite season of most members of our family, we are happy to say good-bye to summer and hello to cinnamon, nutmeg, and apples. Our daughters always loved it when I made this dish, as I would let them have it for breakfast, with a big glass of milk. They weren't allowed a lot of sugar growing up, so desserts were a treat, but this only has 5 teaspoons sugar per portion, probably much less than most breakfast cereals. Serves 12

2 tablespoons butter, softened

Filling

8 medium Granny Smith or pippin apples (2½ to 3 pounds), unpeeled
2 cups pecan halves
½ cup brown sugar, packed
⅓ cup all-purpose flour
2 tablespoons lemon zest (from 2 large lemons)
1 teaspoon ground cinnamon

Topping

¾ cup all-purpose flour
¾ cup brown sugar, packed
¼ teaspoon salt
¼ teaspoon ground cinnamon
¼ teaspoon freshly grated nutmeg
6 tablespoons cold butter, cut into pieces

Preheat the oven to 350°F. Coat the bottom and sides of a 9 × 13-inch baking dish with the butter.

Cut the apples in half, remove the cores, and coarsely chop; place in a large bowl. Add the remaining filling ingredients and toss to coat evenly. Place in the prepared pan.

Wipe out the bowl with a dry paper towel, and add all the topping ingredients except the butter. Stir to combine the dry ingredients, then add the butter and cut it into the flour mixture with a pastry blender or fork, until the mixture is the texture of coarse crumbs.

Sprinkle the topping over the filling and bake for 45 minutes.

LAGNIAPPE Fresh nutmeg is far superior to dried powdered nutmeg. A microplane grater or small box grater makes it easy to grate your own, and you'll appreciate the difference.

Blackberry Peach Pie

We looked forward to this pie each year as summer was ending, and berries and peaches were at their prime. We picked blackberries in the creek next to our house each year, and we began sliding down the banks of the creek weeks before the berries were ripe, to check on them. When they were ready, Dad piled us into the car and we drove over to Half Moon Bay, on the Pacific Coast, and bought boxes of ripe peaches. We would then pick the berries, come home with purple-red hands, and make several of these pies. Why did we make several of the pies? Because our bigger-than-life Dad never did anything in a small way. ***Makes one 9-inch pie***

- 1 quart fresh blackberries (4 cups)
- 1 pound fresh peaches, coarsely chopped, unpeeled
- 1 tablespoon vanilla extract
- 1 cup sugar
- 3 tablespoons all-purpose flour
- ¼ teaspoon salt
- 2 pie crusts, purchased or homemade (page 263)
- 2 tablespoons cold butter, cut into pieces

Preheat the oven to 425°F.

Place the berries, peaches, and vanilla in a large bowl and toss together. Add the sugar, flour, and salt and gently toss to coat the fruit with the dry ingredients.

Place one of the pie crusts on the bottom of a pie plate and gently fit it in, trimming the edges so that they are even with the edge of the pie plate. Moisten the top edges of the crust with water.

Transfer the berry mixture to the pie crust, dot with the cold butter pieces, and top with the second crust, folding the edge of the top crust under the edge of the bottom crust. Gently press on the edge of the crust to form a seal, then crimp with your fingers or a fork. Cut several slits in the top of the crust.

Bake for 10 minutes; turn the heat down to 400°F, and bake for an additional 45 minutes. Allow to cool before cutting; the juices will be completely set after about 4 hours but the pie may be cut after 2 to 3 hours, if desired.

LAGNIAPPE **Almost any berries could be used for this pie, including boysenberries, loganberries, olallieberries, or blueberries. Strawberries and raspberries are best raw, rather than cooked, but they do make a delicious and simple sauce to put on cake, or other fruit. For a simple berry sauce, put 4 cups berries, ½ cup sugar, and ¼ cup fresh orange juice into a blender and process until smooth. Heat gently, if desired.**

Bread Pudding with Bourbon Vanilla Sauce

Bread pudding was originally developed to make use of stale bread, but evolved into something so creamy, crunchy, and decadent that it is now a much loved dessert. As kids, we turned up our noses at the thought of pudding made from old bread, until we tasted Great-Aunt Irma's version. The cardamom, vanilla, pecans, and Bourbon Vanilla Sauce make this a step or two above other bread puddings we have tasted.

The ingredient list is long, but this is a simple recipe to make. Serves 8

Bread Pudding

1 tablespoon softened butter plus 4 tablespoons (½ stick) butter, melted and cooled
1 cup pecan halves
3 eggs
1 cup sugar
2 teaspoons vanilla extract
1 teaspoon ground cinnamon
1 teaspoon ground cardamom
3 cups whole milk
One 8-ounce baguette, cut into ¾-inch cubes

Bourbon Vanilla Sauce

1½ cups sugar
1½ cups cream
½ teaspoon ground cinnamon
½ teaspoon ground cardamom
¼ teaspoon freshly grated nutmeg
2 tablespoons butter
⅓ cup bourbon
1½ tablespoons cornstarch
1 teaspoon vanilla extract

Preheat the oven to 350°F. Spread the 1 tablespoon soft butter on the bottom and sides of a 9 × 13-inch baking dish.

Toast the pecan halves in a dry frying pan over medium-low heat for 5 minutes, or until fragrant (don't allow to burn). Remove from the heat.

Whisk together the eggs, sugar, vanilla, cinnamon, cardamom, 4 tablespoons melted butter, and milk until mixed.

Place half the baguette cubes in the buttered dish, top with the pecans, then with half the liquid mixture. Add the remaining baguette cubes and top with remaining liquid. Cover with plastic wrap and let sit for 30 minutes, gently pressing the cubes underneath the liquid a few times. Remove plastic, cover with foil and bake for 30 minutes.

Uncover the pudding, gently press the bread cubes down with a metal spatula to moisten them with the liquid, cover, and bake 15 minutes longer. Uncover the pudding, drizzle ½ cup of the warm Bourbon Vanilla Sauce over it, and bake for an additional 5 minutes, uncovered. Let it sit for at least 5 minutes before cutting. Serve the remaining Bourbon Vanilla Sauce with the pudding.

To make the Bourbon Vanilla Sauce, combine the sugar, cream, spices, and butter in a small saucepan and bring to a gentle boil over medium heat. When the butter is melted, combine the bourbon, cornstarch, and vanilla in a small bowl and slowly whisk into the sauce.

Boil gently for 5 minutes, stirring often. Serve with Bread Pudding.

LAGNIAPPE **Bread pudding may be made with any type of unseasoned, leftover bread (unseasoned means not garlic-cheese bread, rye bread, or other flavored savory bread). While the whole purpose of this dessert is to avoid wasting bread that won't be used, I know more than one cook who used a specific leftover bread with such success that they now make that bread, and let it get a bit stale so they can use it in their bread pudding. One such bread was brioche, the other almond croissants.**

Blueberry Pie

Aunt Lorna made this pie every summer from the time she was a little girl in Ashton, Louisiana. She and my dad were routinely sent down to the bayou behind the house at Home Place to pick blueberries for a fresh pie. Like most Cajuns, they were able to rely on the productive land and seafood-laden waters for most of their food. ***Makes one 9-inch pie***

- 1 quart blueberries (4 cups)
- 1 cup sugar
- 2 tablespoons all-purpose flour
- 2 tablespoons fresh lemon juice
- 1 tablespoon cornstarch
- 1 teaspoon vanilla extract
- ¼ teaspoon salt
- 2 pie crusts, purchased or homemade (page 263)
- 1 tablespoon cold butter, cut into pieces

Preheat oven to 425°F.

Place 3 cups of the berries in a large bowl. Place the remaining cup of berries in a blender or food processor with all other ingredients, except the crusts and butter. Process for a few seconds until fairly smooth. Pour over the berries in the bowl, and mix well. (Okay, Grandma didn't have a blender. To be authentic, put the 1 cup of berries through a food mill, and then mix with all other ingredients, except the crusts and butter.)

Place one of the pie crusts on the bottom of a pie plate and gently fit it in, trimming the edge even with the edge of the pie plate. Moisten the top edge with water.

Transfer the berry mixture to the prepared pie crust, dot with the cold butter, and top with the second crust, folding the edge of the top crust under the edge of the bottom crust. Gently press on the edge to form a seal, and crimp with your fingers or a fork. Cut four or five 2-inch slits in the top of the crust (not too close to the center).

Bake at 425°F for 10 minutes; turn the heat down to 400°F and bake for an additional 40 minutes. Allow to cool before cutting; the juices will be completely set after about 4 hours but the pie may be cut after 2 to 3 hours, if desired.

LAGNIAPPE Berries are very perishable and should be stored, unwashed, in a single layer on a baking sheet in the refrigerator. If you have an overabundance of berries, freeze them in a single layer and, when frozen, transfer to zip freezer bags, or make a berry sauce (see Lagniappe, page 247).

Candied Figs

There were huge fig trees on the family farm, and this was everyone's favorite treatment of them. They were soft and sweet, and just called out for some fresh cream to be drizzled on top (Chekla, the family cow, was apparently very cooperative with the need for cream to garnish the candied figs).
Makes 1 quart figs in syrup

2 cups sugar
¾ cup water
8 cups medium figs (about 2 pounds or 2 baskets, or 2 dozen)
Optional garnish: fresh cream

Place the sugar and water in a large heavy saucepan over medium heat and stir to combine. Cook until the sugar is dissolved and the water is boiling, stirring often.

Add the figs, return to a boil, and then reduce the heat to medium-low.

Cook, uncovered, over medium-low heat for 45 minutes, stirring occasionally (and very gently) with a wooden spoon or heatproof rubber spatula. Remove from the heat and cool in the syrup.

Serve warm or at room temperature, drizzled with fresh cream for the best flavor.

LAGNIAPPE **I suggest serving these figs warm or at room temperature because the flavor does not come through as well when foods are very cold. Even composed salads such as potato, coleslaw, and chicken salad should be taken from the refrigerator in enough time for the chill to leave the dish.**

Coconut Pralines

My grandmother used packaged grated coconut that Uncle Adolphe brought back from shopping trips to New Orleans, similar to what is available today. If you want to grate your own, one medium coconut will yield more than enough grated coconut for 3 cups, although I tested these using the more practical packaged coconut.

Makes 2 to 3 dozen

- 2 tablespoons softened butter plus 8 tablespoons (1 stick) butter, cut into pieces
- 2 cups granulated sugar
- 1 cup brown sugar, packed
- 1 cup whole milk
- 3 cups sweetened grated coconut (10 ounces)
- 1 tablespoon vanilla extract

Cover two baking sheets with parchment or waxed paper. Use the 2 tablespoons butter to coat the parchment paper, the heavy medium saucepan to be used, and the two cereal spoons to be used to dish up and drop the pralines.

Combine the 1 stick of butter and remaining ingredients, except the coconut and vanilla, in the buttered saucepan and bring to a boil over medium-high heat, stirring often. Continue to cook over medium-high heat, stirring often, to 236°F on a candy thermometer—just under the soft-ball stage, about 6 minutes.

Remove from the heat and immediately add the coconut and vanilla (this helps reduce the temperature), stirring vigorously until the mixture loses some of its gloss, about 3 minutes.

Working fast, as the mixture firms up quickly, drop half-tablespoons of the praline mixture onto the prepared paper using the two buttered spoons.

Allow to cool before storing in an airtight container, at room temperature, with pieces separated by waxed paper.

LAGNIAPPE **Buttering the pan before cooking the pralines makes cleanup easier; stirring constantly while the candy is boiling makes a finer-textured product; buttering the spoons for the pralines makes the process faster, so they can be dished up and dropped before the candy gets firm (a cereal spoon holds about 1½ teaspoons, or ½ tablespoon).**

Cupcakes (Old Recipe)

This is "an old recipe," according to Aunt Lorna. The fact that the original recipe makes fourteen cupcakes is a testament to the fact that it wasn't developed for today's muffin tins, which hold twelve muffins. These simple white cupcakes are typical of the desserts people used to enjoy in the afternoon with coffee or tea, although you may frost them if you wish. **Makes 12**

- 1 tablespoon corn oil
- 1 cup sugar
- 8 tablespoons (1 stick) softened butter
- 2 eggs
- 2 cups all-purpose flour
- 1 tablespoon baking powder
- ½ teaspoon salt
- 1 teaspoon vanilla extract
- ⅔ cup whole milk

Preheat the oven to 400°F. Grease a 12-cup muffin tin with the corn oil.

Cream the sugar and butter together in a large bowl with a fork until thoroughly combined. Add the eggs, one at a time, mixing with a fork after each addition, until the eggs are incorporated into the creamed mixture.

Sift the flour, baking powder, and salt together; add the vanilla to the milk. Add one-third of the dry ingredients alternately with one-third of the milk to the creamed mixture, just until combined—don't overmix.

Transfer to the muffin tin and bake for 20 minutes, until the tops spring back when gently touched in the center, or a toothpick inserted in the center comes out clean. Remove and cool the muffin tin on a wire rack until the cupcakes can be removed easily after running a knife around the edges (10 to 15 minutes).

LAGNIAPPE The term cupcake came about because all the ingredients were originally measured out as one cup. A recipe from *La Cuisine Creole, A Collection of Culinary Recipes,* 1885, offers the following cupcake recipe: "CUP CAKES. One cup of butter, three cups of sugar, five cups of flour, one cup of milk, three eggs, one teaspoonful of soda, a little brandy."

Fresh Peach Shortcake

This old-fashioned, simple shortcake is an ideal base for peaches and whipped cream—not too sweet to overpower the goodness of fresh, juicy, summer peaches. We also use this cake and method for strawberry shortcake and blackberry shortcake. Serves 8 to 10

2 tablespoons softened butter plus 8 tablespoons (1 stick) butter, melted and cooled
2 eggs
1 cup whole milk
2 tablespoons vanilla extract, divided
2½ cups all-purpose flour
1½ cups and ¼ cup and ¼ cup sugar
1 tablespoon baking powder
½ teaspoon salt
6 medium peaches (about 2 pounds) unpeeled
2 cups heavy whipping cream, chilled

Preheat the oven to 375°F. Grease a 9 × 13-inch baking dish with the softened butter.

Whisk the eggs, milk, 1 stick of the melted butter, and 1 tablespoon of the vanilla together in a large bowl.

Sift the flour, 1½ cups of the sugar, the baking powder, and salt together in a medium bowl, and add to the egg mixture, stirring just until blended.

Pour the batter into a prepared pan and bake for 30 minutes, or until the top springs back when touched in the center, or a toothpick inserted in the center comes out clean.

Chop the peaches and toss with ¼ cup of the sugar. Set aside.

Let the cake sit in the pan for 5 minutes, then turn out onto a rectangular serving tray. Slice horizontally into two layers; remove the top layer and set aside.

Whip the cream, and when soft peaks form add the remaining ¼ cup of the sugar and 1 tablespoon of vanilla, and continue whipping until stiff peaks form.

To assemble the shortcake, drain the peaches, cover the cake layer on the serving tray with half the peaches, then with half the whipped cream; repeat with the second layer, remaining peaches, and cream.

LAGNIAPPE **Light whipping cream is 30 to 36 percent butterfat and will whip; heavy whipping cream is 36 to 40 percent butterfat and whips better, doubling in volume.**

Lemon Pie

This was something Dad would make when there wasn't any dessert or, seemingly, any ingredients with which to make dessert. We always had sugar, flour, cornmeal, eggs, butter, milk, and, almost always, the wonderful Meyer lemons on the trees in the yard.

The eggs, milk, and butter should be at room temperature or the filling may curdle. This is also known as Chess Pie when made without the lemon.

Makes one 9-inch pie

- 1 pie crust, purchased or homemade (page 263)
- 4 eggs, at room temperature
- ½ cup whole milk, at room temperature
- 1½ cups sugar
- ¼ cup yellow cornmeal
- 1 tablespoon all-purpose flour
- ⅛ teaspoon salt
- ¼ cup fresh lemon juice
- 2 tablespoons lemon zest
- 8 tablespoons (1 stick) butter, melted and cooled
- Optional garnishes: whipped cream; additional lemon zest; fresh mint leaves

Preheat the oven to 350°F.

Fit the pie crust into a 9-inch pie plate, fluting the edges and trimming any excess. Place in the refrigerator until the filling is ready.

Whisk the eggs and milk together in a large bowl. Add the sugar, cornmeal, flour, and salt and whisk until well blended. Add the lemon juice, zest, and butter, whisking until smooth.

Pour the filling into the pie shell and bake for 45 minutes, or until a knife inserted in the center comes out clean. Cool on a rack and serve warm or chilled. Add any or all of the additional garnishes, if desired.

LAGNIAPPE **This is by far one of the easiest desserts you'll ever make, especially if you are quick at making pie crusts, or use purchased pie crusts. Garnishing with whipped cream and topping with lemon zest and mint leaves gives the look of a labor-intensive pie with very little work. And it's so good!**

Lorna's Chocolate Sauce

There are two types of people in our family: those who won't serve any chocolate sauce other than this one, and those who just haven't tasted this one yet. You may never purchase chocolate sauce again after tasting this easily made, rich chocolatey favorite.

Makes 2 cups

1½ cups sugar
½ cup unsweetened cocoa powder
1 tablespoon all-purpose flour
1⁄16 teaspoon salt
1 cup whole milk
2 teaspoons vanilla extract

Mix the sugar, cocoa, flour, and salt in a heavy medium saucepan. Add ¼ cup of the milk and stir to a paste.

Stir in the remaining milk and vanilla and bring to a boil over medium-high heat, stirring often. As soon as the sauce comes to a boil, reduce the heat to low and simmer very gently for 5 minutes, stirring often. Cool and store in the refrigerator for up to 1 week, covered.

LAGNIAPPE **Although this basic sauce is delicious by itself, it may be varied depending on its use: add orange liqueur and a bit of orange zest for a chocolate orange sauce; add a couple of tablespoons of bourbon and some dried cherries for a cherry bounce chocolate sauce; add some mint extract and fresh chopped mint leaves for a chocolate mint sauce; or some crushed peppermint for a chocolate peppermint sauce.**

Mrs. Bodin's Fudge Cake (Very Old Recipe)

Aunt Lorna always called this recipe "Mrs. Bodin's Very, Very, Very Old Fudge Cake." It is different from any cake I've ever tasted, and it is absolutely wonderful: fudgy, with a dense cakelike texture, and sweet without being overpoweringly so. I hesitated when it was time to add the raisins, as I didn't think raisins belonged here, but they are indiscernible, yet an integral part of the sweetness and texture of this delightful cake. ***Makes one 9-inch cake***

- ½ tablespoon softened butter plus 10 tablespoons (1¼ sticks) softened butter
- 2 cups granulated sugar
- 1½ cups all-purpose flour
- 3 tablespoons unsweetened cocoa powder
- 4 eggs
- 2 cups chopped pecans
- 1¼ cups drained, pitted cherries, home canned or store-bought can (see Lagniappe)
- ½ cup seedless raisins
- 3 tablespoons vanilla extract

Preheat the oven to 300°F. Grease a 9- or 10-inch cake pan with the ½ tablespoon softened butter. (An 8-inch cake pan is too small; the cake rises right to the top of a 9-inch pan.)

Cream the 1¼ sticks of butter and sugar together with a fork in a large bowl until light and fluffy.

Sift the flour and cocoa powder together.

Add the eggs to the butter-sugar mixture, one at a time, alternately with the flour-chocolate mixture, just until the batter is combined—don't overmix.

Fold in the remaining ingredients, just until mixed into the batter.

Bake for 1½ hours.

LAGNIAPPE **Mrs. Bodin undoubtedly used cherries that she, or perhaps a neighbor, canned herself. Since most of us probably don't put up our own cherries, you may instead use one 15-ounce can of pitted cherries.**

While cakes today would be baked at a higher temperature, Mrs. Bodin probably used 300°F to be on the safe side, as the old ovens (and this recipe was from the time of wood-burning ovens) were not nearly as accurate as what we've had in home kitchens for the past eighty or so years. The long cooking time is because of the low oven temperature.

Myrtlettes

This recipe was shared with me by my cousins, Lynn Labauve and Carol Monahan, who said this family favorite of theirs was named for their father's sister, Myrtle. It is a very rich cookie bar—2 to 3 squares are enough for a serving. ***Makes 24 squares***

Filling

1 tablespoon softened butter plus 8 tablespoons (1 stick) softened butter
1 cup all-purpose flour
1 teaspoon baking powder
¼ teaspoon salt
1 cup granulated sugar
2 egg yolks
1 teaspoon vanilla extract

Topping

2 egg whites
1 teaspoon vanilla extract
1 cup brown sugar, packed
½ cup chopped pecans

Preheat the oven to 350°F. Grease a 9 × 13-inch baking dish with 1 tablespoon of the butter.

Sift the flour, baking powder, and salt together in a small bowl.

Using a fork, mix the stick of butter and sugar together in a large bowl until thoroughly combined. Add the egg yolks and vanilla and stir until they are incorporated into the butter mixture. Add the dry ingredients, in thirds, to the butter mixture, folding in just until combined; don't overmix.

Transfer the mixture to the baking dish and pat evenly over the bottom. Bake for 15 minutes. Meanwhile, make the topping by beating the egg whites until stiff. Fold in the vanilla, and then the remaining ingredients.

Remove the dish from the oven and gently spread the topping over the dough (the topping will flatten the bottom a bit as the layers blend together; this is fine). Return to the oven and bake 25 minutes longer. Cool and cut in squares. My cousins prefer these even more the next day, as they become chewy.

LAGNIAPPE **There are many types of sugar, but the ones you'll need to have on hand for all the recipes in this book are granulated (table sugar), confectioners' (powdered sugar), brown sugar (both light and dark, if you like; dark has a stronger flavor). Unless confectioners' or brown sugar is specified, all these recipes use granulated sugar.**

Pecan Brittle

Pecan brittle (or any nut brittle, for that matter) is so good that it seems as if it should be a lot of trouble to make, but it isn't. In fact, one year as my family was preparing to go to my parents' house to celebrate Dad's birthday, our then-little girls were upset because they hadn't made him a present. So we quickly made pecan brittle, let it cool, and were out the door forty-five minutes later (with a very happy grandpa on the receiving end of his favorite candy, made by his three granddaughters). ***Makes 1 pound***

2 teaspoons butter
2 cups pecan halves
1½ cups sugar
½ cup light corn syrup
Pinch of salt
1 teaspoon baking soda

Place a piece of foil on a baking sheet, and butter it.

Combine the pecans, sugar, corn syrup, and salt in a heavy saucepan and bring to a boil over medium heat (this takes about 5 minutes). When the mixture boils, reduce the heat to medium-low and continue cooking, uncovered, for about 30 minutes, until the mixture reaches 300°F on a candy thermometer.

Immediately remove from the heat and vigorously stir in the baking soda. Pour the pecan brittle onto the foil-covered baking sheet. Allow the brittle to sit until it is cool and breakable; break it into pieces and store in airtight containers.

LAGNIAPPE **Some people choose to make their own candy, but it hasn't been necessary for a long time. Many of the candy bars we enjoy now have been around for more than 75 years:**

The chocolate bar (since 1894)

Tootsie Roll (since 1896)

Hershey's Kisses (since 1907)

Life Savers (since 1912)

Clark Bar (since 1914)

Baby Ruth (since 1920)

Mounds (since 1921)

Milky Way and Peanut Butter Cup (since 1923)

Snickers (since 1930)

Pecan Pie

There has never been a Thanksgiving or Christmas meal at my father's house or my house that didn't have pecan pie on the menu. When someone asks, "What kind of pie do you want for dessert on Thanksgiving?" they are really asking, "What kind of pie do you want for dessert on Thanksgiving in addition to pecan pie?" This is one of our favorite versions, so rich that we cut it in eighths, rather than in the usual six pieces we serve from a pie.

Makes one 9-inch pie

- 1 pie crust, purchased or homemade (page 263)
- 1½ cups white corn syrup
- 1 cup dark brown sugar
- 8 tablespoons (1 stick) butter, melted and cooled
- 3 eggs, beaten
- 2 teaspoons vanilla extract
- ¼ teaspoon salt
- 2 cups pecan halves or chopped pecans (about 8 ounces)
- Optional garnish: freshly whipped cream

Preheat the oven to 350°F. Bring the pie crust to room temperature.

Fit the pie crust into a 9-inch pie plate, fluting the edges and trimming any excess. Leave at room temperature until the filling is ready.

Whisk together the corn syrup, brown sugar, melted butter, eggs, vanilla, and salt in a large bowl until blended. Stir in the pecans, and pour into the pie shell.

Bake for 55 minutes. Remove and cool on a rack.

LAGNIAPPE **As rich as this pie is, a dollop of freshly whipped cream cuts the sweetness and is a welcome addition. Pecan halves are more traditional in this pie, but chopped pecans can sometimes be much less expensive, and they are fine.**

Pecan Praline Bites

As these are quick and easy to make, they were one of our Friday Night Candies with storytelling time. In spite of his good intentions, Dad didn't really know much about making candy, but these never revealed his lack of expertise! ***Makes 3 cups***

- 2 teaspoons corn oil
- 5 cups pecan halves
- ¾ cup brown sugar, packed
- ½ cup granulated sugar
- ⅓ cup heavy whipping cream
- 1 tablespoon vanilla extract
- 1 teaspoon ground cinnamon
- ½ teaspoon ground nutmeg

Preheat the oven to 350°F. Grease a 9 × 13-inch pan with the corn oil.

Place the pecans and brown and granulated sugar in a large bowl and toss to combine.

Whisk the cream, vanilla, cinnamon, and nutmeg together and pour over the pecans and sugar. Toss to mix well and transfer to the pan. Bake for 30 minutes, stirring every 5 minutes. Remove from the heat, stir once more, and allow to cool a bit before eating.

Within a short time after they are completely cooled, transfer to an airtight container and store at room temperature.

LAGNIAPPE **Due to the high sugar content, and low water content, spoilage by bacteria or mold is not usually a consideration with candy. Texture and flavor, however, can be diminished by the wrong storage method. Pralines, and especially these praline bites, should be stored in an airtight container (after being completely cooled). They may soften or otherwise change texture if left out at room temperature.**

Pecan Pralines

These have more of a crisp texture than the chewy coconut pralines. We used to make them with the pecans from the family farm that Uncle Adolphe sent us each fall. As we sat around the kitchen table shelling pecans, it always made us feel connected with Home Place. Connected or not, however, shelling the pecans got very tiresome after the initial first few minutes. But Dad wasn't going to get stuck shelling the nuts all by himself. His mantra was, "If you want pralines, help shell the pecans." **Makes 4 dozen**

2 tablespoons softened butter plus 1 tablespoon butter
4 cups brown sugar, packed
¼ cup water
2 tablespoons whole milk
½ teaspoon salt
2 cups pecan pieces or halves (about 8 ounces)
1 tablespoon vanilla extract

Cover two baking sheets with parchment or waxed paper. Use the 2 tablespoons of butter to coat the paper, the interior of the medium saucepan to be used, and two cereal spoons (which hold about 1½ teaspoons, or ½ tablespoon, in volume).

Combine the remaining ingredients, except the pecans and vanilla, in a medium saucepan and bring to a boil over medium-high heat, stirring often with a long-handled wooden spoon. Continue to cook over medium-high heat, stirring often, to 236°F on a candy thermometer—just under the soft-ball stage (about 6 minutes).

Remove from the heat, immediately add the pecans and vanilla (this helps reduce the temperature), and stir vigorously until the mixture loses some of its gloss, about 3 minutes.

Working fast, as the mixture firms up quickly, drop half-tablespoons onto the prepared paper using the two buttered spoons.

Allow to cool before storing in an airtight container, at room temperature, with the pieces separated by waxed paper.

LAGNIAPPE **Put *unshelled* pecans in a damp place overnight to make them less brittle, and to make it easier to extract the nuts in halves rather than broken; place in a bowl, pour boiling water over them, and let sit for 10 minutes before shelling. Spread *shelled* pecans out in a single layer to dry for 24 hours before packaging in an airtight container; they may be kept in the freezer in a zip freezer bag.**

Pie Crust

People seem to either whip up their own pie crusts effortlessly, or purchase them. Here is a recipe in case a "purchaser" wants to come over to the other side. Of course, my ancestors made their own pie crusts, as there wasn't even a dream of purchasing one ready to place in the pie plate, but I bet they would have been thrilled if there had been. I'm giving the recipe here that my family has always made—if you don't want to use lard, use butter or shortening, but it won't be quite the same—still good, but not quite the same. *Makes 1 crust*

2 cups all-purpose flour
1 teaspoon salt
⅔ cup lard
3 to 4 tablespoons cold water
Flour for dusting

Sift the flour and salt into a large bowl. Add the lard and cut into the flour with a pastry blender or fork, until the mixture is the texture of coarse crumbs.

Add the water, starting with 3 tablespoons, and lightly mix with a fork until the dough holds together. Form into a ball, and chill for at least 30 minutes. Divide in half.

Transfer each half of the dough to a floured board. Flour a rolling pin and roll out the dough to about ⅛-inch thickness. Use as needed.

LAGNIAPPE "Blind baking" is the baking of a pie crust before the filling is added. This is the procedure when a cooked crust is needed for a fruit tart or cream pie, for example, that is not going to be baked in the oven. The pie crust should be pricked in several places so that it doesn't blister and rise unevenly. Additionally, placing foil on top of the crust and adding dried beans or rice on top of the foil prevents the crust from rising. You can purchase "pie weights" that will achieve this purpose, but I keep a bag of dried beans (about 2 cups) that I use over and over again to blind bake my pie crusts. A blind-baked crust is usually baked in a 425°F oven for about 15 minutes. The foil with the weight should be removed for the last 5 minutes so the crust will brown evenly.

Syrup Cake

This traditional Cajun cake is made with cane syrup. We use Steen's Cane Syrup, which can be ordered from Abbeville, where some of the Labauves still live (see Sources, page 267). A substitute may be made with 3 parts dark corn syrup to 1 part molasses.

Makes two 9-inch cakes

- 2 teaspoons softened butter plus 8 tablespoons (1 stick) softened butter
- 2½ cups all-purpose flour, plus some flour for dusting
- 1 teaspoon baking powder
- 1 teaspoon baking soda
- ½ teaspoon salt
- 1 teaspoon ground ginger
- 1 teaspoon ground cinnamon
- ½ teaspoon ground nutmeg
- ½ teaspoon salt
- ¼ teaspoon ground cloves
- 1 cup cane syrup (or ¾ cup dark corn syrup and ¼ cup molasses)
- 1 cup boiling water
- ½ cup sugar
- 2 eggs
- ½ cup chopped pecans
- Optional garnish: freshly whipped cream

Preheat the oven to 350°F. Grease two 9-inch cake pans with 2 teaspoons of the butter and dust them with flour.

Sift the 2½ cups flour, the baking powder, baking soda, salt, and spices into a small bowl; mix the syrup and boiling water in a small bowl and stir to combine.

Mix the remaining 1 stick of a butter and sugar with a fork in a large bowl until light and fluffy. Add the eggs, one at a time, mixing with a fork until incorporated. Add the dry ingredients alternately with the syrup mixture, mixing gently after each addition. Fold in the pecans and pour the batter into the pans. Bake for 40 minutes, or until the cake springs back when touched in the center, or a toothpick inserted in the center comes out clean.

LAGNIAPPE **This cake is a bit like gingerbread, but has much more flavor, and the pecans give it additional texture. Whipped cream is a wonderful contrast in color, texture, and temperature with the cake—especially when the cake is served hot.**

Orange Cream

Great-Aunt Irma had a pitcher of this beverage made up one Sunday to serve after dinner, when her sister, Great-Aunt Alice, snuck an abundance of cayenne pepper in Irma's remoulade sauce and ruined it. (Irma and Alice had a long-standing battle over which of them made the better remoulade sauce.) Irma got her revenge by whisking up a bunch of eggs and substituting the raw eggs for the orange cream in the pitcher, then offering a tall glassful to Alice who, thirsty from the Louisiana heat, gulped it down. This was part of the "remoulade wars," a family legacy that is apparently genetic, as my sister Lorna and I will never agree about how remoulade sauce should be made. Neither of us, however, will drink a glass of orange juice offered by someone without carefully inspecting it. Serves 6

4 cups fresh orange juice
½ cup half-and-half
4 teaspoons confectioners' sugar

Combine all the ingredients in a bowl and vigorously whisk to combine. Chill or serve over ice.

LAGNIAPPE **This is a bit like the popular drink Orange Julius. It is very refreshing, a nice way to end a meal when you don't feel like having a heavy dessert but want a bit of something sweet.**

Sources

B & T Enterprises of New Orleans, Inc.
1100 24th Street, Kenner, LA 70062; 866-243-6092; marlinseafood@yahoo.com; www.crawfish.cc (Cajun food products)

Blum & Bergeron, Inc.
P.O. Box 549, Houma, LA 70361 800-875-2548; www.driedshrimp.com; blumbergeron@bellsouth.net;

Cajun Grocer
116 Alley 3, Lafayette, LA 70506; 888-272-9347; support@cajungrocer.com; www.cajungrocer.com (Cajun food and nonfood products)

Comeaux's Inc.
709 Park Way Drive, Breaux Bridge, LA 70517; 800-323-2492; ray@comeaux.com; www.comeaux.com (Cajun food and nonfood products)

Crazy Cajun Enterprises, Inc.
877-862-2586; orders@crazycharley.com; www.crazy-charley.com (Cajun food products)

Louisiana Fish Fry Products
5267 Plank Road, Baton Rouge, LA 70805; 800-356-2905; info@louisianafishfry.com; www.louisianafishfry.com (Cajun food products)

Randol's Seafood Market
2320 Kaliste Saloom Road, Lafayette, LA 70508; 800-YO-CAJUN; randols@aol.com; www.randols.com (Cajun food products)

Shoppinglouisiana.com
P. O. Box 97, Clinton LA 70722; 800-221-8060; shop@shoppinglouisiana.com; www.shoppinglouisiana.com (Cajun food and nonfood products)

Steen's 100% Pure Cane Syrup
119 N. Main Street, Abbeville, LA 70510; 800-725-1654; steens@steensyrup.com; www.steensyrup.com (Cajun food and nonfood products)

Note: Two helpful Web sites are
www.gumbopages.com
www.louisianacajun.com

Bibliography

Ancelet, Barry Jean, Jay D. Edwards, and Glen Pitre. *Cajun Country: Folklife in the South Series*. Jackson, MI: University Press of Mississippi, 1991.

Angers, Trent. *The Truth About the Cajuns*. Lafayette: Acadian House Publishing, 1990.

Arsenault, Bona. *History of the Acadians*. Ville Platte, NE: Hebert Publications, 1988.

Bernard, Shane K. *The Cajuns, Americanization of a People*. Jackson,MI: University Press of Mississippi, 2003.

Brasseaux, Carl A. *Scattered to the Wind, Dispersal and Wanderings of the Acadians, 1755–1809*. Lafayette, LA: Center for Louisiana Studies, University of Southwestern Louisiana, 1991.

Conrad, Glenn R. *New Iberia, Essays on the Town and Its People*. Lafayette, LA: Center for Louisiana Studies, University of Southwestern Louisiana, 1986.

Cormier-Boudreau, Marielle, and Melvin Gallant. *A Taste of Acadie*. New Brunswick, Canada: Goose Lane Editions, 1991.

Dormon, James H. *The People Called Cajuns, An Introduction to an Ethnohistory*. Lafayette, LA: Center for Louisiana Studies, University of Southwestern Louisiana, 1983.

Gutierrez, C. Paige. *Cajun Foodways*. Jackson, MI: University Press of Mississippi, 1992.

Herbst, Sharon Tyler. *Food Lover's Companion*. New York: Barron's Educational Series, 1990.

Johnson, Pableaux, and Charmaine O'Brien. *World Food New Orleans*. Victoria, Australia: Lonely Planet Publications, 2000.

Keyes, Frances Parkinson. *Blue Camellia*. New York: Julian Messner, 1957.

———. *The Frances Parkinson Keyes Cookbook*. New York: Doubleday & Company, 1955.

Labensky, Steven, Gaye G. Ingram, and Sarah R. Labensky. *Webster's New World Dictionary of Culinary Arts*. Upper Saddle River, NJ: Prentice Hall, 2001.

La Cuisine Creole, A Collection of Culinary Recipes. New Orleans: F.F. Hansell & Bro., 1885.

Los Isleños Heritage & Cultural Society. *Los Isleños (Canary Islanders) Cookbook*. Gretna, LA: Pelican Publishing Company, 2003.

Rushton, William Faulkner. *The Cajuns, From Acadia to Louisiana*. New York: Farrar Straus Giroux, 1979.

Tannahill, Reay. *Food History*. New York: Stein and Day, 1973.

Time-Life Books. *American Cooking: Creole and Acadian*. New York: Time-Life Books, 1971.

Index

C

H

I

J

K

L

M

N

O

P

Q

R

S

T

V

W

Y